GENE HOWARD

I0023423

ALABAMA
Republican Party
—1867-2010—

Notes and Observations of a
DEEP SOUTH STATE

Lower Peach Tree Press, LLC

Alabama Republican Party - 1867-2010
Notes and Observations of a Deep South State
All Rights Reserved.
Copyright © 2020 Gene Howard
v1.0

The opinions expressed in this manuscript are solely the opinions of the author and do not represent the opinions or thoughts of the publisher. The author has represented and warranted full ownership and/or legal right to publish all the materials in this book.

This book may not be reproduced, transmitted, or stored in whole or in part by any means, including graphic, electronic, or mechanical without the express written consent of the publisher except in the case of brief quotations embodied in critical articles and reviews.

Lower Peach Tree Press, LLC

Paperback ISBN: 978-0-578-23765-7
Hardback ISBN: 978-0-578-23766-4

Cover Photo © 2020 www.gettyimages.com. All rights reserved - used with permission.

PRINTED IN THE UNITED STATES OF AMERICA

Conservatives in a Deep South State

This is a different viewpoint about Alabama politics. It differs because the story begins with the origin of a nontraditional political party in post-Civil War Alabama. Organized by a coalition of unskilled political factions, each with their own agenda, Alabama Republicans made a noble attempt to establish the antislavery Party of Lincoln in the Yellowhammer State, only to have it flounder under the rage and scourge of Democrat violence during Reconstruction and decades of intense political conflict.

The history of the Republican Party intends to be an informative and interesting story that helps explain the fundamental reasons for founding an opposition party in a proslavery state. What began as a curiosity by the author developed into a search for factual information about a century of Democrat rule. Further, it is offered to readers in a casual, unconventional style. This account provides critical details about how Republicans fared through the lean years until the GOP breakthrough in the 1980s—and thereafter in 2010.

Previously published works by the author, *Death at Cross Plains*, and *Patterson for Alabama* (University of Alabama Press), served as reference information for the Reconstruction period and the Folsom-Patterson-Wallace era of state leadership.

Considering that this story is an original work, and numerous wide-ranging sources have been consulted and cited, any unintentional errors are the fault of the author. Hopefully, there are few.

Table of Contents

The Alabama Reconstruction Legislature – 1867

(The Alabama Department of History and Artchives)

A Proper Preface: Beware of Great Expectations

Books are written about many things. This book is about only one thing, and it maintains that simple theme from start to finish. The intent is to help explain (and explore) the historical origin of the Alabama Republican Party from 1867 through the Riley administration, and the 2010 GOP takeover of the Alabama Legislature.

Heeding the advice of Sir Winston Churchill, though not a Republican and born in Blenheim Palace to his American mother, Churchill is recognized for his keen insights into human behavior. He addressed something essential in writing: "If you have an important point to make, don't try to be subtle or clever. Use a pile driver." He further recommended hitting the point over and over. That, we shall do, without fail.

Republicans should not read this story with starry-eyed expectations. The first Republican Party in Alabama stood firmly against slavery. Still, some white conservatives were not accepting of ex-slaves in the state government, which was necessary for a successful party.

Though Republicans had people qualified to lead, for over a

century, they never firmly established a fully functioning party until the 1980s and '90s. During that time, Democrats maintained their trademark churlish behavior, all but obliterating Alabama's Grand Old Party.

From the beginning of statehood, Democrats have had a clear field to do as they pleased until an opposition party organized. The coming of the Party of Lincoln after the Civil War threatened Democrat control of the state.

Democrats were protective of their brutal history of slavery, their brotherhood with the KKK, the discriminatory 1901 Constitution, opposition to civil rights, Jim Crowism, and denying women equal rights.

Contrary to Democrats, Republicans promoted the individual freedom of equality for all.

GLH

CHAPTER ONE

Shouts and cheers for the new Republican Party

Organizing an antislavery party in Alabama came as no surprise. The South had lost *The War* and understood *why* they lost a war that both sides believed would not last but a few months. Two Union conventions met in Montgomery on June 4–5, 1867, to organize the Alabama Republican Party. Delegates gathered in the same House chambers, where on January 11, 1861, the Secession Convention declared Alabama a "sovereign and independent state." This time, Union Republicans and the Union League met to reconstruct a defeated state and its people.

In spring meetings, the Union League and the Freedman's Bureau recommended that Republicans and Unionists call a joint convention in the state capitol to organize the Union Republican Party of Alabama. Unionists and Freedmen were pursuing official standing with national Republicans so that Alabama could be reconstructed as the first interracial state government in the South, knowing that it would be a strained and foreboding task.

North Alabama Hill people were classically dissatisfied that Alabama left the union despite strong conservative opposition. The push for secession came almost entirely from wealthy planters in South Alabama, who voted for rebellion to protect the cotton kingdom. It is reasonable to believe that if secession had been voted on by the people—it would have failed.

The South, governed solely by Democrats, had been severely punished by the Union Army because of its slave culture. The *Montgomery Mail* editorialized that people were so traumatized by the experience that "no man would revive it." The most challenging issue facing the convention was creating a political alliance between former slaves and native white conservatives. Hard feelings and memories ran deep on both sides. Troubled by its greatest failure, Southerners remained suspicious of the racial policies of the Republican Party.

The delegate profile reflected the difficulty of organizing a new party after the war. There were more black delegates than white; a hundred blacks outnumbered seventy white delegates. It was the delegates themselves who provided grist for Democrat newspapers reporting on the convention. The *Montgomery Mail* referred to the rare gathering as the "radical" convention and reported that it was the "most perfect farce" in Alabama history.

Forty-five of the state's sixty counties (six congressional districts) sent delegates. When the gavel fell at precisely noon the first day, Francis W. Sykes, a Unionist physician from Lawrence County, was elected chairman pro tempore. Addressing fellow delegates, Sykes claimed that equality was not a new thing with him. Equality, despite Sykes's boast, did not explain why black delegates were segregated to one side of the House chambers. Republicans may have been antislavery, but they were not "pro-Negro."

A sense of bitterness existed among Union loyalists because of secession. Union sentiments were evident in the 61-to-39 secession vote, the closest margin in the Confederacy. The Union League in Washington had been successful at organizing secret societies in Alabama that were loyal to the Lincoln administration. Republicans and Unionists in Alabama were one and the same, especially in opposition to the plantation economy that created disproportionate wealth and political power in Alabama and the South.

The Freedman Bureau under Union General Wager Swayne (Ohio attorney, Yale) helped coordinate Union League activities with Secretary John C. Keffer, bureau director in Montgomery. The league stressed loyalty to the federal government, fair treatment of freed slaves, equal rights for all citizens, and the end to the exploitive plantation system.

With that known, Republicans and their Union League collaborators convened in the state capitol to formally create a multiracial government in a state that had prospered by slave labor as far back as French landowners in the 1700s. Republicans were charting a course fraught with risks and danger. Democrats were equally determined to defend their homeland against the racially mixed party led by their sworn enemies.

For two long, hot summer days in the state capitol, spectators, curiosity seekers, newspapermen, and political opportunists looking to align themselves with the new government crowded the rotunda and main halls of the capitol. Ambitious men not invited to speak to the convention gathered crowds outside the House chambers and shouted out their political opinions. James T. Rapier, a wealthy free black planter from Florence (Lauderdale), mingled with the crowd. (The "**History of the Alabama Republican Party**" [online] cites elected African American Republicans prior to the 1900s.)

The *Montgomery Advertiser* encouraged the new party to return to the Union as soon as possible. The capitol newspaper wrote that the Republican Party was "a mighty party big enough to control the state." Delegates applauded Dr. Sykes when he announced that Alabama must "comply with Reconstruction by Congress through the Republican Party."

Elsewhere throughout Alabama, Democrat newspapers published unflattering articles about the proceedings and sent dispatches around the state from the "Radical Convention." Reporters described the shoddy appearance of white delegates, noting that the "negroes looked and dressed better and had cleaner faces than the whites."

Despite a diversity of interests, the convention was orderly and civil and black delegates rarely interrupted the proceedings. That changed in the afternoon session when the motion was made to grant Judge Richard Busteed (New York) a seat to the convention, which caused black delegates to revolt. Black delegates were aware that in a previous speech in Lowndes County, Judge Busteed had cautioned blacks about voting in elections because they could not make intelligent decisions. The motion caused a near riot on the convention floor, which one newspaper described as "perfect bedlam." When the motion was put to a vote, Busteed was denied a seat at the convention by a convincing 143–25 margin.

A committee of thirteen delegates (seven whites and six blacks) introduced a slate of permanent convention officials. Judge William Hugh Smith of Randolph County was named convention chairman. Smith had resigned a Democrat judicial appointment to help organize the new party. He formally recognized Alabama's sitting governor, Robert M. Patton, to address the convention. Patton was a slave-owner Whig from Lauderdale County and Alabama's governor, serving under the authority of General Swayne. Patton cooperated with Republicans the same as he was quick to oblige the commanding Union general.

Judge Smith formally announced what was already known about the purpose of the convention: Reconstruct Alabama under the authority of the Republican Congress. Reconstruction could not be done without organizing a Republican Party. "Let us accept the name of the Republicans," Smith said from the podium, "and go to work in earnest and without distinction of race, color, or condition." With those declarations, Alabama became the first Southern state to sanction Congressional Reconstruction.

The committee further nominated thirteen vice presidents and four secretaries. The most prominent person nominated was John Keffer of the Union League. Except for Keffer from Pennsylvania, convention officials were residents of the state. At least, they were current residents. Charles Pelham (Talladega) was one of four secretaries elected.

The convention then moved to organize the Alabama Republican Party. Delegates chose John C. Keffer, the aggressive director of the Union League, as the first chairman of the Republican Executive Committee. C. S. G. Doster was elected secretary, and Thomas O. Glascock, treasurer. Sara Woolfolk Wiggins, in her book, *Scalawags in Alabama Politics*, lists the names of fourteen Southern whites, five Northern whites, and six blacks who served on Alabama's first Republican Party Executive Committee (pp. 143–45).

Delegates later endorsed full civil and political rights for all citizens, repeal of the federal cotton tax of $0.03 per processed pound, and abolished the discriminatory poll tax. An indication of the deep division within the party compelled a man from Marengo

County to call for striking "Union" from the party name. It passed. A black delegate suggested that Republicans should go to the plantations and teach them about their new rights and freedoms.

After adjourning, Judge Smith and General Swayne met with black delegates to resolve the conflict over the attempt to seat the controversial Judge Busteed in the convention.

General Swayne had appointed Judge Smith to coordinate voter registration in preparation for statewide elections, with black and white officials serving as the board of registrars. Between July 1 and August 20, 1867, 160,991 men registered to vote—72,748 white and 88,243 black. It would be the first time black men voted.

By the next election in 1868, the highly esteemed **William H. Smith** ascended from his role as the former chairman of the organizing convention to the governor. Chester Arthur Bingham (Talladega) had ambitions for governor and lobbied the party leadership for the nomination. (The Bingham family of Mercer, Pennsylvania, was strict abolitionists who aligned with the new Republican Party as early as 1856. John A. Bingham, also from Mercer, was the principal framer of the Fourteenth Amendment that gave citizenship to former slaves.)

Democrats chose to sit out the 1868 election without nominating a candidate for governor. When no elections were held, Congress appointed Judge Smith as the first Republican governor of Alabama. The boycott left other top state offices vacant. Over in Georgia, Democrats boycotted state elections, and Republicans filled those state offices.

Ohio native Andrew Applegate, former Union Army captain, became Alabama's first lieutenant governor, although Applegate lacked the popular support of the highly regarded Smith. He was referred to critically as "Jack Appletoddy," a well-earned slur due to his taste for strong drink. Historians said that he was good at "speechmaking" and made good use of the word "rebel." He died before serving out the two-year term of office. (William Warren Rogers Jr., *The Alabama Review*)

Other Republican state officials were: Charles A. Miller, secretary of state; Robert M. Reynolds, auditor; Chester Arthur Bingham, treasurer; Joshua Morse, attorney general; John C. Keffer, superintendent of industrial resources; and Noah B. Cloud, superintendent of schools.

The political circumstances of Gov. William Smith's appointment by Congress in July 1868 enabled Alabama Republicans to inaugurate the first Republican governor during Reconstruction. (Michael Fitzgerald's article about W. H. Smith for the *Encyclopedia of Alabama* explained the many details involved in Judge Smith's path to Alabama's top office.)

The General Assembly first met on July 14, 1868, when the Reconstruction Legislature took office with a hundred members in the House and thirty-two in the Senate. Twenty-seven Freedmen sat in both Houses of the legislature. Gov. Smith vetoed the first bill that would have given legislators a salary increase. Republicans further signaled new leadership in Alabama by once again raising the American flag atop the capitol dome.

The South had no way of anticipating the harsh political and economic turmoil following the Civil War. Cotton that sustained the national economy had made the South the wealthiest region in America—based on slavery. But the war left the people destitute and fiercely defensive. The Klan reflected the anger of the people by aggressively keeping the Union Army occupied with endless violent outrages, the most sensational a mass hanging in July 1870 of seven men in the village of Cross Plains in northeast Calhoun County. One of the victims was a white missionary, William Luke, from Artemesia Township, Ontario, Canada. The reason for Klan attacks was all the same: terrorism against Republicans, black and white. The KKK functioned as the terrorist wing for Alabama Democrats, carrying out vicious racial warfare against Republicans and their allies. (Howard, *Death at Cross Plains*)

Carpetbaggers and scalawags

The profile of Republican leaders was comparable to Democrats, according to Sarah Wiggins. Most scalawags were more interested in helping their state survive military defeat and the curse of economic devastation from having lost the war. Combining forces with ex-slaves, scalawags, and carpetbaggers formed an influential political force that defended Republicans against absolute Democrat rule.

The National Republican Party itself was barely rooted in American politics. Organized in 1854, at Ripon, Wisconsin, over the national debate about which states would be admitted into the Union as free or slave state, Republicans held their first convention in 1856 at Lafayette Hall, Pittsburgh, Pennsylvania. (Horace Greeley named them Republicans.) By 1860, Abraham Lincoln, former Whig and antislavery activist, was elected as the first Republican president. Lincoln's political views set in motion Southern secession and the Civil War.

Governor William Smith served a hectic two-year term only to lose a close reelection in 1870 (by 1,439 votes) to Democrat Robert Burns Lindsay, in a campaign marred by widespread Klan violence. Gov. Smith claimed election fraud and remained in office for almost a month after Lindsay's inauguration, protected by a squad of black Union soldiers bivouacked on capitol grounds. Smith and State Treasurer Chester Arthur Bingham barricaded themselves in the governor's office and survived on food handed to them through the windows. Lindsay (Colbert) camped down the street at the Exchange Hotel during the dispute, and the two governors communicated by letter. Smith's intractable defiance rankled Democrats who had celebrated Lindsay's election with a big parade through downtown Montgomery led by a brass band.

Smith's legal defense was led by Charles Pelham and Lewis Parson, who filed a series of injunctions alleging fraud by Democrats. The "flimsy farce," as the matter was known in newspapers, drew national attention until Smith exhausted all of his official options and left the capitol. Bingham lost his position as state treasurer and the state printing business, as well. Gov. Lindsay finally moved into the governor's office in the first week of December.

But Democrats were only temporarily successful at removing Republicans from office. Gov. Robert Burns Lindsay (a native of Scotland) served a two-year term until Republicans elected **David P. Lewis**, Huntsville attorney, as Alabama's second Republican governor. Lewis became governor in 1872 in an election overwhelmed by violence that required a recount.

Lewis lost his reelection bid in 1874 to Democrats, and he and many of the original Republicans returned to the Democratic Party. Public opinion was so harsh against Republicans that newspapers substituted the names of Republicans, black and white, with the term "radical." Voters understood the language of Reconstruction and were determined to remove what they believed was an illegitimate government enforced by the Union Army. (*Advertiser*)

To that end, two elections changed the balance of power that reverted political control to the Democrats. A combination of good fortune and misfortune began when Alabama Democrats elected George S. Houston as governor in 1874 and took control of the legislature. The election, heavily marred by Klan violence, essentially ended radical Reconstruction early in Alabama and the Republican strategy of remaking the state into a biracial government. It also ended the seven-year period where Republicans were often competitive in elections, overseen by the Union Army until the Republican Party collapsed under the force of Democrat terror.

Still, Congressional Reconstruction oversight remained. But the 1876 presidential election changed that too. Reconstruction officially ended when Republican President Rutherford B. Hayes (Ohio) negotiated the withdrawal of federal troops from the South following the 1876 presidential election. Hayes lost the popular vote to Samuel L. Tilden (New York), one of five such elections in American history (1824, 1876, 1888, 2000, and 2016).

Desperate to keep the White House after Ulysses Grant, Republicans conceded the remnants of radical Reconstruction with an agreement to remove federal troops from the South in exchange for a handful of disputed electoral votes. Some twenty votes, primarily from Southern states (Oregon, Florida, Louisiana, and South Carolina), were needed to secure a 185–184 Electoral College victory for Republicans. The compromise was reached only two days before the inauguration. A year later, President Hayes returned control of the South to the Democrats. The two elections crushed Republican ambitions in Alabama, although it had been a Republican president who recalled the Union Army in 1877. (Alabama voted for Tilden.)

General Wager Swayne stepped to the podium late Wednesday afternoon, June 5, 1867, and made the final motion to adjourn the convention sine die. Thrilled with organizing a party that challenged corrupt Democrats, delegates stood and raised three rousing cheers for the Union and the new Republican Party. (*Montgomery Advertiser*)

As it was, a decade after the organizing convention met in the same room in the state capitol, there was little to celebrate. The future did not look promising for Republicans in Alabama.

CHAPTER TWO

The Democrats' long, cruel reign of white supremacy

Indeed, the acclaimed organization of a biracial political party did not bode well for Republicans in Alabama or the South. The general population quickly discovered that the new party was not capable of leading the state, pointing to their signature Reconstruction experiment. The state fell into an immediate crisis as Republicans struggled with too many demands and expectations for a major governing party. The South lost the war over the issue of slavery, and Congressional Republicans required Southern states to involve ex-slaves in reconstructing state governments. That, alone, earned Alabama Republicans the scorn of the people and the wrath of Democrats eager to reclaim power.

Democrats, contrary to their frontier-style politics, did not always have cooperative relationships. Infighting plagued Democrats from the beginning of Alabama statehood in 1819. The hated Republicans, under the protection of the Union Army with former slaves taking a prominent role in state matters, unified Democrats. Democrats created identity issues for Republicans by claiming that they wanted to achieve black-and-white racial equality by law. Republicans did legislate political opportunities for ex-slaves, but they stopped short of calling for social equality. The Democrat solution was to organize a stronger opposition party.

Convening at the state capitol in Montgomery on July 29–30, 1874, the Democratic and Conservative Convention knew that Republicans were vulnerable, as they plotted to take back control of the state government from the "radicals." Democrats set a determined course to "redeem" Alabama from the biracial government. Meeting in the House chambers in the capitol, Democrats adopted a powerful message that the majority of the state population understood—*white supremacy*. Democrat newspapers reporting from the floor of the convention delivered a message that damned the very existence of Republicans.

Convention Chairman James L. Pugh (Barbour), a member of the old Confederate Congress and former US Senator, made the intent of Democrats very clear. Pugh said that the convention would be a "splendid exhibition of the brainpower of the Caucasian Democrats of Alabama." In his remarks, Pugh further claimed that white people had a higher capacity for intelligence and were more honest than blacks. (*Montgomery Advertiser*)

Less than a month later, August 20–22, 1874, a weakened Republican Party staged a three-day convention in the new Bullock County courthouse in Union Springs, a bit over thirty-seven miles due east of Montgomery. It would be the longest and largest state Republican convention until the 1960s. Even as they met, Republicans were counting their losses. And for a good reason. The convention was a mirror of the David Lewis administration: ineffective under pressure, weak on human rights, and lacking cohesive leadership within the party.

Even worse, it was an uproarious convention. Delegates

wasted the first day arguing over credentials and seating. Then there was the infamous Richard Busteed whose bluster and threats created unnecessary dissension. Too many lengthy resolutions consumed time, as did the debate over Charles Sumner's Civil Rights Bill under consideration by Congress. Democrat newspapers reported all of it and telegraphed articles throughout the state. The convention was really messy from the start and made the GOP leadership seem confused and disorganized.

Democrats were confident that they could overwhelm Republicans on their well-practiced issue of race, and they launched a vicious crusade to return Alabama's white civilization to sovereign rule. Alabama Democrats followed this strategy for the next hundred years. (Allen Going, *Bourbon Democracy in Alabama, 1874–1890*)

The scorched earth racial strategy and the manifest shortcomings of Republicans enabled Democrats to deliver the fatal blow to the upstart Republican Party. Observers said that the GOP had been compromised by its members, particularly Northern carpetbaggers who plundered the party and exploited the misery of Southern people. Republicans were further weakened when many members became disgusted and returned to the Democratic Party.

Republicans could have built a successful party if white conservatives had collaborated with the ex-slaves the way they did with other political factions. In the end, the first Alabama Republican Party failed because of its members and the liberal racial policies of the new party.

Democrat George S. Houston was elected to consecutive two-year terms, ending Republican rule enforced by the Union Army. An attorney from Lauderdale County in North Alabama, Houston had opposed secession and quietly waited out the war with most of the Hill Country people in the Tennessee Valley. An avowed Unionist, even so, Houston was welcomed by Democrats because of his success as an eight-term congressman in the US House.

Houston campaigned as a conservative in the 1874 gubernatorial election. The Democrats had a simple strategy: appeal to white voters for racial unity while blaming Republicans for the poverty and turmoil of Reconstruction. The strategy worked. Houston defeated Governor David Lewis by a vote of 107,118 to 93,934.

The Klan worked hand in hand with Democrats, night riding and intimidating blacks that suppressed the Republican turnout. The Democratic Party's return to power only sensationalized Alabama's troubles, as Democrats asserted political and economic control over Republicans and the black population. Democrats moved quickly to overturn the Reconstruction Constitution of 1868, which had expanded voting rights for African Americans.

Eager to once again dominate all phases of the state government and courthouse politics throughout Alabama, Democrats grasped racial vengeance not only as government policy but also as a way of life. Decades after the Reconstruction Era, Alabama's rural majority population often focused on race and elected those who shared their political and social ideals.

Republicans endure a century of defeat

The issue of white supremacy essentially broke the Alabama Republican Party and elsewhere in the South. With race as the dominant factor, freedom and equality were not given the opportunity to influence the affairs of state or inspire people. Republicans who ran for public office were not well regarded or were ignored outright. Historical accounts during that period consistently saw Republicans as almost nonexistent.

(The remainder of this chapter reflects the compromised position of Alabama Republicans and the effects that the 1901 Constitution had on Alabama.)

The 1876 election was a critical test for Republicans after the bruising 1874 loss. Rival GOP conventions met at the capitol in May, because the party was unable to agree on a candidate for governor. The press referred to the internal squabble as a matter of "the outs against the ins." In a move to resolve party differences, a conference was arranged in July at Blount Springs, a resort with three large hotels over 127 miles north of Montgomery. Republicans eventually compromised and nominated **Noadiah Woodruff** on the "Independent State Ticket." A planter and cotton merchant in Selma (Dallas), Woodruff had been mayor of Selma for three terms and had business and family ties in Talladega. The party lost big in November with Woodruff as their compromise candidate getting only 34 percent of the vote.

Republicans were a beaten party in 1878 and did not nominate a candidate for governor to oppose Democrat Rufus W. Cobb. However, Republicans endorsed Greenback candidate **James L. Pickens** (Lawrence) in 1880. Pickens only received 24 percent of the vote in Cobb's reelection. It is worth noting that Republicans in the Black Belt consistently lost elections even though they outnumbered Democrats. Democrats taunted Republicans: "You can outvote us, but you can't outcount us." Democrats brazenly threw out thousands of Republican votes in each election to remain in power.

July 4, 1881—was founding day for Tuskegee Normal School for Colored Teachers during Rufus Cobb's second administration.

Booker T. Washington (Republican) was hired as the first president. Tuskegee opened with thirty students in a building described as a "shanty."

By 1882, the only option for the still-weakened Republicans was another endorsement for governor. Greenback Party candidate **James L. Sheffield**, a native of Lawrence County, was active in the Greenback and Independent movement. Sheffield tallied over 31 percent of the vote in Democrat Edward A. O'Neal's first election for governor. A prewar Democrat and a colonel in the Confederate Army, Sheffield represented Marshall County in the Alabama Legislature and helped write the 1861 and 1865 Alabama Constitutions. With Sheffield heading the ticket, the Greenback-Republican coalition elected twenty-two conservatives to the legislature.

Thomas Seay, Hale County Democrat, faced two Republican opponents in consecutive gubernatorial elections. In 1886, **Chester Arthur Bingham** did not pose a serious threat to Seay; Bingham polled 37,118 votes compared to 145,005 for Seay. Bingham, from Pennsylvania, served as state treasurer during the first Republican administration in 1868–1870, and again during the David Lewis administration, 1872–1874. He edited a Republican newspaper in Montgomery, the *Alabama State Advocate*, and won the state printing business during both Republican administrations. Bingham, who helped organize the Alabama Republican Party, chaired the Alabama GOP for fourteen years—1874 to 1888.

Republicans nominated **Whitley Thomas Ewing** for governor in 1888 to oppose Thomas Seay. Ewing polled just over 22 percent of the vote. Ewing was described as a "mild Reconstructionist" who was a delegate to the 1867 constitutional convention. The Republican Party offered a progressive platform that supported education, new election laws, abolishing the infamous convict lease system, and cooperation with the temperance movement. Republicans did not win a single legislative seat in 1886 or 1888. (Allen Going)

After Bingham's failed campaign for governor, Republican leadership passed to the very capable **Dr. Robert A. Moseley Jr.,** Montevallo native. A physician and druggist in the Confederate Army, Moseley switched to the Republican Party in 1872. He founded five newspapers, including *Our Mountain Home* in Talladega, when he was the mayor. Dr. Moseley obtained federal appropriations to purchase land for Tuskegee, Montevallo, and the University of Alabama. He was a delegate to National Republican conventions in 1876, 1880, and 1884. Moseley also chaired the Alabama Republican Party from 1888 to 1896.

The voting trend did not change in 1890 when Democrat Thomas G. Jones defeated Republican **Benjamin McFarland Long** with 76 percent of the vote. A wealthy coal industrialist from Walker County, Long founded the city of Cordova and built a splendid mansion there that still stands today. He had a distinguished war record serving under Robert E. Lee in the Mexican War and as a captain for the Confederacy despite his opposition to secession. He was a member of the 1865 constitutional convention and the Alabama Legislature. Long had been active in Republican politics since the Smith and Lewis administrations. His son, Pope Long, chaired the Alabama Republican Party in 1916.

Reuben Kolb opposed Democrats Thomas Goode Jones (1892) and William Calvin Oates (1894) as the Populist candidate for governor. A courageous and bold speaker, Kolb came close to winning with over 47 percent of the vote against Jones and almost 43 percent against Oates. The Populist-agrarian forces profoundly angered Democrats and jeopardized their control of the state, particularly in the Black Belt. Kolb's relentless success forced Democrats to draft a new exclusionary constitution to defend the party against populism.

Democrats take away the vote of the poor

Democrats struck back with a two-pronged attack against Republicans and the surging Kolb movement. Their chief objectives were eliminating the electoral power of blacks and protecting the political influence of Alabama's property owners against another uprising by poor whites, the equally dangerous Populists.

Thus, the outcome of the 1900 governor's race created the political context that further weakened equality and freedom among common folks. The path to a new constitution came when Democrat William J. Samford, Opelika attorney, beat Republican **John Anthony Steele** in the governor's election with over 71 percent of the vote. A Princeton graduate and circuit judge originally from Tuscumbia, Steele was a member of the Alabama Secession Convention (Lauderdale) and the Alabama House in 1878.

Samford's election prompted calls for a new state constitution now that Democrats were in control of the legislature. Democrats convened a constitutional convention for May in the capitol. On opening day, May 21, 1901, the *Montgomery Advertiser* heralded the event with a page one headline in bold type: "*Constitution Framers Assemble in Alabama's Historic Capitol.*" An impressive photograph of convention Chairman John B. Knox centered the article. The paper reported that the old House chambers, a venue to so many historical events, had been transformed into a "comfortable" meeting place. (The reporter did not describe "comfortable.")

In a dramatic turn of events, Gov. Samford, already suffering from failing health when elected, died unexpectedly June 11 while attending a University of Alabama trustee meeting in Tuscaloosa. State leadership shifted to William Jelks, president of the Senate, who served as governor until the next election. Jelks was the ultimate white supremacist. A newspaper publisher in Eufaula, he penned numerous editorials that suggested relocating Southern blacks elsewhere in the United States and bringing white European immigrants to Alabama.

The gathering of leading Democrats was determined to remove easy access to elections for ex-slaves, which also affected poor whites sympathetic to the Populist movement. John B. Knox, a corporate attorney from Anniston (Calhoun), had solid credentials with Democrats, having served a term as chairman of the state party. Knox was direct and emphatic in his opening address to the convention. He said that a new constitution was necessary for resolving the ongoing "Negro problem." Knox explained that the purpose of the convention was to "establish white supremacy" in Alabama. Knox further offered an explanation if Democrats were charged with racism. He advised delegates that disfranchising blacks due to their intellectual and moral condition, and not their race, were reasons for a new constitution.

The 155 delegates were the political and professional elite of Alabama, including two former governors; ninety-six lawyers, and thirty-eight Confederate veterans. Future governor William W. Brandon (1923–1927) served as reading clerk. The convention remained in session eighty-two days that summer from May 21 to September 3, reshaping state politics and concentrating power in the state legislature. Gov. Samford's sudden passing made it necessary to restore the lieutenant governor's office.

The 1901 Constitution protected "the intelligent and the virtuous vote" of qualified white people. It further established the cumulative poll tax and literacy test—a twenty-page test that mystified illiterate blacks and whites alike. V. O. Key recorded the details of the poll tax in his original research on Southern politics.

The *Advertiser* returned in September on signing day for the new constitution. The reporter described it as a "Love Feast." Signing the parchment alphabetically, many delegates were so moved emotionally after having taken care of the "Negro problem," that they wept, as did ladies in the gallery. Delegates applauded their work and broke out in song. Each member received an ink pen and a stand. Chairman Knox was honored with a "handsome watch."

Promoted in part as an "honest election Constitution," voters ratified the document 108,613-to-81,734, with evidence of extensive election fraud by Democrats to guarantee the final passage. Booker T. Washington brought two lawsuits against the state in an attempt to overturn the racially biased constitution. (Wayne Flynt, "Alabama's Shame," *Alabama Law Review*)

The Democrat constitution did, indeed, suppress the voting rights of the poor. Their political influence fell dramatically by the next statewide election when only 5,000 black Republicans were eligible to vote out of 181,000 registered black males. The 1901 Constitution was absolute dominance of the state's electoral process. It restored Democrat rule by whites, even though less educated and impoverished white males were adversely affected. A useful change in the new constitution extended the official term of office from two to four years.

Roosevelt rides rough over lily-whites

Some Republicans were not immune to spats of racism, either. Prior to the 1902 Republican convention, the Republican executive committee met in Engineers Hall in Birmingham and adopted a resolution (17–10) that betrayed black Republicans by removing them from the party. Ad Wimbs, the "colored" secretary, resigned and left the meeting.

The resolution was introduced by GOP Chairman William Vaughn, Southern "Lily-White" movement activist. To the amusement of Democrats, the press reported the details of the convention meeting in the armory of Birmingham city hall. The Vaughn faction of the Republican Party was deep into lily-white schemes that originated in Texas and spread across the South. Vaughn and his followers were hell-bent on removing blacks from the party. Tickets were required, and armed guards refused entry to black Republicans at the door. Over one thousand people attended the annual Republican convention. (*Birmingham News*)

The lily-whites were in top destructive form. Chairman Vaughn announced that the meeting was the "proudest day of his political life." Charles P. Lane, the editor of the *Huntsville Tribune* and candidate for lieutenant governor, told delegates in his welcoming remarks that he was "happy to greet you as the white man's party." But it was Dallas Smith of Opelika, the future Republican nominee for governor, who made a case for lily-white Republicans. He said for thirty years, "the negro has been a millstone around the party's neck." Another delegate claimed that "there weren't five hundred true Republican negroes registered in Alabama."

Vaughn and Julian Bingham, son of Chester Arthur Bingham,

had gained control of the state executive committee with the intent of kicking black members out of the party. The resolution passed by the GOP executive committee, specified only qualified white voters defined by the Democrats' 1901 Constitution were allowed in the hall.

Apprised beforehand about the radical plot against black Republicans, Booker T. Washington did not attend the convention. Instead, he walked down the street in Tuskegee and discussed the matter with Republican leader Joseph O. Thompson. Washington and Thompson had active political ties to President Theodore Roosevelt. Both men informed the White House and national Republican officials about the growing crisis in the Alabama Republican Party.

The national party acted quickly and decisively. The GOP ordered the readmission of aggrieved blacks back into the party, removed Vaughn from his patronage position as US Attorney, and Bingham as an internal revenue collector for Alabama. That was not all. At the next national Republican convention in Chicago (June 1904), the party refused to seat Alabama's lily-white delegation, forcing Republicans across the South to stop discriminating against black members. (Glenn Feldman, *The Disfranchisement Myth*)

The attempted removal of blacks created yet another celebrated election flop. Ridiculed by the state press as the "Lily-White Party," Democrats routed Republicans in November. *"True to Faith, Democrats of Alabama bury the Lily Whites Under Ballots,"* headlined the *Montgomery Advertiser*. William Vaughn chaired the party from 1896 to 1904.

The first Alabama governor to serve a four-year term of office was William D. Jelks, elected in 1902. Democrats saw the election as a complete vindication of the controversial constitution when Jelks trounced Republican nominee **John A. W. Smith** by a 74 percent margin. Not a "straight" Republican won election to the legislature, and Republicans lost sixteen legislative seats from the previous election. The *Advertiser* editorialized that the election was a "sorry showing" for Lily-White Republicans.

John A. W. Smith had a political pedigree. He was the son of William H. Smith, the first Republican governor of Alabama. Born in Randolph County Rockdale community, young Smith practiced law in Birmingham but was not involved in the politics of his father until he attended the Republican convention that year in Birmingham. He polled a modest 26 percent of the vote. "Rough Rider" Theodore Roosevelt, the Progressive Republican from Oyster Bay, New York, became president after the assassination of William McKinley, September 14, 1901.

The legislature passed Alabama's first comprehensive primary law in October 1903, although primary elections were held the previous year. Written exclusively for Democrats that changed from nominating conventions, primaries were held at the expense of the state but denied state-funded primaries for competing parties that did not poll more than 25 percent of the total vote in the previous general election. That provision blocked Republicans from holding their own primaries funded by the state. Democrat control over state government could be seen in listing the entire roster of Democratic Party Executive Committee officers and members in Alabama's annual statistics published at state expense.

Democrats dropped the word "conservative" from the title of the party for the 1906 election. The name change came at the request of industrialist B. B. Comer, who regarded himself as more progressive than conservatives in North Alabama Hill Country.

Comer, in 1906, won the election with 85 percent of the vote. A wealthy cotton farmer and textile manufacturer from Barbour County, Comer owned 30,000 acres of land in East Alabama. Republican **Asa E. Stratton**, a former Confederate cavalry officer, garnered only 14 percent of the vote. *"Republicans Wiped off Map"* headlined the *Advertiser*. Socialist candidates ran stronger in some counties than Republicans.

Stratton resigned a county judge position in Texas and served in the Texas state Senate. He moved first to Walker County, then to Montgomery as a bankruptcy judge before opening a law practice there. An indication of the numerical strength of the Republican Party was seen in a letter Stratton sent to the national party in 1905. In the letter, Stratton complained about the large number of federal employees on the Republican executive committee. He said that the state party had only thirty-eight members and that twenty-nine of them were postmasters.

The 1906 election saw another major political change for the state. Voters elected two "alternate senators" to replace Alabama's sitting senators in the event of their death. The Seventeenth Amendment required that United States senators be elected by popular vote. Initially, the US Constitution required state legislatures to elect senators. John Tyler Morgan had been an Alabama senator since 1877 and Edmund Winston Pettus since 1897. Both men were from Selma, and both died within weeks of one another in 1907. John H. Bankhead and Joseph E. Johnston, "alternate senators," took their seats in Congress. It was known as the "dead shoes" primary. (Alabama didn't officially ratify the Seventeenth Amendment until 2002.)

Booker T. Washington, the esteemed leader of black Republicans in Alabama, addressed a throng of 3,000 African Americans at "Negro Day at the Alabama Agricultural Fair," in Montgomery prior to the November 1906 elections. Washington urged black communities to organize law-and-order leagues to combat rising crime among blacks. Gov. Jelks, appearing on stage with Washington, said, "negroes needed to respect the law."

Democrats elected Emmet O'Neal governor in 1910. O'Neal was the son of Edward O'Neal, Alabama governor in 1884. Republican **Joseph O. Thompson** ran under the Republican emblem, an American Eagle surrounded by the words: "Publicity, Progress, and Patriotism." Residing in an expansive mansion in Tuskegee, Thompson was a prosperous businessman and owner of a 25,000-acre multipurpose plantation operated by some 1,200 men and their families. It was reported that over 200 miles of fencing were required to enclose the plantation. Johnson chaired the Macon County Republican Party and the Alabama Republican Party from 1904 to 1912. He was also appointed postmaster of Tuskegee. Thompson proposed Republican primaries and supported the rights of blacks. Despite his popular appeal, Thompson received only 20 percent of the vote against O'Neal.

The Rosenwald Schools

Help for African American communities often came from outside of Alabama, providing support for black children deprived of equal education. What is regarded as the most ambitious black education project in Alabama during that period was the Rosenwald Schools, developed by Dr. Booker T. Washington, president of Tuskegee Institute. When Julius

Rosenwald, CEO of Sears and Roebuck, joined the Institute's trustee board in 1912, he helped expand Dr. Washington's rural school program. As early as 1904, Tuskegee started a public school building program through the generous philanthropic funding of Henry Huttleston Rogers of Standard Oil Company. Forty-six schools were built in Macon County before Rogers died in 1909.

Julius Rosenwald donated part of the funding for each building, requiring matching funds from local black communities. The schools were an unprecedented project in the development of black education in the South. Rosenwald Schools meant better buildings, trained teachers, and improved health conditions for black children. Although Booker T. Washington died in 1915, Tuskegee Institute continued the Rosenwald School building program.

By 1932, a quarter of all black schoolchildren in the South (5,357 schools) were taught in Rosenwald Schools. The first eighty Rosenwald Schools were built in Alabama. Between 1913 and 1932, 407 schools, shops, and teachers' homes were built in the state. Both Washington and Rosenwald were Republicans who helped struggling blacks in the hostile environment of the segregated South. (*Alabama Heritage*, Dorothy Walker; spring, 2012. *The Journal of the American Institute of Architects*, "Remembering the Rosenwald Schools," September 2015)

The next decade of Alabama politics was dominated by Democrat business and industry leaders. In 1914, Democrat Charles Henderson beat Republican **John B. Shields** by almost 84 percent of the vote. Shields, who was more Greenback than

Republican, had been probate judge in Walker County. A native of Sevier County, Tennessee, Shields came from an industrialist family that did business with Alabama's first Republican governments. He was an officer in the Confederate cavalry and won a seat in the Alabama Legislature as an Independent.

Anniston industrialist Thomas Kilby was elected governor in 1918 on the strength of an 80 percent victory over Republican businessman **Dallas B. Smith** (Opelika) of "Lily-White" fame. Republicans could muster only 19 percent of the vote for Smith, remembered for saying that black Republicans were a millstone around the party's neck. Smith had been active in the Alabama Republican Party as early as 1870 and understood that the black-and-white factions in the party disagreed more than they agreed.

Kilby was recognized for his progressive leadership: increased spending for education, expanded services for the mentally ill, and funded and staffed enforcement of child labor laws. He attempted to abolish the convict lease system. During the Kilby administration, Alabama followed the trend of Southern Democrats and turned thumbs-down on the Nineteenth Amendment that gave women the right to vote. Having taken voting rights away from blacks and poor whites in 1901, Democrats were not willing to give women the same rights in 1919.

William W. Brandon beat Republican **Oliver D. Street** in the 1922 governor's race. Street, a lawyer from Guntersville in Marshall County, had a distinguished professional career as an author of early American life in Alabama and trustee of the Alabama Department of Archives and History. In 1914, Republicans nominated Street to run for governor, but he declined. He served as US Attorney for the Northern District of Alabama from 1914–1920 during the Woodrow Wilson administration.

The KKK in the National Democratic Party. The 1924 National Democratic Convention held in New York City's Madison Square Garden revealed a party divided by race. Democrats were at odds over prohibition and a Ku Klux Klan plank in the Democrat platform; the Klan was a major voting bloc in the party. Broadcast for the first time over national radio, the convention cast a legendary 103 ballots over sixteen days to nominate John W. Davis of West Virginia for president. Newspapers styled Southern delegates as "turd kickers" and the convention as a "Klanbake." Forney Johnson, son of Alabama Governor Joseph Forney Johnson (1896–1900), openly advocated rejecting the Klan plank. It passed. On the sixty-sixth ballot, some 20,000 Klansmen wearing white hoods and robes met in protest across the Hudson River in New Jersey. Republican Calvin Coolidge of Plymouth Notch, Vermont, was elected as the nation's thirtieth president. Alabama voted Democrat.

Alabama elected Democrat Bibb Graves from Hope Hull, Montgomery County, in 1927, preceding the Great Depression. Republicans nominated **John Arthur Bingham** of Talladega, yet another son of an original GOP organizer, Chester Arthur Bingham. Young Bingham made a less-than-average showing with 18 percent of the vote. Graves had a reputation as the ultimate white supremacist—once serving as Grand Cyclops of the Montgomery Klavern of the KKK. Graves's primary support came from World War I veterans, the Klan, and organized labor. He abolished the convict leasing system, initiated the first state sales tax for education, and a two-cent gas tax for a state road-building program.

Grover C. Hall, the editor of the *Montgomery Advertiser*, won a Pulitzer Prize for his 1928 editorial writing calling for Gov. Graves to end Klan violence. Klansmen were flogging whites and blacks, men and women. The *Advertiser* published the names of fifty-six people in Talladega flogged by the Klan over three years. Hall wrote so glowingly about the Miller administration that Gov. Miller appointed him probate judge of Montgomery County.

Graves appointed his wife, Dixie Bibb Graves, to fill the unexpired term of Senator Hugo Black after FDR appointed Black, who also had Klan ties, to the US Supreme Court in 1937. Senator Graves defended the practice of lynching by staunchly opposing national antilynching legislation in Congress. She made a grandiose statement on the Senate floor opposing lynching legislation: "Do not sear the brows of your sister states with this brand of shame."

Republicans offered no opposition for Benjamin Meek Miller in 1930. First- and second-ballot choices for Democrats were eliminated under Miller in 1934, replaced by the primary runoff system. When unrepentant Klansman Bibb Graves ran for a second term in 1934, Republican **Edmund H. Dryer** polled an unimpressive 12 percent of the vote. Dryer, from Birmingham, authored a booklet: "Origin of Tuskegee Normal and Industrial School" in 1938. Dryer had been a Republican candidate for state Senate in 1926 and lost.

Alabama Republicans elected two members to the House in 1934, from Winston and DeKalb Counties. Percy M. Pitts of Chilton County was elected to the Alabama House in 1938. His wife, Myrtle Reynolds Pitts, was a member of the Republican National Committee from 1945–1956. (*Journals of the Alabama House*)

Frank M. Dixon became governor in 1938 with only nominal Republican opposition. **Dr. William Addington Clardy**, Roanoke (Randolph) dentist, did no better than 12 percent of the vote (16,513). Clardy had active professional careers in dentistry and Republican politics. He served as probate judge of Randolph County. *Alabama* magazine featured Dr. Clardy on the cover of its 1938 Fall issue.

Governor Dixon reorganized the state government that eliminated many duplicate functions similar to the state government today. Dixon was a member of the Christian Americans—an anti-labor, Klan-influenced political organization. Like some Democrat governors, Dixon was conservative; yet, he failed to extend the equality and fairness to minorities.

In the 1942 general election, Chauncey Sparks led the Democrat ticket with an 89 percent romp over Republican **Hugh McEniry**. From Athens in Limestone County, Hugh's father, John Thomas McEniry, served as mayor of Bessemer from 1894 until 1898. Few details are known about Hugh other than he was a graduate of Birmingham-Southern College and was active in Republican politics with his father. During the 1942 election, Frank M. Johnson, Winston County, father of Republican federal judge Frank M. Johnson, won a seat in the Alabama House. Republicans opposed FDR's New Deal strictly as a socialist program.

Spark's term was a calm prelude to the 1946 election of what is known as the most entertaining governor in state history—James E. "Big Jim" Folsom. The Republican nominee was the distinguished educator **Dr. Lyman Ward**, founder of the Southern Industrial Institute in Camp Hill (1898), Tallapoosa County, later, Lyman Ward Military Academy. The school for poor white children had been established on a 400-acre plantation. Dr. Ward also served as the minister of the Camp Hill Universalist Church for over fifty years.

There was a strong semblance between James E. Folsom and

V. O. Key's view of Alabama politics in his 1949 classic, *Southern Politics in State and Nation*. He described Alabama's political-social mind-set this way: "There is wholesale contempt for authority and a spirit of rebellion akin to that of the Populist days to resist the efforts of big farmers and 'big mules' . . . to control the state." Key believed that the people of Alabama retained a frontier independence and the inclination to defend life and liberty.

The Gordon Persons administration introduced the advent of the Alabama Education Television system atop Mount Cheaha, the first state education television network in America. APTV was authorized by the Alabama Legislature in 1953 and began broadcasting in January 1955. Some twenty-five other states eventually developed their own public television system similar to the Alabama station. Persons won the general election in 1950 over token Republican opposition. **Dr. John S. Crowder** won a scant 9 percent of the vote—only 15,127 compared to 154,414 for Persons. From Tuscaloosa, Crowder attended the 1948 national GOP convention. Republicans were overwhelmed in every state office in 1950.

Jim Folsom regained the governor's office with the thoroughly corrupt Democrat primary in 1954, after Phenix City mobsters assassinated Attorney General-nominee Albert Patterson on the night of June 18, 1954. The Patterson murder attracted more attention than usual to the Republican Party. Still, **Tom Abernethy** received only 26 percent of the vote in the general election. Abernethy had an outstanding career as a teacher, journalist, and editor of the Talladega *Mountain Home* and other state newspapers. Abernethy was a Dixiecrat in 1948 and became a Republican after the movement failed. He was elected as a delegate to three national Republican conventions. Abernethy and his wife, Ludie, had few financial resources. They campaigned in a borrowed car and stayed overnight with friends while traveling.

John Malcolm Patterson, the youngest governor of Alabama at thirty-seven, was swept into office by public sentiments over Albert Patterson's murder, gunned down on the mean streets of Phenix City, the infamous crime city on the Chattahoochee River. Voters only gave **William L. Longshore** about 11 percent of the vote against Patterson. Longshore, from Birmingham in Jefferson County, served as US Attorney for the Northern District of Alabama, 1956–'61. He also ran for the US House of Representatives in 1956. Longshore descended from a highly respected Shelby County family active in Republican politics in the early 1900s.

Political observers at the time believed that Patterson could have beaten George Wallace without relying on the racial issue. Nevertheless, Patterson's campaign resembled a nineteenth-century white supremacy election, complete with Klan involvement.

Alabamians, with the specter of Albert Patterson ever present, gave their support to Patterson with a 314,353-vote win over Wallace's 250,451. It was the only race Wallace ever lost in Alabama. Patterson said that his campaign organization, led by successful Birmingham businessman Charlie Meriwether, believed that the candidate who took the strongest opposition on the forced integration of schools would be the people's choice. Either way, Patterson won.

GOP: *civil rights champions*

The present-day quest for racial equality changed dramatically when President Dwight Eisenhower's administration passed the

1957 Civil Rights Act, the first such legislation since 1866. The 1866 law, enacted by the Republican Congress, gave the legal rights and privileges of American citizens to African Americans, but the law had minimal effect in the South. Democrat President Andrew Johnson refused to enforce civil rights laws in Southern states, which resulted in few benefits for blacks in the Old Confederacy.

The 1957 Civil Rights Act had far-reaching effects throughout the nation, more so in the South where blacks had been systematically discriminated against since slavery. (The US Supreme Court struck down a similar Civil Rights Law passed in 1875.) The 1957 Act also neutralized much of the offensive language in Alabama's 1901 Constitution, enacted by Democrats in Governor William J. Samford's brief administration. The act gave women the right to vote and serve on juries, which previously had been the sacred right of white males.

President Eisenhower's position on equality deeply angered Democrats in Alabama. The president believed that the legislation was "moderate and conciliatory" following the 1954 US Supreme Court ruling on school desegregation. Eisenhower explained in a news conference that he was severely disappointed that some people believed the civil rights program was intended to "disturb the rights or social order of a particular section of the country."

Republicans should not have been surprised by Eisenhower's actions. During the campaign, he differed little from Democrat Adlai Stevenson on some issues, and that included civil rights. Eisenhower favored integration, gradually. He brought no conservative credentials to the presidency; in fact, Eisenhower was not a registered Republican or a registered voter. Political writer Russell Kirk summed it up with the comment that the general "was a golfer." He stood with minorities in America the same as he did in the military and vowed not "to turn the clock back—ever." Eisenhower was immensely popular and won the election overwhelmingly, with over 55 percent of the vote. (Winston Du, Vanderbilt)

But Alabamians were highly provoked at the liberal racial policies of the president and congressional Republicans. Lieutenant Governor Guy Hardwick of Dothan said, "The Civil Rights bill will mean federal troops sooner or later in the South." Senator Sam Engelhardt from predominately black Macon County said the bill was comparable to the "Hitler regime," and a "despicable way to pick up Negro votes."

The anger of Alabama Democrats during the civil rights furor only worsened. During the filibuster on the legislation, Southern senators, led by Lyndon Johnson (Texas), claimed that the act was a "legislative lynching bee." Former US Rep. Laurie Battles, addressing a rally in Birmingham, had a religious revelation that Northern Republicans and Northern Democrats were like the Pharisees in the Bible: "They stand on house tops and shout for civil rights while at the same time they're taking away the civil rights of others."

State legislators warned that unless the state was reapportioned, the Black Belt would rule the Alabama senate. Etowah County Senator E. L. Roberts said that "Negroes easily could win seats in the chamber where negroes now are admitted only on errands." Sam Engelhardt introduced legislation to reduce the black voting population of Tuskegee from 420 to a meager ten, setting off a black boycott around Tuskegee's famed Confederate Square business district.

(When John Patterson became governor amid civil unrest

throughout the nation, he made a historic contribution to democracy in Alabama. Under the threat of federal lawsuits, Patterson called a special session in June 1960, to reapportion the Alabama Legislature for the first time since the passage of the controversial 1901 Constitution. Prior to that, some sixteen counties in the Black Belt controlled over 80 percent of the votes in the legislature—a flagrant abuse of the people's right to fair and equal representation.)

Legislators became more aggressive when the senator from Wilcox County introduced a bill resurrecting the highly discriminatory cumulative poll tax. In 1953, voters had placed a two-year limitation on the $1.50 annual poll tax. The bill would have reinstated the tax to accumulate at the same levels prior to the statewide vote. The poll tax was applicable from ages twenty-one to forty-five and could accumulate up to thirty-six dollars, high enough to keep equally poor blacks and whites away from the polls on Election Day.

President Eisenhower and the National Republican Party attempted to convince Southerners that the signature Civil Rights Act did not discriminate against the South. Still, in the South, where varying forms of race dominated political and social life, people believed that they were, again, victims of Northern aggression.

John B. Knox, Chairman, Alabama 1901 Constitution Convention.

(Birmingham Public Library Archives)

CHAPTER THREE

❧❧❧

Beating the big
drum of racism

*The chronology of the Alabama Republican
Party briefly reviews the Wallace influence
on Alabama politics in its entirety.*

By 1962, George C. Wallace had learned a hard lesson about Alabama politics and captivated the attention of voters with his defiance of the federal government (which he referred to as the "central government"), specifically, the forced integration of schools. He is famous for saying that he would not be beaten on the racial issue again—and he wasn't. Republicans may have lacked a sustainable political organization to compete in state elections, but they were quick to recognize the futility of opposing Wallace. In 1962, State Senator **Frank P. Walls**, Tuscaloosa, proved that point. Walls had the distinction of polling the lowest vote total of any Alabama gubernatorial candidate—3.73 percent, or 11,789 votes. Walls was listed as either Independent or Republican. He later ran for Congress on the Alabama Conservative Party ticket. That would indicate that Walls was more Independent than Republican. It was during this period that Wallace had the Confederate battle flag returned to the Alabama capitol.

The larger strategy of Republicans hinged on waiting out Wallace, and they had reason to be encouraged. The Wallace administration would end in 1966, but more importantly, in 1964, Republicans elected four congressmen, the first since Reconstruction. A political whiz named John Grenier, the innovative director of the Alabama Republican Party, instilled optimism and excitement in the party with his exceptional leadership.

To the dismay of Republicans prepping for a serious run for governor, the political community realized that Wallace had no intention of giving up the governor's office without creating absolute turmoil in state politics. The rapacious, power-hungry Wallace, not content as a one-term governor, first attempted to ram through the legislature a succession bill that would allow him to run for a second term. In the viciousness of trying to force change, Wallace fomented hatred among Democrats and left a deeply embittered party in the wake.

Wallace opponents, including John Patterson and Tuscaloosa State Senator Ryan deGraffenried, focused solely on Wallace's dictatorial succession plan, convinced that people had had enough of his antics that were hurting the state. Ultimately, the bill failed in the Senate, but soon after the governor's race, it took a dramatic turn. On February 10, 1966, Ryan deGraffenried's small Cessna plane slammed into Lookout Mountain outside Fort Payne on a campaign flight to Gadsden, killing deGraffenried and the pilot. DeGraffenried was leading in the polls and drawing huge crowds in rallies throughout the state. (More details are found on page 54.)

Wallace immediately devised another scheme to sidestep existing election laws. In a matter of two days, Wallace qualified his

wife, Lurleen, for governor. "She ain't all that sharp," Wallace said
of his wife, "but she can take care of herself." Lurleen Wallace
was given a pass as the proxy and escaped the harsh criticisms of
other candidates. She blew through the Democrat primary with 54
percent of the vote—no runoff. Patterson ran sixth, and Big Jim
Folsom finished dead last. (Georgia elected Lester "Ax Handle"
Maddox governor in 1966.)

Another pivotal event marked the 1966 election. Richmond
Flowers ran a weak second to Mrs. Wallace, yet more than 80 percent of his votes were black, the result of the 1965 Voting Rights
Act. President Lyndon Johnson signed the legislation into law
in August 1965. It banned discriminatory literacy tests and poll
taxes, which were intended to suppress blacks and poor whites
voting in Alabama. For the first time since Reconstruction, blacks
voted in large numbers without intimidation or violence. Some
African Americans in Wilcox County went to the polls in their
Sunday best. The new voting rights law, with specific advantages
for minorities, attracted still more blacks to the Democratic Party.
President Johnson pushed for passage of the Voting Rights Act
for that exact purpose—to create long-term loyalty among African
Americans to Democrats.

Anne Manie

**Outsiders wanting to make a positive social-humanitarian
impact on the plight of blacks in the South tended to focus
primarily on education. This was the case when the United
Presbyterians of North America (UPNA) made a missional
decision in 1894 to build six schools in Wilcox County. The
intent was to provide free education for blacks in Alabama's**

isolated Black Belt. William Henderson, former Union Army officer, sold 600 acres to the UPNA to build Prairie Mission Schools, including the school at Anne Manie. The community was the only place in the county where former slaves could own property.

The school project, initially named the Arlington Literary and Industrial Institute, was comparable with education facilities that the state provided for white students at the time. Large dormitories for male and female students, a two-story central classroom building, cafeteria, principal's residence, and gymnasium were situated amid a grove of oaks. Two black Presbyterian churches were organized in the community, one for the elite black educators, another for common black folks—and a cemetery. (Darrell Prescott, *The Harvard Crimson*, 1970)

Conflict arose when civil rights demonstrations erupted across the Alabama River in Camden, the county seat, and the Klan made night raids on the school to intimidate blacks, firebombing one building. To further discourage black participation in the 1960s protests, Democrat county officials halted ferry service crossing the Alabama River to Camden. It was a one-hour alternate route into town. The school at Anne Manie survived Klan raids but closed in 1969 when county and city schools were integrated. The sewing ladies at Gee's Bend, who organized the Gee's Bend Quilting Bee to earn money for their families, were deprived of a way to cross the river. A modern ferry returned to the river crossing service in 2006. (*Prairie Mission*, Alabama Historical Commission, 2000)

The wife-husband Wallace campaign completely disordered

the 1966 governor's race. The tragedy and their quick claim for control of Alabama shattered the Republican election strategy, especially **James D. Martin's**. Martin, a prominent Gadsden businessman, had designs on running for governor after his election to Congress in 1964.

In 1962, Martin came close to pulling off an upset, racking up 49.1 percent of the vote against incumbent Democrat Senator Lister Hill. Without question, Martin was the most attractive Republican in Alabama. Yet, he was outgunned in the general election against Lurleen Wallace. Martin's race against the Democrat machine crushed what could have been a promising opportunity for Republicans to end the century-old pattern of Democrat domination.

Ignoring the enormous odds, Martin made a noteworthy attempt to represent good government in Alabama, but he polled a disappointing 34 percent of the vote against Mrs. Wallace, who was battling cancer at the time. After Martin's crushing loss, Republicans had to reevaluate their objective of winning Alabama's top office. (Chapter 7 has more details.)

Governor Lurleen Wallace faithfully followed George's agenda in his battles against the federal government, forced integration being the federal government's most hated policy. Gov. Wallace lost her battle with cancer less than two years after taking office, and Lieutenant Governor Albert Brewer, a moderate, completed the remainder of the term.

Wallace intimates said that by the 1970 election cycle, Wallace was more subdued after the death of his wife and did not plan to run for governor, content with Brewer's positive leadership. Jaime Etheredge, mayor of Greenville, said he spoke with Wallace in late 1969, and the governor told him that he was not going to run again. "George had been out of office for the previous two years, and Gov. Brewer had led a reform program that satisfied him." Brewer's performance didn't matter to Wallace insiders who wanted him back in power. They persuaded Wallace to run for another term despite having promised his support to Brewer.

Brewer held his own against the old segregationist, winning the primary by a single percentage point against five Democrat opponents. The Wallace organization attacked Brewer in one of the dirtiest campaigns in state history, viciously smearing Brewer and his family. Wallace won the Democrat runoff 51.56 percent to Brewer's 48.44 percent. The Wallace victory essentially killed any hope for genuine reform in Alabama.

Wallace won a third term in 1974 against Republican Elvin McCary, Anniston real estate salesman and former Democrat state senator for Calhoun County. McCary ignored the better judgment of Republican officials and challenged Wallace. He brushed aside the best advice of the party because of his disgust over the Wallace-for-president political nonsense. Many people may have agreed with McCary, but only 15 percent voted for him.

Wallace won an unprecedented fourth term in 1982. Emory Folmar, the former longtime mayor of Montgomery, made a strong run for the office with almost 40 percent of the vote. The 1982 governor's race was believed to be the first competitive two-party gubernatorial campaign in recent Alabama history. Folmar later served as the chairman of the Alabama Republican Party from 1985 to 1989. Between his two final terms, Wallace ran for president twice and, in 1972, survived an assassination attempt in Maryland. It was believed that Wallace kept the governor's office because state resources were essential to his presidential campaigns.

By 1986, the final year in office for Wallace, the true measure of his self-serving dominance became apparent, because very little had been done to lead the state through the kind of positive change that other Southern states were experiencing, especially industrial development and education reform. Historians say that Alabama remained much the same as it was during Wallace's first term in 1963. Throughout multiple administrations, Wallace and his cronies exercised authority over the legislature and state agencies with few substantial benefits for the people. Wallace ran for Wallace, specifically.

Then too the Wallace administrations helped facilitate growth for the powerful Alabama Education Association's (AEA) forty-year reign that extended control of the state government beyond the Wallace era . . . George Wallace and the legislative influence of AEA that, for decades, kept Republicans from developing into a viable political organization.

Frank M. Johnson, Wallace nemesis

Juxtaposed against loudmouthed George Wallace, the lone Alabamian with the courage and legal power to keep George Wallace in check was **Frank M. Johnson**, Republican federal judge from the old Unionist Hill Country of Winston County. Wallace was the perfect antagonist for Johnson. Only weeks after becoming the federal judge for Alabama's middle district, Judge Johnson began handing down decisions that made him an icon for justice in the Deep South.

Johnson and Wallace had been classmates at the University of Alabama Law School, where Johnson referred to Wallace as "Little George." But Wallace's defiance of federal law, starting with his refusal to turn over voting records to the Civil Rights Commission, forced Johnson to dismiss their old school relationship. Jack Bass's book, *Taming the Storm*, provides deeper insights into Judge Johnson's judicial impact on Alabama and Southern history.

Frank M. Johnson's Hill Country roots had thoroughly prepared him to confront racial discrimination and out-of-control despots like Wallace. Raised on a farm in Haleyville, his father set an example for integrity as a lawyer, probate judge, and at one time, the lone Republican in the Alabama Legislature. In 1955, Eisenhower appointed Frank Johnson at age thirty-seven to the federal court. Johnson favored President Eisenhower's government policies.

Wallace pursued headlines, but Judge Johnson followed the US Constitution for his legal decisions, modestly claiming that he was a "hillbilly conservative." Klansmen hated Frank Johnson equally with Martin Luther King; yet, it was the combination of Johnson and King who brought change to Alabama and the South.

Where Wallace and the Kluxers were belligerent and violent, Johnson reflected the stern character of his Winston County ancestors, frustrating those who resisted progress and change. Judge Johnson dismantled Wallace's "Peace Commission" that the governor pushed through the Alabama Legislature in 1963 to spy on anyone seen as a threat to Alabama's segregated society. The list included civil rights activists, anti-Vietnam War demonstrators, people thought to be communists, and professors at state colleges. The commission operated for twelve years until Judge Johnson ruled it illegal in April 1976. Wallace even had paid spies on King's staff and was kept informed about Martin Luther King's most sensitive operations.

The Peace Commission was directed by Birmingham attorney Edwin Strickland and investigator R. Y. Ball. Strickland reported directly to Wallace and the Alabama Legislature. The commission essentially reported on people with different political views than Wallace and the Democrats. Strickland coauthored a book about Phenix City and the assassination of Albert Patterson that was quickly made into a movie.

Johnson and Wallace had extended careers in a critical era of national importance. Wallace remained on the political stage as the defiant governor of Alabama, and Judge Frank Johnson's rulings were important in forcing social change in Alabama and the South. Comparatively, with the wisdom of time, Judge Johnson had earned the best historical legacy for lasting progress.

George Wallace admitted later that his law school friend Frank Johnson had been right, and he had been wrong. Frank Minis Johnson judged with confidence because he held the high moral ground on civil rights with the support of the US Supreme Court and US Congress. This is why the intemperate Wallace lost many of his battles against progress.

Booker T. Washington, President, Tuskegee Institute

CHAPTER FOUR

John Grenier and the party of loose ends

T_{ime} magazine described twenty-two Young Republican operatives recruited by the Republican National Committee as "The New Breed," serious, button-down, college-educated amateur politicians who would eventually take control of state party organizations in the South from its aging leaders who were content with summer conventions and candidates who consistently lost elections. The recruits were the core operatives for "Operation Dixie" in 1960, a central part of the national Republican organizing strategy to cut into the Democrat stronghold in the South. "The New Breed" lived up to the expectations of national Republicans, and the party reaped huge dividends throughout Southern states. More importantly, the RNC's Southern election strategy helped regenerate Alabama's anemic Republican Party.

The most capable Young Republican in Alabama fitting the profile of new conservatives was John Edward Grenier, a New Orleans transplant who came to Birmingham in 1959 as an attorney with Southern Natural Gas Company. Handsome, urbane, educated, Grenier presented himself as a social elitist with the cultivated tendency during conversations to casually slip into French, expressly for himself. His easy language skills tended to impress people. Raised in a life of privilege by his banker father, Charles Desire Grenier Jr., John Edward came across much too often with ordinary folks as arrogant, an off-putting liability in the world of dirt-road politics.

Yet, the dapper Louisiana Frenchman had a surprisingly competitive edge. Playing sports at Jesuit High School in New Orleans, he lettered in track, football, and baseball. After earning undergraduate and law degrees from Tulane University, he qualified as a pilot in the Marine Corps stationed in South Korea. Captain Grenier flew more than a hundred patrols with the VMF-312, the "Checkerboard Squadron." Returning from military service, Grenier enrolled at New York University in New York City, where he earned an LLM degree in taxation. He practiced law briefly on Wall Street before moving to Birmingham.

More importantly, John Grenier's cool reserve, a natural trait of his patrician upbringing, conveyed self-confidence and the innate will to excel that was important throughout his professional and political career. People may not have favored his *Grand d'Espagne* personality, but they were drawn to his competent approach to the business at hand—legal and political.

Grenier turned to politics when he read, out of curiosity, the 1960 national Democratic Party platform leading up to John F. Kennedy's presidential victory. The Democrat platform was the longest at the time that condemned the Eisenhower administration's success in social, economic, and foreign policy. Repulsed by the unrivaled liberalism, he contacted the rather small Young Republican organization in Birmingham and volunteered. He was not yet thirty. And so, the anger of one man over the fictional criticisms of Democrats became the first step in resurrecting the near dormant GOP.

Grenier and the Young Republicans were immediately useful to the party. State GOP Chairman Claude Vardaman enlisted their help in turning out a crowd for Vice President Richard Nixon's visit later that summer. The party was hosting a major campaign rally in downtown Birmingham. The national GOP nominating convention had been held in the Chicago International Amphitheater in July, and Nixon, unopposed, had selected Henry Cabot Lodge Jr. of Massachusetts as his running mate.

Nixon left a huge rally in Atlanta on Friday, August 26, 1960, for the short flight to Birmingham. Grenier and the energetic Young Republicans escorted the vice president on a brief walking tour of Birmingham city hall as motorcades from across the state converged at Woodrow Wilson Park, to hear Vice President Nixon address the Republican rally covered by the national media. Nixon had reason to court Southerners. On May 6, President Eisenhower signed the Civil Rights Act of 1960 that struck down remaining discriminatory laws in the still-segregated South. The primary roadblock to equality in Alabama had been the old state Constitution. (Reference pages 24–26)

Congressional Republicans had introduced the 1960 Civil Rights Act to correct weaknesses in the 1957 Act, the first such federal legislation in eighty-two years. Senator Lyndon B. Johnson (Texas) and Senate Democrats staged a record-setting filibuster trying to derail the bill. Journalist Robert Novak said that civil rights legislation was mostly a matter of historical necessity: "The Supreme Court's 1954 decision against segregated public schools had unleashed generations of black frustration." Republicans speculated that the black exodus to the North after World War II indicated that the rising black middle class was also interested in civil rights. The GOP would learn that they had badly misread the interests of black America.

Nixon reminded the crowd that no presidential candidate had visited Alabama for the past thirty years. "Democrats need to stop taking Alabama and the South for granted," Nixon told the cheering throng filling the downtown park. Despite two historic civil rights acts, blacks voted overwhelmingly for John F. Kennedy in 1960, evidence that the black vote was not so much about politics as it was about money and federal benefits that reached back to FDR's New Deal. (Republicans later supported the 1965 Voting Rights Act, when Democrats reversed their racial position to attract the African American vote.)

The rally was a rare success for Alabama Republicans, especially for John Grenier and the apostolic twelve-member Young Republican organization. The Nixon visit was a warm-up for the 1960 presidential election. Alabama Democrats would eventually split its electoral votes between Senator Kennedy and an unpledged segregationist slate that supported former Klansman Harry F. Byrd, senator of West Virginia.

Republicans in Alabama were emerging from decades of political isolation—a ghost of a party. The party rented a house in Birmingham for the state headquarters, which enabled Manyon Millican, Republican state organizational director, and a staff of mostly female volunteers to do busywork for the party. Virginia Garrett (Montgomery) helped organize Republican Women's Clubs in Alabama in 1962. The GOP naturally attracted women voters that Democrats ignored. (J. L. Sledge, dissertation, Auburn University, 1989)

Grenier's work did not go unnoticed or unrewarded. The next year, he was elected chairman of Young Republicans in Alabama, an important step forward for Grenier and the party. The position allowed him to introduce himself to county organizations, where he found a lack of interest and an aloofness uncommon in real-world politics.

But there was more. Grenier's official relationship with the RNC "Operation Dixie" put him on salary so he could devote more time rebuilding the party. When he was not traveling, he coordinated Young Republicans out of his corporate office. At every meeting—north, south, east, west—sometimes held in crossroad grocery stores, he installed a new, energetic Republican as a precinct leader. In the year that he chaired Young Republicans, Grenier personally organized sixty-four of Alabama's sixty-seven counties, placing new leadership at the county level.

What he found in random pockets in Alabama were many Post Office Republicans, a throwback term from the era when party loyalists sought patronage appointments during Republican administrations, often as postmasters. County organizations were intentionally small and suspicious of outsiders, Grenier discovered, because too many Republicans preferred exclusivity and lacked the political skills to campaign for public office. Party meetings usually numbered fewer than twenty, and often members were Northern transplants who had been active in Republican politics back home. Worst still, Grenier found that Republicans rejected new people in the party. It wasn't much by a stretch, but his findings established the basis to energize the weak and ineffective Alabama Republican Party.

By the time of the 1962 state Republican convention, Grenier's organizational work for the RNC had laid the groundwork for his election as state chairman. It would be a historic event for Alabama Republicans. Bypassing the stubborn old guard, Grenier had 675 of 866 delegates committed to his election at the June 8 convention, over 200 from Jefferson County alone.

Republicans in Alabama were like a political organization of another era. Claude O. Vardaman, the bookkeeper for Alabama Power in Birmingham, had been chairman since 1942. He was known as a close friend of President Eisenhower. Dr. Joseph C. Swann (Randolph), Wedowee physician and bank president, led the party from 1932 to 1942.

A surge of grassroots enthusiasm had been building throughout the state, making it necessary to change the convention site from the Tutwiler Hotel downtown to the Birmingham Municipal Auditorium to accommodate a record crowd expected to exceed 5,000. The city welcomed the surging Republicans in grand style. The *Birmingham News* publicized the event extensively. A cartoon depicting the symbolic Republican elephant drafting a plan for a two-party system in Alabama made a huge political statement on the editorial page.

Ninety miles south down State Highway 31 in Montgomery, Bob Ingram, the resourceful *Montgomery Advertiser-Journal* political writer, scooped Republicans three days before the convention was gaveled into order. In a page-one story, Ingram announced from the capital city, where politics and race were the two most popular topics of conversation, that John Grenier would be elected chairman of the Alabama Republican Party and James Martin would challenge Lister Hill for the US Senate. The paper further reported that George Wallace was already selecting his cabinet prior to the November general election, confident that the Democrat nominee would be the next governor—a political tradition since 1874.

Ingram further explained the statistical strategy for the Senate race. Grenier noticed that in the May 1 Democrat primary, over 143,000 fewer people cast their ballots in the three-way Senate race—Lister Hill, Donald Hallmark, John Crommelin—than the governor's race. A lack of interest in the Senate race, in the minds of Republicans, indicated some level of arithmetical discontent with the incumbent. The strategy was simple: a well-organized campaign and a big Republican turnout in November, compared to a light voter turnout for the Democrats, would give Martin an outside chance for a possible upset. Martin's race against Hill would be the premier campaign for Republicans. Ingram's crystal ball reporting in the *Advertiser* had Republicans scratching their heads before the auditorium opened its doors.

In a place where square dancers do-si-doed, all-night gospel singings lasted into early Sunday morning, symphony orchestras rhapsodized the elite, and high schoolers held annual proms— Republicans met to conduct party business in a new and exciting fashion. Beauty queen Jane Virtue from Sheffield (that's what the paper reported), riding an elephant draped with a GOP banner, led a parade of exuberant, well-heeled Republicans to the Municipal Auditorium for the morning session.

The first order of business was electing a convention chairman, an honor that went to Young Republican Joe Farley, Birmingham attorney and Grenier's top assistant. Ingram, reporting from the convention, wrote: "Alabama Republicans were as zippy as a new model auto as they convened to choose their warriors against the Democrats." Grenier gave a rousing speech that delegates cheered and applauded even though his election was not contested.

James Douglas Martin's official nomination for the US Senate opposing Lister Hill brought delegates to their feet in a loud floor demonstration. Martin took the podium escorting his wife, Pat Huddleston Martin, from Clanton. Mrs. Martin, a beautiful and talented soprano, had won the Miss Alabama crown in 1955. Martin took the podium and excited the convention with a rousing speech that formally launched his first political campaign.

Speaking extemporaneously in an impressive stentorian voice, his natural communication skills held the rapt attention of convention delegates. Martin was interrupted repeatedly by cheers and standing ovations. He reminded Republicans how the Kennedy administration had run roughshod over the South and was busting the national budget with liberal spending. They heard front-page issues come alive through Martin's speech. Republicans were convinced they had a winner in the Senate race. At forty-four, Martin was one of the new faces of Alabama's reinvigorated Republican Party.

Martin's nomination was the climactic conclusion of weeks of meetings, vacillation, restless nights, intensive discussions, and poring over Grenier's campaign data. A successful oil distributor in Gadsden, the previous year, he joined the Associate Industries of Alabama (AIA) and attended AIA meetings in Birmingham. He was chosen to attend a meeting with a delegation of businessmen who chartered a special train to Washington D.C., to meet with Alabama's nine-member congressional delegation. More importantly, Martin spoke for the group that numbered over a hundred business leaders.

The meeting with the Alabama congressional delegation had been specifically arranged to discuss the concerns of AIA. The differences between business and Congress were stark and specific: Alabama's congressional delegation was voting against the interests

of the business community. Senator Lister Hill, distinguished states-
man that he was, spoke for the delegation. When Martin began quoting specific reasons for their trip to the Capitol, Hill explained that
they were voting with the Kennedy administration, both Democrat
and liberal. Regardless, Martin insisted that the congressional delegation was voting against Alabama business.

There was only one woman in the meeting—Mignon Comer
Smith, the opinionated, outspoken heiress of the Avondale Mills
fortune and lifelong Republican, even though her great-grandfa-
ther, B. B. Comer, was the Democrat governor of Alabama from
1907–1911. Smith kept one foot in Alabama politics while living at the Watergate Towers in Washington. At the conclusion
of the meeting, Smith asked Martin about his party affiliation:
was he Democrat or Republican? Martin explained that he voted
Republican in national elections and Democrat in local elections
because there were no Republican candidates in his county. It was
the same dual voting tendency of many Alabamians, where political involvement was mostly through the Democratic Party. Miss
Smith suggested bluntly, with Lister Hill looking on, that if he
wanted to change things in Alabama, then he should run for the
Senate against Senator Hill.

The suggestion startled Martin, as it did others who overheard
the conversation. He explained to Miss Smith that he had no political plans beyond the meeting. Martin said that with a business
to manage, a growing family, and a modest bank balance, politics
was not a personal ambition. But Smith continued to press Martin
that they were obligated to do more than come to Washington and
make their case—they should run for public office and change
things. Still, Martin declined further comment about running for
public office.

Nevertheless, Mignon Smith's pointed remarks became the initial declaration for the Senate race against a man that Republicans didn't particularly dislike; they wanted conservative representation in Congress. The next day, the *Birmingham News* reported that James Martin would oppose Lister Hill for the Senate. The announcement shocked Martin because he had made no such decision. He learned later that Smith had a journalist relationship with the *News,* and that she had been the source for Bob Ingram's prophetic convention reporting.

Two days later, Mignon Smith and John Grenier arrived at Martin's home in Gadsden to discuss the Senate race. Grenier, who Martin held in high regard, had the numbers from the Democrat primary that showed a 143,000 undervote in the Senate race. They agreed that it revealed a lack of interest in Hill's election, who spent most of his life in Washington. At the end of the meeting, Martin still wasn't convinced that a Republican could attract Democrats to vote for him. It took time, more phone calls, and personal visits with Smith and Grenier before Martin agreed with them. He would run for the Senate against Senator Lister Hill.

In interviews shortly before he died in 2017, Martin said he recognized that the South was going through tremendous change with the Kennedy administration and issues surrounding civil rights. "People were restless and angry." He said that by the time of the 1962 Republican convention, he was emotionally prepared for his first political campaign.

At the nominating convention, Martin thoroughly denounced the Kennedy administration to the cheers of the capacity crowd. When Senator John Tower of Texas rose to speak, delegates were still standing and applauding Martin. Tower was the first elected Republican senator from the South since Reconstruction. (Tower won LBJ's former seat in 1961.) "I have nothing against Harvard," the diminutive Tower explained to delegates. "It's a great institution, especially since the faculty left and came to Washington. But what has been good for Harvard has been horrible for the country." He said that the Kennedy administration "feel themselves messiahs."

The 1962 GOP convention was not without controversy. Tom Abernethy (Talladega), chairman of the Resolutions Committee, caused a minor revolt when he reported that the party would not nominate candidates for governor or lieutenant governor. Julian Elgin jumped to his feet in protest. Elgin, a large-scale farmer and cattleman from Montgomery, had designs on running for governor against Wallace. He was outraged.

Elgin's outburst changed the tone of the convention. Still, the resolution illustrated the party's predisposition of avoiding a confrontation with Wallace. The Republican brain trust knew Republicans could not win a fight with Democrats. Elgin was vehement in his protest over the resolution. "It's the most asinine action I have ever heard of. If we are going to sit back and let the big mules in Birmingham—who control the Democrats' candidates—to also control this party, then we are just fools." Grenier's convention strategy was in jeopardy of being second-guessed by Elgin, and many delegates clamored for candidates to oppose Wallace and Jim Allen of Gadsden, the Democrat nominee for lieutenant governor.

A foolhardy mind-set gripped some delegates, who stubbornly refused to change the tendency to oppose Democrats in major elections. Grenier and Mignon Smith had Jim Martin positioned as the top-tiered candidate for Senate and believed that staging uncompetitive races would weaken Martin's campaign against Senator Hill.

Convention Chair Joe Farley called for a voice vote to approve the resolution and end the controversy. When he ruled that it had passed, Elgin and his supporters protested loudly and demanded a roll call vote. The vote confirmed Farley's ruling—462 for the resolution and 243 against. The vote was John Grenier's first victory as chairman. Republicans would not field a candidate against Wallace and Allen, whose elections were well-nigh certain.

Republicans were playing an unfamiliar game, but they had the wisdom to avoid Wallace, who had a considerable following in Alabama and across the South because of his fiery defiance of the federal government and opposition to integration. Wallace measured success by media attention when he challenged the government, calling the Washington crowd "liberal pinkos." It was the elixir that the little governor craved. The Wallace factor, even in the Republican Party, was illustrated anecdotally when one delegate boldly announced, to a loud chorus of boos, that he intended to vote for Wallace in November.

Extreme opposition to racial change was seen statewide when Birmingham police chief and Democratic Party National Committeeman Eugene "Bull" Conner turned water hoses and police dogs on black marchers only blocks from the auditorium. Wallace's racial strutting and Bull Conner's fire-hose diplomacy against peaceful demonstrators would easily overwhelm Republican candidates. Grenier believed that Republicans would fare better campaigning against a Washington politician rather than Alabama's firebrand governor.

Charles Wilson (Tuscaloosa) exhorted delegates to remain

committed to the strategy of supporting Martin for Senate: "We must accept the leadership and affirm what we did this morning when we elected John Grenier." In a conciliatory gesture to Elgin, Republicans staged a floor demonstration and offered him the nomination for commissioner of agriculture. Elgin didn't want the nomination, but he reluctantly accepted the opportunity to oppose A. W. Todd, winner in the Democrat May primary. Todd's victory was as sure as Wallace's election.

The historic effort to resurrect the Alabama Republican Party concluded with the nominations of a scattering of Senate and House candidates for the fall general election, mostly from Mobile, Jefferson, and Montgomery Counties. Grenier said that twenty Republicans would run for the Alabama House and four for the Senate. Guy Hunt, from Holly Pond, was nominated to run for the state Senate in Blount, Cullman, and Winston Counties. One House candidate was identified as a member of the ultraright, anticommunist John Birch Society (JBS), an indication that the right-wing Birchers had infiltrated the party.

At the banquet that night, US Representative Donald C. Bruce from Indiana gave the keynote address for the final event of the convention. Rep. Bruce poured steam on the convention by challenging fellow Republicans to make Jim Martin the first senator from Alabama in a hundred years and force the nation to look favorably on the South. National Democrats generally assumed the traditional support of the South and tended to accommodate Southern attitudes, while national Republicans had the habit of writing off Southern states as solid Democrat. The two strategies were well reasoned.

The convention was more than Grenier and his coterie of Young Republicans, "The New Breed," had imagined. In the shake-up following John Grenier's election, only ten former executive committee members remained in the party. Voted out were a few members on the committee who had supported Grenier for chairman.

CHAPTER FIVE

Jim Martin discovers the key to conservative success

John Grenier took a firm hand in party leadership, and Alabama Republicans set a more enterprising course against their archenemies, the Democrats. The next election cycle loomed two years away in 1964, and the young, energetic chairman set about recruiting Republican candidates for as many county and state offices as possible.

But first things first. Republicans took a major step by nominating a formidable candidate in James D. Martin to challenge Listen Hill. Conceding the top offices to the Democrats, Republicans invested their modest resources in the first viable candidate capable of doing what John Tower did in Texas—send a Republican senator to Congress.

Martin was a genuine American success story: humble roots, World War II veteran, and a self-made millionaire in an oil distribution business. Republicans had, from time-to-time, nominated candidates with exceptional public records, but Martin compared with the best the party had to offer since Reconstruction and fit Grenier's profile of a conservative businessman.

Born September 1, 1918, in the Boils community near Tarrant

in Jefferson County, the eldest son of a schoolteacher mother and a railroad-engineer father, he was raised in a home without electricity or running water and attended schools lacking even modest conveniences. Preparing for a law career when World War II broke out in 1941, Martin volunteered for the US Army, eventually earning a second lieutenant commission as a "Ninety-Day Wonder." He rose to the rank of captain, commanding an artillery battery in the Third Army under General George Patton, and fought Hitler's army across Europe with the renowned American general.

Captain James D. Martin was one of the first Americans to discover the greatest hidden horror of the Third Reich: Nazi concentration camps. At Ohrdruf, Martin opened the gates to the ghastly scene of dying men and women—starvation, disease, gas chambers, and crematory ovens. Notifying the chain of command, Martin eventually led inspection tours of the camp with Generals Dwight Eisenhower, George Patton, and Omar Bradley. Discoveries of Nazi concentration camps had a powerful impact on Allied forces and world opinion. Martin said he would remember the gruesome scene with anger for the rest of his life.

Contrasting Martin's rugged life story, Lister Hill was the heir to an upper-class lifestyle in Montgomery, the son of distinguished surgeon Dr. Luther Leonidas Hill. Born in 1894, Joseph Lister Hill had the advantage of a law degree from the University of Alabama and law degrees from the University of Michigan and Columbia University. Lister Hill had academically prepared himself for a career in politics.

Elected to the US House of Representatives in 1923, he became an Alabama senator in 1938, following Dixie Graves's resignation. He stood for election in 1938, 1944, 1950, and 1956 and qualified for a fourth term in 1962, nearing the age of sixty-eight.

A moderate Democrat, Hill had a laudable political career and is best known for the Hill-Burton Act that provided health care for rural Americans. He was an icon to the national health-care profession, and he was seen as a major force in national politics.

Hill was as much a national figure as an Alabama senator. This would be Hill's final campaign—extremely demanding for the aging senator more comfortable in the environs of Washington than a long summer campaigning in Alabama. Jim Martin and the Republicans knew that and would exploit the disconnect.

John Grenier activated the GOP election strategy immediately in counties where he had installed new leadership. The party had four months to convince a majority of Democrats to make a daring choice and vote for a Republican.

James Martin got busy building a campaign organization as John Grenier, now operating out of Republican headquarters in Birmingham, guided the election strategy. In the meantime, Martin bought a new red Ford station wagon and had a big gray loudspeaker mounted on top. In preparation to be away from his home and business, Martin hired a manager for the thriving oil dealership that he had built from scratch. It was a costly but necessary arrangement that protected his family and business.

Then he hit state highways and farm-to-market roads full time with a driver and "*Martin for Senate*" signs on both sides of the station wagon. Often, the red Ford station wagon was filled with volunteers. It was a rudimentary-style campaign, at best, but Martin and Republicans could not afford headline country bands or gospel singers as could Democrat candidates.

His first campaign tour across North Alabama was met with a collective shrug. The Hill people, Unionists who rejected secession and voted conservative, showed little interest in Martin. He was unable to draw sizable crowds, even in the larger cities like Huntsville, Decatur, and the tri-cities of Florence, Tuscumbia, and Sheffield. The press shrugged as well. Jim Martin began second-guessing his decision to run for public office and thought that he had made a mistake by agreeing to oppose the legendary Lister Hill.

But Martin's success changed once he turned toward south Alabama. He was more encouraged with each campaign stop in central and south Alabama. People were more accepting of a Republican candidate, and the crowds were larger. Initially, Martin was surprised by the pyramiding effect of his campaign appearances. A speech, always extemporaneous filled with current political facts, generated more invitations to other towns and civic and social organizations. It was an aftereffect that kept the campaign continually moving to even larger, more receptive audiences. Those who heard Martin speak were quick to tell others about his dynamic speaking style.

Things began to fall into place for Republicans after that. In Thomasville, White Smith underwrote the cost of badly needed television exposure in the Birmingham market. In the studio, Martin set a chair with Lister Hill's name taped to it and talked for thirty minutes, casting occasional glances to the vacant chair. The TV speech generated more invitations and donations that kept the campaign moving. Martin stopped the Ford station wagon at every radio station along the way, and he walked in unannounced and did an interview, adding his itinerary at the end of the program.

The one-vehicle caravan was not alone. Working from state headquarters, John Grenier phoned precinct leaders to raise money for billboards and remained in contact with other Republican campaigns. Martin may have been the headliner, but other Republican candidates were also campaigning at a record pace. Three congressional candidates worked their respective districts—John Buchanan in Birmingham, Tom Abernethy in Talladega, and Evan Foreman down in Mobile. Kay Thomas opposed Agnes Baggett for the secretary of state.

With television as the new communication medium, Martin adapted to the mostly unrefined fundamentals of live broadcasts. It was easy getting TV news coverage. At the time, stations lacked the staff and news-gathering sophistication. Jim Tom Norman in Pike County, sawmill and restaurant owner, contacted the Montgomery television station and arranged for thirty minutes of prime-time exposure. At the TV station, Martin watched Norman count out sixty-eight hundred-dollar bills for the telecast.

By September, once-confident Democrats were taking a more serious look at Martin and Republican candidates. They were both threatened and angry. During a Democrat rally in Montgomery, with most of the congressional delegation on stage, Hill made exaggerated statements to the cheers and applause of fellow Democrats. He bashed and berated Republicans as "a bunch of scoundrels," saying that if Martin were elected, he would have to "find a window to crawl through when he got to Washington." Martin refused to respond to Hill's fits of extreme name-calling.

The Democrat congressional delegation was occupied with their own election concerns, however, forced to campaign state-wide under the "9–8" plan to eliminate the congressman with the lowest vote total. The plan was developed by Gov. John Patterson to comply with court-mandated reapportionment following the 1960 US Census. The hard-charging Martin and the "9–8" plan brought Democrats together to champion Hill and the Democratic Party.

Democrats were essentially campaigning as an extended political team, attempting to overwhelm Martin by the sheer number of elected officials, raising their voices and shaking their fists at Republicans who dared to challenge their political sovereignty.

Jim Allen, a Democrat nominee for lieutenant governor, and Congressman Albert Rains, both from Gadsden, double-teamed Martin in his own hometown. Union workers at the huge steel and tire facilities added the influence of organized labor—unions that were equally antagonistic toward Republicans. Martin said it was discouraging campaigning in Gadsden.

But the issue that overshadowed the 1962 campaign developed over in Oxford, Mississippi, where James Meredith was admitted to the once-segregated university. President Kennedy created a major controversy in the South when he ordered troops to control race riots. In taking that dramatic step to preserve peace, President Kennedy and his brother, Bobby, gave Republicans and Democrats a common issue—federal intervention.

The Martin-Hill campaign turned into a back-and-forth routine on civil rights at that point. Martin slammed the Kennedys for sending troops to Mississippi, while Hill and the Democrats protested that they had consistently opposed civil rights legislation, pointing out that President Eisenhower sent federal troops to help integrate Central High School in Little Rock, Arkansas. By one degree or another, Democrats and Republicans in much the same way railed about the Oxford controversy, aware that Democrats were getting the worst of a thorough media thrashing. The rage against the intrusion of the federal government into local affairs, which began earlier in Alabama as the result of the riotous Freedom Rides in Birmingham and Montgomery, became major issues at the approach of the November general elections.

By comparison, there were stark differences between Martin and Hill on integration. Hill had signed "The Southern Manifesto" in 1954 that condemned the Supreme Court decision in *Brown vs. Board of Education* and ordered school desegregation (nineteen Southern Democrat senators signed the anti-integration document). On the other hand, Martin avoided typical Southern racial reactions and saw the issue as a matter of state's rights. Quoted in the *Southern Courier* (Montgomery), Martin said that he would not discourage black children from entering white schools, and he opposed closing white schools to avoid integration. It was a principled alternative to the endless racial attacks by segregation-obsessed Democrats.

Jim Martin looked beyond Alabama and the South as the origin of the national debate on the school issue changed the tone of the Senate campaign. Walter Dean Burnham, a political science professor at the University of Texas, described Martin's campaign as radically different from other elections in the South. He said that Martin became the "pacesetter" for subsequent Southern elections in that his campaign was waged over national issues, stressing local control, individual freedom, and criticism of big government that shifted emphasis from desegregation to state's rights.

A political sideshow unfolded at the Wallace headquarters when the *Montgomery Advertiser* published a story about a controversial research paper that suggested racial differences between blacks and whites, complete with a photo of Dr. Wesley Critz George and George Wallace. The paper was an eighty-seven-page opinion about the "inferiority of negroes." George's work originated in 1959 with Gov. John Patterson, who paid George $3,000 for much the same opinion. Patterson published, at state expense, 5,000 copies of the book that asserted the moral and intellectual inferiority of blacks and their "tendency to criminality." Patterson intended to use the controversial genetic research in court litigation. The book was never used by Patterson or seen publicly, for that matter.

During the hectic final week of the general election, Martin and his Republican counterparts were storming across the state, making last-minute appeals to voters. Jim and Pat Martin were the guests of a $5-a-plate dinner at Morrison's Cafeteria in Mobile that drew a crowd of 400. Pat Martin entertained the gathering with several songs. Mobile and Baldwin County developed into Republican strongholds in the general election, turning out crowds and hosting successful functions for the Martins.

The press and pundits, however, did not give Martin much of a chance of winning the Senate seat. Bob Ingram, *Montgomery Advertiser* political writer, polled newspapers around the state and heard much the same opinions: Jim Martin and the Republicans were energizing their base down to the precinct level, but they would not win. Barrett Shelton, the publisher of the *Decatur Daily*, said Martin would not receive more than the Republican usual 35 percent of the vote. Yet, all acknowledged that Republicans had been more aggressive than in past elections. George Wallace joined Hill late in the campaign to guard against a last-minute collapse and the possibility of the aging senator losing the election.

On election night, Democrats were astounded when national broadcast news reported what was happening in Alabama. Jim Martin led in the early returns but soon fell behind Senator Hill, but only slightly. In the end, Martin would poll 49.1 percent of the total vote—a near upset of stunning proportions. Hill took the populous counties in the Tennessee Valley, except Walker and Winston, including Martin's home county, Etowah. He won the "Yellow Dog" Democrat and black vote. African Americans were already voting in increasing numbers in large cities like Montgomery, Mobile, and Birmingham, portending a major demographic shift within the Democratic Party.

Martin was stronger in central and southern counties, winning thirty of the sixty-seven counties. Republicans battered the one-party system in South Alabama for the first time since Reconstruction, polling more votes than Hill in twenty Black Belt and Wire Grass Counties, where Democrat control was absolute. Remarkably, Martin won Barbour, George Wallace's home county.

It wasn't easy assessing Jim Martin's success in a state dominated by Democrats, because the Democrats and the press had badly misread the election. But it was not a mystery to Jim Martin, John Grenier, or Mignon Comer Smith and Republicans who listened to the concerns and anger of the people. Martin did not run against Lister Hill. He ran against the New Frontier, and in doing so, became one of the most admired and prominent political figures in Alabama and the South. He had come a long way from the Boils community in Jefferson County and brought the Alabama Republican Party with him. Thought to be little more than another also-ran Republican candidate, Martin came close to defeating one of Alabama's most revered political personalities. (LBJ personally sought out Martin in a Washington meeting and asked him how he almost defeated Hill.)

Bob Ingram in the *Montgomery Advertiser* summed up Martin's achievement this way: "It was Martin and the exuberant Republicans of 1962, who contributed most to the political revolution which brought about a two-party system in this state."

That did not hold true for Republican congressional candidates— all three lost.

Random GOP success

John Andrew Posey from the Free State of Winston was first elected to the House in 1922, reelected in 1930 and 1934. R. L. Tolbert from DeKalb County was elected in 1934, but Democrats challenged the election. Percy McGraw Pitts from Chilton County was elected to the House in 1926 and reelected in 1930. In 1962, Republicans Tandy Little, Montgomery businessman, and Donald Lamar Collins from Jefferson County served in the legislature. They were joined in 1964 by Alfred Goldthwaite, descendent of a prominent Montgomery political family. Goldthwaite became the first elected Democrat office holder in the modern era to switch to the Republican Party. (*Journals of the Alabama House*)

Bert Nettles, Mobile County, won a special election in 1969 and served until 1974. Doug Hale, the Huntsville engineer, joined Nettles in 1970. Progressive minded with a reputation for integrity, Nettles advocated bringing African Americans into the party. He said forming a coalition with African Americans would help the GOP win elections. Nettles won two legislative elections in the Mobile area with heavy black support. He further said that having blacks in the party was "healthy" because they could speak to their "sphere of influence."

CHAPTER SIX

High drama at Cow Palace

On the heels of Jim Martin's startling campaign against Senator Lister Hill, Republicans were anticipating greater success in the 1964 election cycle. Vastly encouraged by John Grenier's leadership, Republicans launched an extensive recruiting campaign for candidates that reflected the GOP emerging youth movement.

George Deyo, the descendant of one of Anniston's founding families and chairman of Calhoun County Republicans, worked closely with Grenier to identify candidates throughout the east Alabama congressional district. "The chairman had over 250 candidates ready by the next election," Deyo explained. That included Deyo, who ran for the Senate in Calhoun County. "People looked at us like we were communists when we introduced ourselves and told them we were Republicans." Candidates ran rudimentary self-financed campaigns against entrenched Democrats, facing preexisting resentment from voters and severe criticism from Democrats.

That was much the same reaction Republicans got in towns and communities throughout Alabama, except for Winston and Walker Counties. Statewide, the ruling Democratic Party had so imprinted itself on the population with their white supremacist style of government that Republicans represented a political ideology that people found perplexing. The language of Republicans was about business and education and not race. People in the South had been told never to vote Republican, a transgenerational proverb from the long-remembered Reconstruction era and Hoover days. For that reason alone, most Southerners would not have voted Republican if there had been a ballot box on their front porch.

The 1964 Alabama GOP convention was held in Montgomery with registration and committee meetings at the Whitley Hotel downtown. The plenary executive committee session convened in the sprawling Garrett Coliseum. Delegates were excited. Barry Goldwater was the keynote speaker.

Nationally, the Goldwater candidacy was rejected by many mainstream Christian denominations. The *Christian Century*, the leading national Christian news agency at the time, published a continuous stream of editorials and articles critical of Goldwater and the Republican Party. Extremism, "a doctrinaire not based on practical politics," was cited as the central reason for supporting Lyndon Johnson and the Democratic Party.

Alabama's constitutional offices were not up for election in 1964, and Republicans focused on challenging the eight congressional seats. John Grenier and Jim Martin were encouraged to run for Congress. Grenier declined, citing his duties as party chairman, and simultaneously serving as the Goldwater coordinator for eleven Southern states. Dr. Tom Brigham (Birmingham) assumed the role of acting GOP chairman assisting Grenier in managing multiple party functions during the hectic election year. Martin, fresh off the near-miraculous Senate race in 1962, readily accepted the nomination to run for Congress.

Nominated with Martin for Congress was a combination of political veterans and novices: John Buchanan of Birmingham, William Dickinson of Montgomery, Jack Edwards of Mobile, Glenn Andrews of Anniston, Bob French of Tuscaloosa, Charles O. Smith of Russellville, and Marvin Prude of Ensley. Martin, Buchanan, Andrews, and Edwards had previous political experience and firsthand knowledge about running a broad-based campaign. As it happened, Goldwater canceled his speaking commitment to the Alabama convention, and Senator John Tower of Texas, keynoter at the 1962 convention, subbed for Goldwater.

Alabama Republicans plotted their next moves as Gov. George Wallace was deep into his first run for president as an Independent. Wallace had national ambitions that created problems for the state. Turmoil arose within his own party because Wallace was ignoring the "little people," who he insisted were just as "cultured" as anyone in the nation.

National politics had a role in Alabama when Jim Martin agreed to do George Wallace a personal favor as Republicans gathered for the national convention on July 13–16 in San Francisco. One sunny day as Martin worked in the yard, his wife, Pat, called out to him that Gov. Wallace was on the phone and wanted to speak with him. Wallace wouldn't say what he wanted on the phone, only that he had dispatched an airplane to the Gadsden airport to pick up Martin. Martin told Pat goodbye without totally understanding what Wallace wanted or changing out of his work clothes. He drove immediately to the Gadsden airport arriving almost simultaneously when the state plane landed on the small airstrip.

At the Montgomery airport, a state trooper escort sped Martin to the Jefferson Davis Hotel down the street from the state capitol.

He was led to a room on the third floor where Wallace and confidants Seymore Trammel and Bill Jones waited. Wallace explained, with little discussion, that he had a mission for Martin. He wanted him to fly to San Francisco and personally inform Barry Goldwater that he wasn't going to launch a third-party campaign for president, but he would be willing to run as Goldwater's vice presidential nominee.

Martin attempted to talk his way out of the spontaneous trip to the San Francisco convention, but Wallace would have none of it and insisted that there was little time for other arrangements. Trammel handed Martin an airline ticket. When Martin insisted that he was not prepared to travel, Trammel opened a bag stuffed with money, counted out a thousand dollars in hundred-dollar bills and handed it to Martin. With the travel essentials taken care of, state troopers drove Martin to Dannelly Field, where he caught his flight west. Only then did he have time to phone his wife Pat back home and explain Wallace's diplomatic mission.

After Martin left for San Francisco, Jones told the governor that the money was wasted. Wallace exploded: "Well, goddammit, it ain't the first thousand we've pissed away, and it won't be the last."

Jim Martin caught up with Goldwater in the crowded lobby of the stately Mark Hopkins Hotel on Nob Hill, but Goldwater was reluctant to talk openly and suggested that they go up to the hotel roof for privacy. On hearing the Wallace proposal to run as his vice presidential nominee and the willingness to switch parties, Goldwater told Martin that he couldn't make that kind of agreement because he did not have the official nomination. The entire incident illustrated how Wallace forcefully pursued a more prominent role in national politics.

On the return trip back to Alabama that afternoon, Martin heard a radio report on the plane that Wallace had just announced on *Meet the Press* that he wasn't going to run for president. Back in Gadsden, Martin phoned Wallace and gave him Goldwater's short answer about being his running mate. Wallace thanked him for making the trip. Martin's reward was a new suit that he bought at a men's shop near the hotel but didn't have time for the tailor to alter the pants. He had the store clerk pin the pant legs so he could wear the suit to meet Goldwater.

The table was set for Senator Barry Goldwater to lead the Republican Party. The convention at the Cow Palace was raucous and divisive for traditional conservatives. Goldwater's *The Conscience of a Conservative* portrayed him as militant-minded and prone to say exactly what he thought. Strongly independent, Goldwater's nomination created a bitter clash between conservatives and moderates with the Civil Rights Act of 1964 as a hot topic. The KKK and John Birch Society endorsed Goldwater.

The 1964 convention had a lasting effect on the Republican Party. The hard-line policy positions of Goldwater would determine conservative standards for two Republican presidential campaigns: Richard Nixon in 1969 and Ronald Reagan in 1980. It was called the "revolution from the right," where Goldwater essentially realigned the Republican traditional Eastern base led by Nelson Rockefeller of New York.

Dr. Tom Brigham chaired Alabama's thirty-nine-member convention delegation to the 1964 GOP convention and cast the first twenty votes for Goldwater. The Goldwater conservative movement deeply divided national Republicans, but in Alabama, party loyalists like Jim Martin and John Grenier maintained control of

Republicans. The *Montgomery Advertiser* and the *Birmingham News*, the two largest newspapers in Alabama, endorsed Goldwater.

In Richard Morris's memoir of Reagan, **Dutch**, Morris wrote that the National Republican Party persuaded Reagan, who had switched parties in 1962, to record a television address and help shore up Goldwater's controversial campaign. The speech that Reagan gave, "A Time of Choosing," launched Reagan's political career more than it rescued Goldwater's. Reagan talked about mainstream American values that generated money for the party, and Republicans realized that they had a viable future candidate in the very popular Reagan.

In the end, Goldwater carried only six states: his home state of Arizona, plus a vast swath across the Old South—Louisiana, Mississippi, Alabama, Georgia, and South Carolina. Avoiding the racial language trap common to Democrats, Goldwater campaigned on "state's rights," a message understood by Southerners, Republicans and Democrats. Goldwater had opposed the Civil Rights Act of 1964, LBJ's signature legislation, which laid claim to the black vote in the South, aided by the Selma-to-Montgomery march. Goldwater called Johnson a "phony" and a "faker" for switching positions on Civil Rights expressly for black voters. Goldwater's opposition was based on the intrusion of the federal government in state affairs, and that the act interfered with the rights of citizens to do business with whomever they chose.

Earl and Merle Black (twin brothers) in their book, **The Rise of Southern Republicans**, attributed Republican success in 1964 to race, not conservatism. The Black brothers further defined Republican victories in the South as shifts in white voting trends. Southern voters were more accepting of the Goldwater message that the rest of the nation found objectionable.

The Goldwater sweep resulted in electing five of eight members of the Alabama delegation: James Martin, John Buchanan, Glenn Andrews, William Dickinson, and Jack Edwards. To a man, the five Republicans campaigned on the Goldwater theme of state's rights. Even more remarkable for a Deep South state, the Democrats, avowed segregationists, supported the Southern Manifesto call for massive resistance to integration. Martin and Andrews, both businessmen, served one term in Congress. Edwards served until 1984, and Dickenson served until 1993. Both were lawyers. Buchanan, a Baptist minister in Birmingham, served until 1980. He was the finance director for the Alabama Republican Party in 1964.

When President Lyndon Johnson championed the Civil Rights Act of 1964, he was stealing a page from the Republican playbook. Stigmatized by history as the party of American slavery that legislated segregation and opposed civil rights, Democrats changed their stripes and sponsored civil rights legislation in 1964 and 1965. Republicans voted for both laws by a higher percentage than Democrats. Democrats and the liberal media labeled Republicans as racist and made false accusations that the Rs and the Ds had switched sides.

George Wallace was blamed for the GOP victory in Alabama. Bob Ingram wrote in the *Montgomery Advertiser* that Wallace had "gutted the Democrat Party." Ingram said that Republicans won in Alabama because Democrats had only Wallace to "anchor" their party. Wallace did not respond. He had lost his populist appeal to Goldwater's conservatism.

Whatever influence that galvanized the unusual election change, ramping up the Alabama Republican Party was part of a changing demographic pattern in the South. Professors Byron

Shafer and Richard Johnston explained a more comprehensive view of the evolving political parties in their book, *The End of Southern Exceptionalism*. "Economic development came to the American South in the years following World War II, in a manner that it had not experienced since well before the Civil War," their research showed. "Economic development proved to be directly associated with partisan change, most especially by way of the prospects, at long last, for a Southern Republican Party."

The Goldwater ideology indicated that conservatism had significant appeal in the South that created a proven path for the GOP to win elections without getting mired in racial battles with Democrats. During the 1980 presidential campaign, Reagan endorsed state's rights in a speech at the Neshoba County Fair in Mississippi. "I believe in state's rights," Reagan explained, "where people do all they can at the community and private levels." The media followed the Democrat script and called him racist.

The South had a new conservatism, suggested Gordon MacInnes in his book, *Wrong for All the Right Reasons: How White Liberals Have Been Undone by Race*. MacInnes said, "Republicans were perfectly positioned to take advantage of the large, rapid changes in public opinion as the televised image of black America shifted from prayerful victims of racist Southern police to rioters and looters." Riots broke out in New York in the summer of 1964 for six straight nights, the first race riots outside the South that spread to other Northern cities.

Early that same year, Dr. Billy Graham held a Gospel crusade in Birmingham's famed Legion Field, where some of the nation's top universities competed in football games. Graham announced that the Easter Service would be integrated. Barely six months earlier, the nation saw images in Birmingham of police dogs and fire hoses, where four little girls were killed in a bomb blast at the Sixteenth Street Baptist Church.

Graham told how the Klan had torn down signs about the crusade, and authorities were concerned there would be a race riot. Ignoring threats, Graham and his evangelistic team moved forward with the racially integrated service, and Graham preached a simple message of love, repentance, and faith. "The racial problem is not limited to Birmingham, Ala.," Graham said on his *Hour of Decision* program that Sunday. "As long as man continues in his sins, there is no hope for solving our political and social problems."

CHAPTER SEVEN

Republicans fool themselves

Alabama Republicans continued their strategy of waiting out Wallace before moving forward with the next phase of making the party more competitive. Once Wallace eventually vacated the governor's office because of constitutional succession, Republicans reasoned that they had an outside chance at finally taking the governor's office in the 1966 election.

George Wallace, however, would eventually crush the political ambitions not only of Republicans but also a long string of formidable Democrats who had designs on the top office. John Patterson yearned to be governor again, following his near-magical election following his father's political assassination in Phenix City. Then there was Big Jim Folsom, a two-termer who wanted another shot at glory, with thoughts of living in the new Governor's Mansion that the state had purchased in 1950 from the Ligon family. Folsom and his growing family resided in a stodgy old brownstone just down Perry Street during his first term. The house was later demolished for the new interstate route through Montgomery.

Republicans were not the only political organization preparing for the 1966 elections. Ten Democrats were running for governor, and Republicans had Jim Martin positioned as their strongest contender. But Wallace would change the dynamics of the election as the result of a tragedy. Democrats and rising Republican ambitions could only watch helplessly as their hopes faded while Wallace turned a fatal mishap to his advantage.

Ryan deGraffenried, Tuscaloosa attorney, who lost to Wallace in the 1962 Democratic primary by 10 points, was the top contender for Democrats in 1966. He had thoroughly prepared his organization for the next election. But Wallace was not about to leave the governor's office without a fight. In the summer of 1965, Wallace called a special session with the intention of forcing the Alabama Legislature to change the state Constitution, so he could succeed himself. Patterson and deGraffenried formed an alliance to deny Wallace the necessary twenty-one votes in the Senate to pass the bill. Wags around the capitol city labeled Wallace's aggressive tactics as the "Succession Session." Wallace went so far as to campaign in the home districts of opposing senators to leverage support for passage of the bill. It didn't work.

DeGraffenried, more than Patterson, was the more attractive personality favored to succeed Wallace. Accomplished, handsome, principled, and popular, he was the next-generation candidate, the best Alabama Democrats had to offer during dramatic social and political change. DeGraffenried detested Wallace, routinely referring to him as a "loudmouthed demagogue." And contrary to Wallace and his Klan support, deGraffenried favored school integration. The son of a US Congressman, deGraffenried was better organized with a precinct captain in every box and crossroads village in the state.

In February, the day after qualifying for governor began, deGraffenried boarded a small Cessna plane in Fort Payne amid a severe thunderstorm against the advice of friends and set off for a scheduled campaign appearance in Gadsden. Shortly after takeoff, the small plane crashed into Lookout Mountain outside of Fort Payne in blinding wind and rain, killing deGraffenried, age forty, and the pilot. The people of Alabama were stunned when the evening news about the fatal crash flashed across their television screens. The tragedy immediately changed the political plans of Democrats, particularly the power-hungry Wallace organization.

The bereavement period in the Wallace camp lasted exactly two days before George Wallace qualified his wife Lurleen for governor, a political rarity even in the unpredictable politics of the Deep South. (There were false claims that Wallace took weeks to make the decision.) With the Wallaces now firmly entrenched as the top contenders for the Democrat nomination, the campaign for governor changed in their favor all the way to the November general election. Only Republican Congressman James D. Martin stood in the way of four more years of compromise and demagoguery.

Campaign ads in state newspapers pictured the Wallaces side-by-side, topped by the slogan—"Keep a Good Administration." It was a "twofer" deal, a bargain for some Alabamians desperate to keep their political champion in office. Lurleen Wallace eventually made a sixty-one-county walk over nine opponents without a runoff that attracted national attention to Alabama's colorful election.

For Republicans, the tragedy created an internal squabble. Winton Blount and Jim Martin flew to Gettysburg seeking advice with ex-President Eisenhower, then on to New York to talk with Richard Nixon and seek his wisdom about running against the Wallaces. Both party elders advised caution campaigning against Mrs. Wallace.

However, in the meantime, a behind-the-scenes drama was

unfolding for Republicans as the result of the deGraffenried tragedy. In the brief interval following his death, while candidates were
reassessing the new political landscape, Lurleen Wallace's sudden
entry into the election also created havoc in Republican ranks.
Martin's first intention had been to run against deGraffenried, the
anticipated Democrat nominee for governor, with John Grenier
set to challenge John Sparkman for the Senate.

Bert Nettles said Republicans were "fooled" by previous elections. Following Jim Martin's close call in 1962 and the success
of the 1964 US House elections, Nettles said in an oral history interview with Walter DeVries that Republicans thought they could
"run and win elections just by being Republican." Martin, for one,
was confident he would win in 1966.

With front-running deGraffenried out of the picture, Mrs.
Wallace was set to mangle the Republican nominee. Yet, the talk
among GOP leaders rationalized that Martin would have a better
than even chance of beating Sparkman, and Grenier could shift to
the governor's race. But the suggestion created instant controversy, particularly between the candidates. Further, the sensitive topic
of race favored Republicans after Alabama's entire Democrat congressional delegation signed the 1956 "Southern Manifesto" opposing racial integration. Some Democrat candidates sported big
white resistance buttons that declared "Never."

Martin would not consider changing races, and Grenier deeply resented the suggestion. Grenier had intended to run against the
sixty-four-year-old Sparkman, and he did not want to change races any more than Martin. The party was roiled by dissension and
a who's-on-first routine prior to the July 29–30, 1966, Republican
State Convention at Garrett Coliseum in Montgomery. Rumors
persisted, even in the media, that Republicans were planning a

major floor demonstration to draft Martin for Senate. But Martin wouldn't even discuss it publicly, although the Senate nomination was his for the asking. Without question, the possibility of defeating Sparkman would have enabled Republicans to realize their goal of electing a first-rate conservative to represent Alabama in the US Senate.

Other factors complicated the controversy even more. The party had poll numbers showing Martin leading Sparkman—45 to 43 percent. Knowing this, it was reported that the Wallace camp sent word through back channels that they would support Martin over their own senator. It was a tacit understanding that strongly suggested Martin had an edge against Sparkman. The drama concluded only days before the convention when Martin announced that he was running for governor and would oppose any change otherwise.

While the debate over getting the right candidate in the right race dominated Republican strategy, the sweltering heat and humidity at Garrett Coliseum forced Republicans to shed their coats and fan themselves while taking care of party business. Over 2,000 delegates filled the large arena as the nation grappled with civil unrest and riots in northern cities, and stories about the Vietnam War dominated the daily news. Racial unrest prompted President Lyndon Johnson to comment that the riots in large cities were hurting the "negro cause."

Montgomery Representative Alfred Goldthwaite, a Grenier ally and the first public official to defect to the Republican Party, presided over the convention as the new chairman of the Alabama Republican Party. Goldthwaite discouraged changing horses midstream, claiming it would be "calamitous" for the party on the verge of nominations. Thus, the party *and* Martin failed to exploit the breathtaking opportunity of Alabama electing a US Senator.

As the matter stood, the Martin-Grenier decisions concerned convention delegates, yet the nominations were made: Jim Martin would be the GOP candidate for governor; John Grenier would oppose Sparkman for Senate. There would be no change in the party lineup.

The *Montgomery Advertiser* pictured the James Martin family on the front page, the Martin children on stage waving. Pat Martin entertained delegates with patriotic songs with encores; in the background, a huge *"Martin for Governor"* banner rippled in a rare breeze in the open doorway of the coliseum. The *Advertiser* eventually endorsed Martin over Mrs. Wallace.

Of course, there was other business. Among the more important was a resolution calling for expanding the seventy-two-seat Republican executive committee and a debate about a Republican primary, but that event was still a few years away. Senator Strom Thurmond (SC), who had switched to the Republican Party after the Dixiecrat movement failed, was the guest speaker.

The GOP did not challenge other constitutional offices but distributed a long list of candidates that Grenier and Goldthwaite had qualified for the general election: sixteen candidates for state office: twenty-seven state Senate candidates; eighty-six House candidates, and 107 executive committee candidates for municipal and county offices. Republicans were decidedly optimistic.

Disregarding long odds, the GOP would challenge Democrat heavyweights for governor and Senate, which many delegates believed was essential for the party growth. The polls had shown the way to victory in the Senate race, and the Wallace camp had signaled their behind-the-scenes cooperation. Still, Republicans had confidence in their top man against the Democrat's strongest candidate. Late-polling data gave a much different picture of the election: Martin could not beat Lurleen. Still, the candidates held their ground.

On the campaign trail, Martin methodically attacked President Lyndon Johnson, avoiding direct criticism of Mrs. Wallace, respectful of womanhood. Voters were angry with Johnson because of the Vietnam War, the high cost of his not-so-Great Society welfare programs, and widespread urban race riots. Martin and Grenier were rewarded for their loyalty when Barry Goldwater and Strom Thurmond made campaign appearances on their behalf. But Republicans seemed oblivious to the imminent Wallace firestorm.

Ignored in the political stew, neither Wallace and the Democrats nor Martin and the Republicans actively sought the support of the new bloc of black voters. Republicans seemed unmindful that the original intent of their party was to give minorities a voice in a free society.

The national media noticed, unlike previous elections, that there was an absence of segregation rhetoric from candidates. The sole reason was an estimated 100 black candidates were running on the Democrat ticket. Republicans noticed but waved it off.

By the November election, 235,000 African Americans had registered to vote. Still, they were more or less disregarded by old-line Democrats, although they would have had a significant impact on the party. Seven blacks made it through the primaries to the Democrat runoff, including Tuskegee civil rights attorney Fred Gray. All of them lost.

The *New York Times* speculated that Martin would actually beat Mrs. Wallace. Journalist and historian Theodore H. White predicted that Alabama would be the first former Confederate state to elect a Republican governor. All the confidence and enthusiasm were based solely on Jim Martin's sensational showing in the 1962 Senate race and his subsequent election to Congress in 1964. White encouraged the lofty expectations of Republicans.

Republicans finished the final weekend of the 1966 general election in grand style. Jim Martin and an entourage of Republicans campaigned by train, the *"Victory Special,"* braving freezing winter weather. The four-day train route stretched 1,300 miles from the mountains of North Alabama to the Gulf Coast—forty-two stops in all. Martin and the Republicans gallantly soldiered on after the *Montgomery Advertiser* released the results of another poll that showed Lurleen Wallace leading Martin by an almost 2-to-1 margin.

On the stump, Martin pointed out that the election had national significance and warned voters not to be misled by Wallace's third-party ambitions, that it would only benefit President Johnson. Despite harsh weather conditions, large, enthusiastic crowds, some estimated as high as five thousand, cheered Martin as he barnstormed from the rear platform of the train.

An indication of electoral change was evident on the November 8 paper ballots. Democrats deleted their signature "White Supremacy" motto. And in the manner of good political jokery, the Wallaces were endorsed by a pair of natural antagonists that illustrated more dissimilarities in the election. A black organization in Birmingham threw their support to Wallace, and the United Klans of Alabama did the same, firsts for both organizations.

On Monday night, Martin made his final appeal to voters via statewide television. Full-page campaign ads in major newspapers suggested that the election was between "A Man or A Woman," with photos of Martin and Lurleen Wallace. *"Don't kid yourself— George Wallace is Grabbing for Personal Power,"* the Martin ads stated. Republicans overspent their $200,000 campaign account .

. . but all of the money in the world would not have changed the election.

Joe McFadden, writing for the *Montgomery Journal*, said that the campaign against the Democrats was a major mismatch despite Republican confidence. "The pleasant traditional Republican facade of pure hearts and ineffectual good intentions," was not expected to threaten the Democrat power structure. McFadden was right. It didn't.

Clearly lacking sophistication about political campaigns, the election was a humiliating defeat for Republicans, just as Bert Nettles had anticipated. Mrs. Wallace did to Republicans what she did to Democrats in winning the nomination without a runoff. She took 64 percent of the vote. Grenier, running against Sparkman for the Senate, courted Democrats by aligning himself with Wallace, but the last-minute feign to the left angered Republicans and created a split among party loyalists. The 1966 elections were a revealing and pointless failure for Republicans. Democrats took every House election, and only Leland Childs, a party switcher from Jefferson County, won election to the Senate.

Lurleen Wallace carried sixty-six counties, losing only to Martin in the Republican stronghold Winston County. The vote total was 537,505 for Wallace and 262,943 for Martin. Sparkman likewise trounced Grenier, but Grenier was pleased that he ran 8 percentage points stronger than Martin.

Disappointment abounded among Alabama Republicans. Martin was devastated by the defeat, and John Grenier believed that the party had peaked during the election despite obvious missteps about candidates and offices. Grenier had anticipated more Republicans would be elected after investing two years recruiting candidates and raising money. He felt, with good reason, that running Martin against Lurleen Wallace was a "disastrous mistake." He said that the big loss returned the party to its long history of decline and failure, attributing a lack of unity among Republicans to internal party issues, which he termed as "internecine war."

Grenier further explained that the John Birch Society had infiltrated the party. Some former Dixiecrats allied with the Birchers to radicalize the executive committee. Yet, without question, the absolute critical issue that defeated Republicans was Wallace and his dominance on race. "The issue of race is everything in Southern politics," Grenier explained.

The wreckage of the failed 1966 campaign created a time of reflection to determine why things had gone so terribly wrong. Yet, the trauma was abundantly clear to experienced political observers. Ray Jenkins, commenting on Montgomery politics in an oral history, said that Republicans were not a political force and predicted that the GOP would not be competitive for some time. "They [Republicans] just don't understand politics for one thing." Jenkins said that the party tended to function as a "closed club that didn't even pretend to engage in political activity." Failure to get the right man in the right race made his point.

Jenkins said Republicans did recognize that change was coming to the South after Dwight Eisenhower won the 1952 and 1956 presidential elections. (Eisenhower campaigned in Alabama.) "That's when they started doing more than country club executive committee meetings that constituted Republican activity." He said that Jim Martin and John Grenier took the party away from the old crowd that Jenkins tagged as the "facade keepers." He said that Martin and Grenier would be remembered for their attempt to organize Republicans into a relevant political organization.

Bert Nettles, Mobile attorney, who later chaired the state GOP convention, said Republicans grew in Alabama and elsewhere in the South by attracting conservative Democrats, who brought more political experience to the party. Nettles also recognized greater racial acceptance among young voters. He said, "The new generation did not follow racial issues, because they saw evidence of racial change throughout the nation that included blacks." Conservative values became the foremost issue for future generations of Republicans.

The many Republican disappointments of '66 did reveal how Jim Martin's groundbreaking-campaign style blazed a clear path that outrivaled the obsolete mind-set of Democrats, starting with the race against Lister Hill. "It was the beginning of the end of the New Deal coalition that had held prominence over American, and Southern politics since the Great Depression," Gordon Harvey, Jacksonville State University history professor explained in a *Birmingham News* article on Martin's passing on October 30, 2017. "Martin introduced national political issues to what had in the past been primarily state-oriented campaigns."

Byron Shafer and Richard Johnston, writing about Southern exceptionalism, further pointed out that by the 1970s, the old South had disappeared as a relic of the agrarian past. Economic development and legal desegregation brought a radical change in the South. "Republicans, not Democrats, became the party of the better-off," they wrote. "Economic development proved relentless for the new Southern Republican Party."

Not everywhere, that is. George Wallace held Alabama in a death grip through his tyrannical dominance of the state and near-unlimited power as governor. When Wallace eventually left the governor's office after an eternal eighteen years, the Alabama Education Association (AEA) continued dominating state politics until the eventual GOP breakthrough decades later.

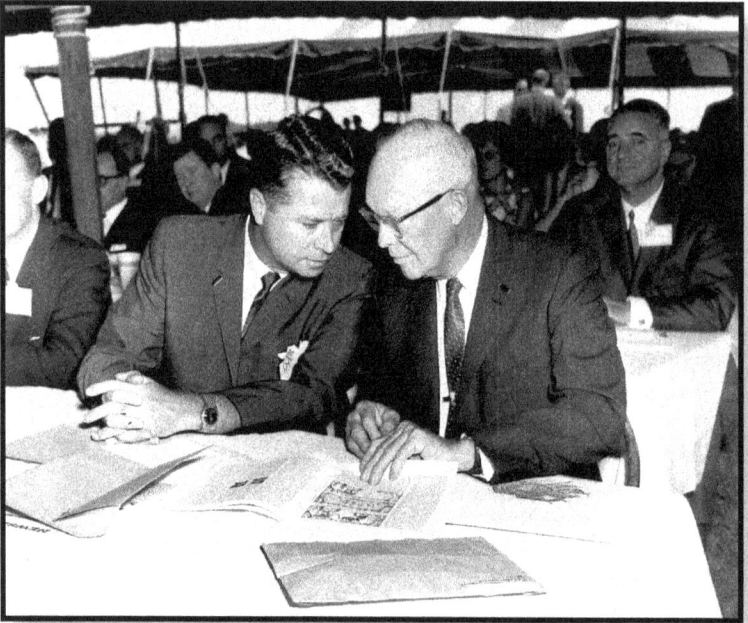

President Dwight Eisenhower and Congressman James Martin
(White House Photo)

CHAPTER EIGHT

The wilderness years

The next two decades—1966 to 1986—saw the Alabama Republican Party flounder from convention to convention, eventually holding its first primary, trying to divine a more successful way of winning the confidence of voters. Yet, no one proved capable of leading the party out of the political wilderness. And a humiliating and frustrating interregnum it was. The first order of business was paying off 1966 campaign debts and evaluating the election disaster.

By the next biennial Republican meeting in Mobile, recovering Republicans had been reduced in number and expectations. Still, some 735 delegates attended the convention, June 29–30, 1968, in the Mobile Civic Auditorium. The six-year burst of energy had greatly reduced the party of any realistic expectations of beating the Democrats. A top concern was air-conditioning. After sweating through two days of unbearable heat at Montgomery's Garrett Coliseum, Republicans sought relief from the humid summer heat for their annual convention. Bert Nettles, a Mobile attorney and temporary party chairman charged with convention planning, welcomed delegates to the perfect venue in his hometown.

When the convention was gaveled open, Gov. Lurleen Wallace had died, Robert Kennedy had been shot, and reports about the

Vietnam War dominated national news. George Wallace, temporarily out of power, created front-page news when Sam Donaldson
and an ABC television crew filmed him shaking hands with
Robert Shelton, Grand Wizard of the United Klans of America.
Wallace ordered staffers to destroy the film, which they did to an
irate Donaldson and the camera crew. Wallace, forever loose with
facts, claimed that ABC had "contrived" to film the incident and
"tie him to the Klan." (*Montgomery Advertiser*)

But Republicans had their own issues. "*Republican Convention
to Bring Party Wrangling to a Head*," the *Montgomery Advertiser*
headlined prior to the convention. The article referenced the power struggle between Jim Martin and John Grenier, with roots in
the nondecisions of the 1966 governor-senate election. Martin had
marshaled his forces that included Jefferson County's 163-member
delegation, to elect him committeeman to the national Republican
convention at Miami Beach in August. The committeeman would
chair the Alabama delegation to the Republican convention, a personal quest of Grenier. Having served as the Southern coordinator for Nixon's failed 1960 presidential campaign, he wanted the
honor of leading Alabama Republicans for Nixon at the national
convention.

Contrary to Grenier's plans, Jim Martin won the right to chair
the delegation. Martin supporters further elbowed Grenier aside
when the former party chairman attempted to win a delegate, or
alternate delegate, seat to the convention. Bert Nettles, chairing
the convention, refused to recognize Grenier during nominations.
Despite the backhanded treatment by his own party, Grenier supported Martin. The *Mobile Press-Register* published a front-page
photo of Martin and Grenier greeting each other at the convention.
Martin's influence in the party remained intact after the disastrous

1966 elections, and he emerged as the dominant leader of the Alabama GOP during the wilderness period.

Again, Republicans walked away from an election battle with Wallace. The GOP's top statewide candidate in 1968 was Perry Hooper, Montgomery County probate judge, nominated to oppose James Allen of Gadsden for the US Senate. Mrs. Bobbie Ames was elected national committeewoman. An attempt to expand the seventy-two-member executive committee failed, but more importantly, delegates passed a milestone resolution led by the Martin camp, establishing a Republican primary by the next election cycle in 1970.

The 1968 convention was not without its own drama. Party unity was severely tested when ultraconservative John Birch Society delegates started a fight for control of the state executive committee. The Birchers were upset with GOP Chairman Dick Bennett over party patronage, controlled by the Patronage Committee composed of Bennett and the three sitting congressmen. With Nixon in the White House, political appointments were prize plums, and the Birchers, for the second time, were unable to incite dissidents to revolt with them and take control of the state party.

Martin, speaking to the *Mobile Press-Register*, said that Republicans had little hope of making progress in Alabama with Wallace in office and Republicans watching from the sidelines. "Once the third-party issue has been settled, Alabama voters are not going to return to the Democratic Party. We need to develop leadership, particularly in rural areas, and broaden the base of our party." Martin's conclusions were insightful but premature.

In the November 1968 Senate election, Perry Hooper lost to James Allen in another lopsided contest: Allen polled 638,774 votes to Hooper's 201,227—which accurately measured Democrat dominance over Republicans.

Alabama voted for Richard Nixon in 1968, who defeated Democrat Hubert Humphrey. Nixon successfully appealed to voters in Sun Belt states on the basis of conservative economic policies. Alabama Republicans were disappointed that Nixon's victory did not benefit the state party in the general election. All Alabama Republicans gained from the '68 election were more losses while George Wallace celebrated another third-party presidential run.

Republican's first primary—failure

The transition from convention-style politics to statewide primaries did not happen as suddenly as delegates at the 1968 GOP state convention had imagined. The party was not prepared for that kind of change, according to Republican Chairman Richard "Dick" Bennett, Greenville timberman. Bennett and party leaders were forced to beat back hard-line right-wingers demanding that the party oppose Wallace, regardless of any damage Democrats could inflict upon their candidates. Bennett felt there were risks for incumbent Republican congressmen if the Wallace organization promoted straight-party voting. GOP leaders were content to plow the middle ground and qualify more candidates for the state legislature.

Republicans also abandoned sketchy plans for a statewide primary in 1970. Again, Wallace staunchly refused to give up the governorship, and Republicans recognized the foolhardiness of challenging the Democrat power structure. GOP convention delegates in 1970, instead, sought to protect three GOP congressmen—Jack Edwards, John Buchanan, and Bill Dickinson.

Republicans further decided to invest their modest resources in candidates for the state House and Senate to challenge solidly entrenched Democrats.

Looking ahead, Republicans were expected to nominate at least one candidate at the state level to qualify for a party primary in 1972. Bob French, Fort Payne attorney, accepted the sacrificial nomination to oppose Jere Beasley for lieutenant governor (the Wallace organization distributed campaign literature with a photo of Beasley and Wallace). French acknowledged, almost apologetically, that his candidacy was a legal maneuver to maintain Republican political status so that the GOP could be on the ballot in the next election cycle. There were erroneous reports in the press that insisted Republican candidates were required to poll a minimum of 20 percent of the total vote in the November general election. French won only 15.50 percent. (See page 17 for primary rules drafted by Democrats.)

With that, delegates nominated forty-one House and four Senate candidates. One House candidate was R. L. Hill from Jefferson County. Hill was a black man employed by VISTA at Miles College. In the Democrat primary, Fred Gray, Tuskegee attorney, had been nominated for the legislature, the first black since Reconstruction. Republicans nominated Doug Hale for a House seat in Huntsville. Hale resigned from an MIT fellowship and returned home to help rebuild the Republican Party. He won the election and joined Bert Nettles in the Alabama House.

The 1970 nominating convention was the final old-style convention for Republicans. At least part of the reason was Bert Nettles brought legal action against the party to force Republicans to hold primaries, the same as Democrats. Party leaders Jim

Martin and John Grenier actively supported the transition to primary elections.

Indeed, all things were new for Alabama Republicans in 1972, but not the magical rise as a top political contender. The GOP desperately wanted to achieve parity with Democrats, but that failed too. Republicans did not have a champion capable of sparring with George Wallace, nor did they have a message that appealed to the emotions and fears of Deep South voters.

Albert Brewer, after losing a brutal battle to Wallace in the 1970 Democrat primary runoff, said that racial politics was not the way he campaigned. Still, neither did racial politics define Ryan deGraffenried or Big Jim Folsom. The lessons in primaries were sobering and specific; if moderate Democrats could not win, neither could conservative Republicans.

The top race for Republicans in 1972 was not the governor's office but the Senate seat held by John Sparkman, sparred by Jim Martin's indecision in 1966. Winton Blount Jr., a multimillionaire with a national profile as postmaster general in the Nixon administration, committed to oppose Sparkman. Known as a civic-minded philanthropist, Blount built the highly acclaimed Alabama Shakespeare Festival in Montgomery and dedicated it to his wife, Carolyn. His résumé included a term as president of the US Chamber of Commerce. Blount had a splendid reputation that should have turned the heads of Alabama voters.

Blount skipped out on Democrats and began keeping company with Republicans in 1952 due to his admiration of WWII hero Dwight Eisenhower. During racial unrest at the University of Alabama, Blount, a university trustee, attempted to calm unrest while Wallace stood in the schoolhouse door. He advocated obeying federal civil rights laws.

The first Republican primary. Three prominent Republicans qualified for the US Senate: Winton Blount, Jim Martin, and Bert Nettles made the 1972 Senate race a milestone for Alabama conservatives. Martin had long advocated state primaries, not party conventions and hand-picked candidates, as the most effective way to build the party. But in the end, Blount's deep pockets overcame Martin and Nettles, and he won the primary in an unspectacular 27,736-to-16,800 victory over Martin with Nettles polling 5,765 votes. The combined total of slightly more than 50,000 votes should have alerted Republicans that the party would not be competitive come November. Subsequently, Republicans stumbled badly in 1972.

As a candidate, Blount found it difficult relating to ordinary working people. Too often, he came across as aloof and abrupt. He had never mastered what Churchill once called the "common tongue." He did splendidly among Chamber of Commerce types but was ill at ease among regular folks. Robert Vance, chairman of the Alabama Democratic Party, said what was on the mind of many voters when he called Blount "an arrogant prick."

John Grenier, the consummate party operative, recognized Blount's shortcomings, as did Ray Jenkins, a political reporter for the *Montgomery Advertiser*. Blount was totally out of his element meeting people that Democrats naturally attracted. "Blount simply couldn't pass himself off as another likable good ole boy running for public office," Jenkins explained.

Matters worsened for Blount and Republicans in May with the attempted assassination of George Wallace in Maryland. News of the shooting, Wallace's hospitalization and eventual return to Alabama for treatment at Spain Rehabilitation Center in

Birmingham, were endless media stories. Even Wallace detractors were sympathetic to the near-tragedy. When Wallace did return to Alabama, it was for one hour, long enough for him to reclaim the powers of the governor's office from Jere Beasley. Then he was off to the Democrat Convention in Miami. President Nixon loaned Wallace a hospital plane for the flight back home and down to Florida for his triumphant arrival at the Democratic National Convention.

The GOP held a much-smaller annual convention in the Birmingham City Auditorium, July 14–15, 1972, on the heels of the Democratic National Convention. The timing was awkward. In the past, Democrat-leaning newspapers provided extensive coverage of Republican conventions, but now, the GOP was given only a brief notice buried deep in the back pages of newspapers and few photos. The Jehovah Witnesses convention got more press coverage than the Republican convention.

Changing the GOP's outmoded nominating conventions to primaries meant that Republicans were no longer a political novelty to the press. The difference being that the primary process had a downside. Conventions were planned and scripted for dramatic effect. With statewide primaries, the GOP had to compete with Democrats and the left-leaning media for the interest of voters. It was a hard lesson; Democrats ruled Alabama.

Republicans, specifically Winton Blount Jr., were thoroughly schooled by the political savvy of Democrats. Sparkman had no trouble neutralizing Blount after the Wallace people gave Sparkman tapes of George Wallace's old campaign speeches, where he upbraided Blount and the Republicans. The Sparkman campaign played snippets of the recorded speeches on radio stations with great effect. The speeches more or less finished off Blount's negative appeal with voters and his ineffective campaign style.

Nevertheless, Blount's brain trust decided that their best alternative was to run on a Nixon-Blount ticket and plastered the message on billboards statewide, hoping that the relationship with Nixon would offset Sparkman's hard-hitting radio ads. Eisenhower lent his personal support from Gettysburg. Blount and a scattering of Republican candidates in state races were optimistic that the presidential election would bring more Nixon voters to the ballot box in Alabama, the way Goldwater did in 1964. Of course, it did not.

Bert Nettles claimed that Blount spent a million dollars, either a figure of speech or a point of fact, in the Senate campaign. When President Eisenhower sent Blount a personal "Dear Red" letter, Blount took out full-page ads in newspapers throughout the state, reprinting the endorsement. Seemingly, it only served to remind many voters that they did not like Blount.

In the end, Sparkman prevailed by a three-to-one margin, though Nixon took Alabama with 72 percent of the presidential vote. Blount carried only two counties, Winston and Houston, with a total vote of 35 percent. The Republicans' first state primary failed to rise above its longtime minority status.

Party Chairman Dick Bennett attempted to explain that ticket-splitting would help strengthen the state's two-party system in the future. "The vote shows that people no longer have strong feelings of party allegiance," Bennett observed in an interview with the *Montgomery Advertiser*, trying to put the best face on the failed election. Nixon's impressive win in Alabama was the first for a Republican president in a century. Nevertheless, Republicans were vastly disappointed that the success of the national party did not influence elections down the ballot in Alabama.

Nixon won the presidency with the standard conservative appeal to voters. Yet, political observers believed that he also benefited from widespread race riots that raged across America. In 1967, there were 159 race riots. Martin Luther King's assassination the next year excited still more riots. During the campaign, Nixon wisely employed a strict law-and-order message.

Political change in Alabama was often led by outsiders moving into the state. Cities like Huntsville, Birmingham, Montgomery, and Mobile became centers that experienced new Republican growth due to industrial development. New GOP committees would join old-line party activists in reshaping Alabama politics.

President Dwight Eisenhower created unimaginable prosperity for Alabama on July 29, 1958, when he signed congressional legislation that created the National Aeronautics and Space Administration (NASA). Operating under the authority of the new space agency was Wernher von Braun and a coterie of 130 German-born scientists at Huntsville's Redstone Arsenal who were developing the Saturn rocket for moon exploration. NASA became part of the new Marshall Space Flight Center that attracted many of the nation's top technology companies and helped usher Alabama and its people into a new age of prosperity and industrial development. Business and population projections indicated that Huntsville was destined to become the largest city in Alabama.

New Republican organizations would rise to challenge the old Democrat-style politics and help usher in a more progressive era of political activism for the emerging Republican Party.

CHAPTER NINE

For governor: thirteen
Democrats, four Republicans

Republicans could not catch a break with George Wallace overshadowing Alabama politics. But neither could ambitious Democrats eyeing the much-too-often vacant governor's office while Wallace exploited state resources for his presidential ambitions. An original routine developed with Wallace campaigns: he would promise to fulfill his duties as governor and not run for president again, but by the time the votes were counted, sometimes the next day, Wallace headed for the airport with state personnel in tow to manage his schedule of appearances. Close friends advised him to stop his foolhardy presidential runs, but after the 1968 election, where he won five states and forty-five electoral votes, Wallace wasn't about to quit.

Any responsible politician with a smidgen of conscience and a reasonably informed electorate would have been aggrieved and embarrassed by promises that Wallace never intended to keep. But Alabamians, like many other Southern states at the time, were more frustrated with Washington and federal intrusion into local affairs than a revolt against their loudmouthed governors. The point being, many Alabamians took more interest in who was elected governor than the president of the United States.

In 1974, Republicans, or rather Elvin McCary, stubbornly challenged Wallace against the wishes of the party. The state senator from Anniston, McCary, illustrated the foolhardiness of running against Wallace by polling less than 15 percent of the popular vote.

Wallace's midcareer eight-year run in the governor's office ended in 1978, clearing the way for head-to-head contests in both primaries. Experts assumed that the Wallace reign was over. The top challengers were Albert Brewer, who Wallace defeated in 1970 employing vicious racial tactics; Jere Beasley, the lieutenant governor with a personal feel for the governor's office; and Bill Baxley, twice-elected attorney general. All three had been in idle mode for two terms, building their organizations while the governor flew around the nation on his delusional quest for the American presidency.

The 1978 elections resembled more of a political stampede than the usual quadrennial election for state leadership. *"Largest field in history facing Alabama voters,"* headlined the *Alabama Journal.* Quoting Philip Rawls, "Come September 5, the voting machines for the Democratic and Republican primaries may resemble the New York City telephone directories." It was a carnival of buttons, billboards, and baloney as candidates bumped into one another, trying to capture the favor of voters. It would not be easy.

The Alabama Legislature had moved the original primary date in 1978 from May to September to avoid the sweltering summer heat and to encourage voters to attend political events without getting dehydrated or sunburned. Changing the primaries to autumn in Alabama made little difference; summer heat in the South tends to linger into September, sometimes October.

For governor, voters had their pick of four Republicans and thirteen Democrats. The lieutenant governor's race attracted almost as many candidates—twelve Democrats and two Republicans. One candidate, Republican Elvin McCary, who foolheartedly ran against Wallace in 1974, qualified for lieutenant governor and the interim Senate seat held by Mrs. Maryon Allen. Senator Jim Allen died of a heart attack on June 1 while vacationing with his family in Gulf Shores. Subsequently, Wallace appointed Allen's widow to complete the final months of her husband's term.

Almost indistinguishable among the thirteen Democrats was a former Republican running as a Democrat—Forrest Hood "Fob" James. James had been an All-American halfback at Auburn University, and his wife, Bobbie, had been homecoming queen. The James family reflected the typical business profile of successful Republicans, and Fob once served on the Alabama Republican Party's exclusive seventy-two-member executive committee. Fob had been a Nixon fund-raiser, and Bobbie James ran for the state board of education—as Republicans.

To help change his political identity, James attended the 1976 National Democratic Convention as a Carter delegate to establish himself as a true Democrat. Still, James's elitist background troubled yeoman-minded Democrats. Party leaders assembled a panel of executive committee members to vet James and determine if, indeed, he was the "born-again Democrat" that he claimed. It was not a very high bar, but James passed muster.

In that election, Republicans wisely scuttled the temptation to try again to build the party from the top down, as in 1966, which resulted in a party without a solid foundation, according to Bill Harris, party chair. Over the past decade, the top-down strategy had weakened the Republican Party, Harris explained to the *Montgomery Advertiser*, resulting in Alabama being the only state in the nation without a Republican in the legislature. The Wallace power structure and the AEA teachers union had outvoted and outspent Republicans to maintain Democrat control of the legislature. In an effort to elect a Republican to the legislature, the party qualified thirty-four candidates for the House and eight for the Senate.

The winner of the statewide Republican primary for governor was another dark horse, **Guy Hunt**, former Cullman County probate judge, farmer, and Primitive Baptist preacher from Holly Pond. He won the Republican nomination by beating Bert Hayes, professor of history from Athens, and Julian Elgin, cattleman and farmer from Montgomery. Veteran political journalist Bob Ingram observed that the 1978 GOP primary failed to excite voters. That was an understatement. Only 25,850 people voted Republican.

Hunt had made an introductory race for state Senate in 1962 and lost. But he shocked the people in Cullman County when he was elected probate judge in 1964, as the last-minute stand-in when the Republican nominee withdrew. Chairing the Cullman County Republican Party, Hunt was not satisfied as a token candidate and made the most of the opportunity. He campaigned relentlessly, knocking on doors and shaking enough hands throughout the county to win two terms. The 1964 Goldwater campaign, no doubt, contributed to his success.

Hunt would eventually leave the probate judge office to lead Ronald Reagan's 1976 presidential campaign in Alabama. Republicans also chose Hunt to chair the Alabama delegation to the Republican National Convention in Kansas City, MO, when the party nominated Gerald Ford for president. Looking less like a governor than anyone running, Hunt, tall and country plain, toured the state in a recreational vehicle with family and friends telling voters that "a new beginning is more than just a promise."

There were other major elections in 1978. Alabama's two US Senate seats were also contested. Jim Martin began the 1978 campaign running for the open Senate seat vacated by John Sparkman, but in early October, he recognized that he was better positioned to run for the seat vacated by Jim Allen. The Democrat nominee for Allen's seat was Donald Stewart, the state senator from Anniston (Calhoun), running with the blessings of George Wallace.

Stewart first intended to run against Howell Heflin before switching to the open seat. In the days following Allen's death, George Wallace casually mentioned to the press that he might run for the Senate himself, but just as quickly, he dropped the notion. Stewart decided to change races when polling showed him with only 6 percent of the vote.

Howell Heflin had served one term as chief justice of the Alabama Supreme Court, defeating John Patterson for the seat. He returned to his law practice in Tuscumbia but was persuaded by friends to run for Sparkman's Senate seat. Heflin led a field of seven candidates in the Democrat primary and beat Walter Flowers in the runoff.

Democrats were comfortable with Heflin, but they had concerns about Donald Stewart, their unproven nominee pitted against Jim Martin. Democrats were alarmed by the steady flow of money that the National Republican Senatorial Committee (NRSC) invested in Martin. Democratic Party Chairman George Lewis Bailes accused Republicans of spending more than the legal limit in a US Senate race. Bailes said the party would protest to the Federal Election Commission. Martin responded that he was sure that the GOP had been within the letter of the law and suggested that the Democrats go ahead and file a protest. The reason for Martin's growing campaign account was that Republicans discovered a loophole that permitted additional funds after switching races.

The *Montgomery Advertiser* reported that when Martin changed from opposing Howell Heflin to Donald Stewart on October 3, GOP strategists in Washington recognized an opportunity: The Martin-Stewart campaign was a totally different campaign committee, which legally allowed the national party to dump more money into Martin's campaign. More money gave new life to Martin's campaign. Changing races also showed more political maturity.

Stewart had been fund-raising for over a year and had raised and spent more than $600,000. Further, as the election neared, his campaign owed another $233,000, most of it to Stewart. Organized labor PACs were his biggest donors, contributing over $100,000. On the other hand, Martin's total campaign receipts from moneyed Republicans and the National Republican Party was more than $500,000. The *Wall Street Journal* reported that the investments in Martin, an "underdog" Republican in a heavy Democrat state, was because he had won a congressional election against Democrats and could possibly win the Senate race.

During the campaign, Jim Martin made an issue of Stewart's medical treatment for a nervous breakdown in 1958, then an eighteen-year-old high school student. Stewart fought back with claims that Martin never did anything for Alabama except campaign for public office. Both candidates benefited from drop-in visits by national personalities. Barry Goldwater came on Martin's behalf; Gregory Peck flew in to lend his support for Stewart. Both national parties invested heavily in the Alabama Senate campaigns, especially the Republican Party, which needed a Martin win to offset anticipated losses in the Senate.

In 1978, votes were more important than money, and Democrats held an advantage in both. Jaime Etheredge, mayor of Greenville and one of twelve Democrat candidates for lieutenant governor, said "Republican" was a "dirty word" among Democrats. He was right. During the Wallace era, few voters took Republicans seriously, or they ignored them outright.

Fob James beat Guy Hunt by about the same plurality as previous Democrat nominees for governor—71.50 percent to Hunt's 25.49 percent—a margin of over 355,000 votes. James had campaigned with an old yellow school bus aptly named, "The Reading Ritin' 'Rithmetic Special." The iconic bus was a hit with voters, and James spoke to crowds from a platform on the back. James ran a tightly scripted campaign advised by Deloss Walker. He was restricted to ads and speeches written exclusively by Walker— nothing more.

Bill Peterson, writing for the *Washington Post*, said there was no Wallace factor in the election, and voters only saw James in slick television commercials as a New South leader capable of changing Alabama's education system. On the stump, James invited voters "to join me in the politics of unselfishness." After his surprising first-place primary finish, James wasn't allowed to debate Bill Baxley in the runoff to avoid potential unscripted gaffes and controversy.

With Wallace out of the picture, the election was primarily about change, a watershed election that foreshadowed future trends for the Alabama Legislature. The state Senate remained solidly

Democrat, but three Republicans were elected to the House, although GOP Chairman Bill Harris had anticipated a 12-to-15 gain after the big push to have a greater presence in the legislature. New Republican legislators were: Ann Bedsole of Mobile, former Birmingham Mayor George Seibels from Jefferson County, and W. J. "Bill" Cabaniss, Mountain Brook, also in Jefferson. It was the beginning of change for Alabama.

Election trends could be seen in women and African Americans picking up one seat each in the legislature, with the number of women increasing to four. African Americans totaled sixteen members with the election, three in the Senate and thirteen in the House, reflecting a major voting trend in Alabama.

Democrats went seeking the black vote in that election, something unheard of among white candidates a decade earlier. Although Democrats had ignored the new African American voting bloc in 1966, the relevance of black influence changed so radically that ambitious politicians were not reluctant to smile and ingratiate themselves to blacks for votes. Some candidates hosted hospitality suites with free food and booze in Montgomery haunts, and that included Howell Heflin running for the US Senate.

Joe Reed, Democratic Party bigwig, observed: "What we're seeing is a lot of people getting political religion. There's one thing politicians love, and that's votes. And they don't count color in the ballot box." (Peterson, *Washington Post*)

Jim Martin, who did not host a hospitality room to ply blacks with freebies, lost to Democrat Donald Stewart 401,852 to 316,170. It was Martin's final campaign.

An even greater change was taking shape in the South and across the nation. The election of Democrat President Jimmy Carter in 1976 from Georgia resulted in a shift in party alignment.

Carter, the first and last evangelical Christian president elected as a Democrat, proved inept in foreign and domestic leadership. Most damaging to the Carter presidency was the energy crisis that saw long lines at gas pumps and interest rates topping 20 percent. Even Democrats were concerned about Carter's careless handling of the national economy.

The Alabama Republican Party had grown out of the anger of conservatives and independents over the liberal trends of the Kennedy administration, and even more under Johnson and Carter. Many conservative Democrats would continue to change their party affiliation in the 1980 national elections.

George Deyo greets President Richard Nixon.
1968 National Republican Convention, Miami
(White House photo)

CHAPTER TEN

An American hero
returns home

Retired Rear Admiral Jeremiah A. Denton Jr. declined when the Republican Party initially approached him about running for the US Senate. Chairman Bill Harris and others in the party were eager to capitalize on Denton's heroic Vietnam War experiences and encouraged him to run for public office as a Republican, like Eisenhower. But the admiral declined. Once retired from the navy in 1977, he moved back to his hometown Mobile with his wife, Jane, and their family. Soon after returning to civilian life, Denton founded the Coalition for Decency and took an activist role in debating his viewpoint about the decline of moral values in America. Busy adjusting to civilian life after a thirty-four-year military career, politics did not interest Denton. That changed in 1980 with the election of Ronald Reagan and the conservative revolution.

But first, Democrat leadership in Washington took a wrong turn that convinced Jeremiah Denton that it was time to get involved in public service. More specifically, Denton was deeply suspicious of Alabama Senator Donald Stewart and his close alliance with the Carter administration. Young Stewart had proven himself capable of congressional work. In his first year in the

Senate, he introduced twelve bills and cosponsored eighty more. He was the only freshman senator chosen as deputy whip by Senate Majority Leader Robert Byrd.

At the same time Jimmy Carter's political reputation began to tarnish, so did Stewart's, who had aligned himself with the president from neighboring Georgia. They were more than political allies in Washington; Carter kin often visited the Stewarts in Anniston. With Carter rapidly losing popularity, so did Stewart in Alabama. The first president from the South since Zachary Taylor in 1849, a slave-owning Whig from Virginia, Carter was marketed for his post-Watergate presidential run by Atlanta advertising executive Gerald Rafshoon.

Carter damaged himself with a tabloidish *Playboy* interview and confessed to "feeling lust in his heart." Lacking a refined political mind, he blamed the nation's problems on people who were "sick at heart." Indeed, they were sick of a president unable to manage a national crisis. In the end, Carter's failings became Stewart's liabilities, and both parties in Alabama began prepping candidates to challenge the freshman senator.

Thus so, Carter's manifest weaknesses prodded Denton to enter the Senate race. A classmate of Jimmy Carter at the US Naval Academy, they graduated together in the accelerated class of 1947. Admiral Denton decided that it was time to run for public office when he saw how Carter had failed to unify the American people during the Iran and Afghanistan crises. A lack of trust and general dissatisfaction in the administration convinced Denton to run against the president's best man in Alabama. Denton made his first move by qualifying for the September 3, 1980, Republican primary.

Denton's personal rancor mirrored a trend three decades in the making, according to Byron Shafer and Richard Johnston in *The*

End of Southern Exceptionalism. Shafer and Johnston explained in their study how changing public opinions were beginning to shape American presidential elections. During the postwar era, the 1960s through the 1980s, when Southern politics was redefining the region, the relationship between party preferences and presidential voting trends shifted. Strong opinions about welfare influenced public attitudes—with liberals clearly Democrat and conservatives favoring the Republicans. Shafer and Johnston further explained that as racial attitudes became more divisive, liberals and conservatives tended to follow the same Democrat-Republican party lines.

In an awkward twist, the top Republican leadership had prematurely promised their support to another candidate for the 1980 Senate race. Party elders had chosen former US Representative Armistead Selden of Greensboro, Hale County, to run against Stewart. The Seldens were a wealthy banker-planter family in old plantation country; Armistead Selden had served seven terms in the House as a Democrat and had been appointed ambassador to New Zealand. He gave up his House seat in 1968 when Lister Hill retired to run against James Allen for the Senate. Selden lost despite Hill's endorsement. Seeking another avenue of political success twelve years later, the GOP welcomed Selden and gave him an opportunity to run for the Senate.

When Selden announced his intentions in April, he was assured that he had the exclusive claim on the Republican nomination. In a press release, Selden said that friends had approached him throughout Alabama about running against Stewart. On a trip to Washington, Selden was introduced to the press as one of several GOP Senate hopefuls. He said he could win, although Alabama Republicans had not won a Senate race in a century.

The hasty blessings by Republicans (Bill Harris was party chairman) gave Senator Donald Stewart an advantage when Admiral Jeremiah Denton entered the Senate race. Newspapers saw the Selden-Denton race as a Republican mistake and that the party had gotten away from its country club-style politics. Republicans tended to give the impression that politics was something Southern gentlemen did as a "summer pastime." That was about to change.

Though Jeremiah Denton ran in opposition to the Republican hierarchy, the admiral had advantages that were entirely new to the party. Denton's life story and moral crusade had created a different kind of candidate. Christian churches, eager to partner in another political crusade after the embarrassing missteps of Jimmy Carter, quickly took up the Denton cause. Over in Georgia, the same religious organizations were equally disillusioned with Carter. Denton's candidacy was another episode in the Reagan populous revolution.

The Moral Majority of Alabama had taken root in Alabama and across the nation as an offshoot of Jerry Falwell's political activism. Membership was restricted to ministers and coordinated by a one-man staff. Concerned Citizens joined the Moral Majority for Good Government, founded in 1977, which had a more diverse group of pastors and laymen based in Birmingham. Concerned Citizens had been active in the 1978 elections of Fob James and Charles Graddick. Christian activism was taking an important role in Alabama politics.

Both Christian groups were nonprofit educational organizations that could lobby, but federal law restricted them from endorsing or making campaign contributions. Likewise, churches associated with Christian activist groups could not endorse candidates under the threat of losing their tax-exempt status. (*The Johnson Amendment*; LBJ, 1954)

The dual organizations promoted a message of God, family, and country that appealed to mostly white, fundamentalist, conservative, evangelical churches. All that stood between Denton and the general election was a primary battle with Selden. The GOP did not anticipate being outdone by Christian conservatives, which included some Democrats. The 1980 election marked a future election trend for Republicans.

At the same time, another battle was brewing in the Democrat primary, where Donald Stewart was facing a formidable opponent in Jim Folsom Jr., son of two-time Alabama Governor Big Jim Folsom. The Folsom name had considerable ballot power in Alabama, particularly in rural counties on the eastern and western regions of the state. Little Jim had a reputation for being a "lightweight" who depended on his father's political success. With both races seen as toss-ups in the polls, it was a guessing game about which Democrat and Republican would emerge from primary battles for the November election.

Of the foursome, Jeremiah Denton had the most impressive life story. His name was synonymous with war heroism, having survived the mental torture and physical horrors of seven years and seven months as a POW in a North Vietnam prison. He described the pain and torture in a book he authored, ***When Hell Was in Session.***

Denton was flying a combat mission from the aircraft carrier *Independence* in 1965, bombing a warehouse complex that was the staging area for North Vietnamese military equipment, when his plane was hit twice by enemy fire, and he was forced to bail out. Fished out of a river, the severely injured Denton began his long ordeal of survival and deprivation. During an interview with a Japanese television reporter a year after his capture, Denton famously blinked the word T-O-R-T-U-R-E in Morse code during the interview. The film was eventually spirited away to America, making him an acclaimed military hero. Denton's prison experience was made into a movie, *Return with Honor*, starring Hal Holbrook. Denton appeared in the movie prominently identified as a POW. Much of the military footage came from North Vietnamese archives.

It was the stuff of American exceptionalism. Denton's refusal to compromise his loyalty to his country was documented and applauded. These were acts of courage greater than politics. The two Christian organizations effectively spread the word in churches throughout Alabama—Reagan for President, Denton for Senate.

Denton easily dispatched Selden by a 2-1 margin in the Republican primary. He campaigned on the issue of American survival, the need for a stronger national defense, and his strong religious beliefs. Voters found Denton more attractive than GOP party elders.

At the same time, no clear winner emerged from the Democrat primary, even though Donald Stewart came agonizingly close to winning the nomination outright with 48.5 percent of the vote. Stewart's runoff opponent was a rerun with Jim Folsom. State Senator Finis St. John and Mrs. Frank Ross Stewart of Piedmont forced the runoff with a combined total of almost 7,200 votes. It would be a much different race the second time around.

To complicate matters for Stewart, he had been hounded in the national press about campaign funds, which muckraking journalist Jack Anderson insisted were illegal. Stewart had accumulated a massive campaign debt in the 1978 short-term election. News reports showed that he took out a $257,000 personal loan to help finance his campaign with financial support from Big Labor. Even though no apparent laws were broken, Anderson thoroughly pounded Stewart about his campaign contributions, calling him "dodgy," creating undeserved suspicion about his character. After the election, Stewart's hometown newspaper, *The Anniston Star*, canceled Anderson's column.

H. Brandt Ayers, publisher of *The Anniston Star*, and the editorial staff recognized what was happening to "their" senator and attempted to moderate his financial controversy. *The Star* sent a reporter up to Cullman to look into Folsom's background and report on his almost-nonexistent civic involvement. The resulting article summarized Folsom's unflattering professional career. He had not held public office in Cullman or managed a local business. He was Jim Folsom Jr., son of Big Jim Folsom, working occasional jobs and running for public office based solely on the family name.

But the Folsom name and Jack Anderson's sacking of Stewart was enough for a Folsom win. A light turnout (the only statewide race on the ballot) gave the advantage to Folsom, and he swept forty-two counties, winning a close race with slightly over 50 percent of the vote. As expected, Folsom won his father's political base in rural Alabama, the "Yonder Boxes." Stewart and Folsom fought over the black vote, and Folsom won that voting bloc too.

Another factor could have possibly influenced the Democrat runoff, however. Veteran political journalist Bob Ingram said in his book of recollections, ***That's the Way I Saw It***, that Republican crossover votes changed the election, and no one is more certain than Donald Stewart himself. Ingram quoted Stewart as saying that "There was never any doubt in my mind what happened. If you look at the returns, it's plain to see." Stewart said that the objective of the crossover voting was to give the GOP nominee, Jeremiah Denton, a weaker opponent in November. Ingram reviewed the Democrat runoff returns and agreed with Stewart.

Though the GOP did not acknowledge coordinated crossover tactics in the Senate race, Alabama Republicans, shut out of state politics for over a century, had a stalwart conservative on the ballot opposing the well-known heir of a political icon. Money solved the problem of name recognition for Denton—money and the rising tide of voter resentment. The national movement to get Jimmy Carter out of the White House added further meaning to Denton's Senate campaign in Alabama.

Democrats did not have an answer for Denton's popular appeal, his stirring war record, his moral crusade, or his personal faith. But it was the chairman of the Alabama Democratic Party, George Lewis Bailes, who made the most outrageous statement of the campaign. Speaking to the Huntsville Press Club only days before the election, Bailes complained. "I've never heard of any flag officer or general officer that was so dumb that he got captured by the enemy anywhere."

The clumsy comment set off a firestorm in the state media. Folsom said he was "very disappointed" in the party chair, and that the attack was "uncalled for." Folsom made an equally critical statement that Denton was putting on a "charade" with his profession of strong moral and religious beliefs. Bailes later apologized publicly to members of the military, but he refused to apologize to Admiral Denton and Republicans.

Denton raised three times as much money as young Folsom, enabling him to saturate the state's larger population centers and rural counties with his message. The most aggressive groups supporting his candidacy, with Ronald Reagan at the top of the Republican ticket, were the Moral Majority and Concerned Citizens of Alabama. The fundamental, evangelical Christian endorsement of Denton, a Catholic, helped broaden the appeal of the Republican Party.

Jeremiah Denton became a US Senator with a 51 percent victory over Folsom, the first Republican senator elected in a hundred years, and the first Catholic elected statewide. He won in the populous urban centers: Montgomery, Jefferson, Madison, Mobile, and Tuscaloosa Counties. In the "Yonder Boxes," Denton undermined the impact of Folsom's traditional rural strength. The Republican victory was important in taking Alabama away from the racial hatred that had so uselessly hindered progress in the state.

At the November 4 election night rally, Denton made the customary comment that the election was "humbling," and graciously expressed his gratitude to the throng of supporters, one of whom was Bobbie James, wife of Democrat Governor Fob James. Mrs. James joined the Denton family on stage as cameras recorded the celebration. She spoke to the crowd and said that she was not bound to the Democratic Party because her husband was the governor. Mrs. James contributed $1,000 to Denton.

The reality of white Christians involved in political campaigns was too much for liberal newspapers that readily accepted the political activism of black ministers and black churches. *The Anniston Star*, which lost big in the reelection campaign of its hometown senator, editorialized on the subject of "Pulpit and Politics." "Brandy" Ayers's lengthy editorial landed squarely on Jerry Falwell and the Moral Majority, which had helped defeat a few prominent political figures throughout the nation in the Reagan victory. *The Star* seemed genuinely offended by the notion that there were "Christian" candidates and "Christian" issues in politics," insisting that politics had always been a secular matter. The editorial misread the emerging involvement of Christian churches and their common evangelical activism. (*The Anniston Star*)

The conservative tide of Republicans and independents took the White House and elected a majority in the US Senate, sending many of the upper chamber's prominent Democrats into early retirement. Reagan won by a 51-to-41 percent margin nationally, surprising out-of-touch Democrats. In Jimmy Carter's home state of Georgia, Herman Talmadge, quintessential Southern senator, lost to Mack Mattingly, chairman of the Georgia Republican Party. George McGovern, a senator from South Dakota and 1972 Democrat presidential nominee, also lost. McGovern said it was the result of a "gang of cutthroats" who threatened "to defeat all of the humane and progressive members of the Senate."

President Carter was equally surprised by his defeat. Only days before the election, polls had him leading Reagan. He accused Reagan and the Republicans of ignoring the poor and all but cloaking Reagan in the white sheets of a hatemongering Klansman, classic infantilisms of the left. But Carter lost Alabama and the South. When told that "it was all over," Carter broke down in tears. He made the face-saving explanation that his defeat did not mean that the American people had an "aversion" to him, confused by the national mandate against his demoralizing administration. Carter left behind a huge national debt that was creeping toward the unthinkable one trillion dollars.

Reagan was an effective populous leader who campaigned

on the themes of hard work, opportunity, strong national defense, and traditional American values—contrasting liberal Democrats' social doctrines of gay rights, welfare entitlements, and big government. Reagan became the most prominent personality of the modern Republican Party as the nation turned to greater influence by conservative principles. There was nothing racial about the Reagan doctrine other than the wild imagination of Democrats.

Merle Black recognized dramatic change for the Republican Party with the Reagan victory. "This was one of the most striking examples of partisan realignment ever, and it was a huge change for the South," Black observed. "At this point, the Democrats really got religion that they were indeed the minority party."

In Alabama, George Wallace got the 1980 presidential election all wrong too. He believed that Reagan's impressive win marked the end of liberal politics in America, giving himself credit that the country was becoming more conservative.

Wallace aligned himself with his Deep South neighbor and campaigned for Carter. Wallace had campaigned in Alabama to build white support for Carter, while Carter concentrated on winning the minority vote. The twofold strategy had worked in 1976, but it proved useless in Carter's populous-versus-liberal race against Reagan in 1980. One thing for sure—Alabama had turned to greater conservative politics in the 1980 election.

Alabama Senator Jeremiah Denton

CHAPTER ELEVEN

The inevitable return of George Wallace

To no one's great surprise, particularly Democrats, Fob James declined to run for reelection in 1982, having temporarily satisfied his ambition to govern. The James administration appeared to operate like a rudderless ship and had not delivered on Fob's promises from the back of the yellow school bus. Gov. James got his education bill through the legislature, the absolute top concern of Alabamians embarrassed by low rankings, but James struggled with the simple matter of being a reform governor. The school bus symbolized education reform, but by the end of his administration, it was seen as just another election gimmick. Parents were sadly disappointed that state schools were still much the same, while James chose to fight personal battles rather than force reform for education.

Gerald Johnson, professor of political science at Auburn University, said in his article, "Montgomery Wars: Religion and Alabama Politics," that during James's first term, the governor took an aggressive role in America's culture wars—religion against politics. Johnson said James challenged federal judicial power and supported displaying Christian symbols in public buildings, specifically the Ten Commandments, all of which, like Wallace outbursts, attracted the national media to the South's somewhat eccentric political way of setting things right.

Gov. James bought a house for his family in Montgomery, an awkward decision for a governor, and only used the Governor's Mansion for official functions. The religious interests of Alabama's First Family became a point of public discussion when the press reported that First Lady Bobbi James was attending faraway religious events in state planes. The James's religious interests concentrated on Israel and their personal ties with Orthodox Judaism.

Fob James's conversion to the Democratic Party did not convince Alabamians that he was a capable leader. Recognizing that James had failed at education reform, voters turned their attention back to Wallace, who had pioneered Alabama's community college system in the 1960s. Almost deaf and paralyzed from the waist down, Wallace prepared for his final election.

In the four-year interim after leaving Montgomery, Wallace had served as head of Rehabilitation Resources at the University of Alabama in Birmingham, a financial safety net created especially for him. Returning to politics, he said that he had repented of his racial sins (he did it personally at Dexter Avenue church), changed his ways, and confessed as much to anyone who may have a vote in the next election. He was no more or no less than his opponents and had proven in the past that he was willing to change his convictions for votes. Hope arose in Alabama that the long primacy of divisive racial rhetoric was finally ending.

Prepping for the 1982 campaign, Wallace was forced to tone down his reckless racial talk for two reasons: scores of black Democrats qualified for public office due to desegregation, but more importantly, people had grown tired of the same old racial grind. Democrats could not oppose civil rights progress because the politics of race had changed.

African Americans in large cities identified as New Deal Democrats, the party of their racial enemies. Blacks, as a new demographic, had shown that they had achieved a measure of political influence. By this time in Alabama history, party alignment had taken shape: African Americans and old-line white loyalists dominated the Democratic Party; conservatives, including party-switching Democrats, rallied around Republicans.

Two contenders of note qualified to run for governor in the 1982 Democrat primary with Wallace: George McMillan, lieutenant governor, and Joe McCorquodale, Speaker of the House. Both were veteran campaigners willing to challenge Wallace, conversion experience and all. After the primary had winnowed out the winner, however, voters would discover that Wallace had not only given up his original sin . . . he had found another.

What the Wallace camp was capable of doing had severely contaminated the 1970 governor's election when Albert Brewer ran first in the primary, and the Wallace machine attacked the thoroughly principled Brewer family. In crossroad villages and hamlets, Wallace operatives showed doctored photos of Brewer's daughter holding hands with a young black man. When the ADC endorsed Brewer, the Wallace campaign took out newspaper ads to inform voters about his favor with blacks. Tactics like this set up another Wallace win.

By the end of the Democrat primary, the two top candidates were Wallace and George McMillan. McMillan had polled 29.62 percent of the vote, edging McCorquodale with 25.05 percent. Wallace had been unable to win the nomination outright with 42.53 percent.

McMillan was worth a second look by Alabama voters. Raised on a Black Belt farm in Greenville, he excelled academically at Auburn and the University of Virginia Law School, eventually establishing his own law firm in Birmingham.

After serving a term in the Alabama House and Senate, McMillan was elected lieutenant governor in 1978, the same year Fob James became governor. McMillan further had the distinction of being named one of the Ten Most Outstanding Legislators in the Nation. Respected among fellow Democrats, he led Alabama's delegation to the 1980 Democrat Convention when Jimmy Carter won the nomination but lost a second term.

With African Americans as an emerging influence in the Democratic Party, the Wallace confederation resorted to another underhanded method of frustrating an opponent—they whispered to the four corners of the state that McMillan was a homosexual. Wallace folks pointed to McMillan's high-pitched voice as proof and said that he was a sissy. With money, power, jobs, and the Wallace legacy threatened, gutter politics scarred the campaign as Wallace and his pals turned their big guns loose for an unprecedented fourth term.

Aware of the gay trash talk and that Wallace lackeys were lurking about looking for fresh gossip, McMillan refuted the carefully planted lies and arranged to have his family accompany him on campaign stops, introducing them to the crowds. Like Albert Brewer, scurrilous slander did not fit McMillan's personal campaign style.

Wallace seriously damaged the state's reputation as early as the sixties when he deliberately placed his political ambitions, characterized by his defiance of the federal government, above the good of the people and the state's economic interests. A vice

THE INEVITABLE RETURN OF GEORGE WALLACE

president of Boeing, which had a huge facility in Huntsville, publicly warned Wallace that Boeing would not add another job in Alabama until something was done about the state's hostile business climate threatened by Democrat trial lawyers.

McMillan came close to pulling off a major upset. Begging the forgiveness of aggrieved blacks and lying about the character of his opponent earned Wallace the Democrat nomination by a very slim 51.19-to-48.81 percent margin. Other than the loss to Patterson, it was a hairbreadth escape, the closest in his political career.

Wallace was facing another trial by fire, however. Counting the days until the general election, Republican nominee **Emory Folmar,** the tough bare-knuckles mayor of Montgomery, waited for Wallace. A rarity in Alabama politics was shaping up, a two-party race for governor.

Emory Folmar represented the best of the Alabama Republicans since Jim Martin in the early sixties. A decorated Korean War veteran, he became wealthy developing shopping centers and had been mayor of Montgomery for two decades, the epicenter of race and politics in Alabama. An article in *Alabama* magazine observed that there was no middle ground with Folmar; people either respected him or hated him. Blacks were dead set against his law-and-order management style, ignoring the fact that Wallace had been their bitter archenemy.

Folmar was noted for being in excellent physical shape, a habit that he developed as a high school athlete and reinforced by a tour of duty as an officer in the US Marine Corps. He was stern, fearless, and dedicated to his responsibilities as the leader of the city, which meant everything that happened in Montgomery was his business. Folmar was known to accompany city employees on routine jobs and often made the rounds with garbage crews. He wanted the citizens of Montgomery to get the best service for their tax dollars. Two ambushes on the streets of Montgomery prompted Folmar to carry a pistol.

No sitting president had been to Montgomery since Jefferson Davis, but President Reagan rewarded Mayor Folmar's loyalty to the Republican Party on March 15, 1982, by addressing the Alabama Legislature. The president spoke about American freedoms and work ethics with a Confederate Flag prominently displayed in the background. Rep. Alvin Holmes of Montgomery did some political grandstanding and walked out during Reagan's speech.

Wallace needed the black vote to win both the primary and the general election. He managed blacks the same way he managed the white vote . . . by telling them what they wanted to hear. A meeting was arranged with the Alabama Democratic Conference, so Wallace could ask for their support against Folmar, who the ADC absolutely hated. J. L. Chestnut, Selma attorney, wrote about the meeting in his book, ***Black in Selma***:

When he beat McMillan in the primary, Wallace came seeking the ADC endorsement in the general election against Emory Folmar, the Republican mayor of Montgomery. Joe Louis Reed, the chairman of the ADC, usually called the shots on the state and national endorsements, but this was one decision he didn't want to make by himself. Joe called about twenty ADC leaders from around the state to come to Montgomery to meet with Wallace the next day in the boardroom of the Alabama Education Association, the state teachers union where Joe worked. We were all

*sitting around the big conference table when Wallace—
smoking a big cigar—came in with a black man pushing
his wheelchair.*

The November general election came down to Wallace running on his record and Folmar reminding voters how Wallace had abused his power. Folmar's unflinching conservatism turned Wallace around and forced him to campaign as a Progressive. Folmar hit Wallace and the Democrats hard with accusations that the Wallace image was hurting the state, but he backed away from mentioning evident health issues, fearing backlash from the press and voters. Republicans were enthusiastic and hopeful, but at the same time, they were careful not to make any rash predictions about the Wallace sympathy factor following the assassination attempt during a Maryland presidential appearance.

Wallace, contrite and confessing, ultimately prevailed with loyal Democrats voting a straight party ballot—winning comfortably 57.64 percent to Folmar's 39.06 percent. Wallace won sixty-four of sixty-seven counties, and remarkably, some 90 percent of black Democrats voted for him. Even if blacks had boycotted the old segregationist, Wallace would have still won. The black vote had been the critical factor for Wallace in the Democrat runoff against McMillan.

Once again, Republican hopes for a breakthrough win against the Wallace-Democrat machine did not materialize. More than anything, Folmar aggressively opposed hard-core corruption in state government and represented conservative values to voters, who did not understand exactly how Republicans could possibly help the people of Alabama.

Republicans were not shut out in the 1982 election, however.

The GOP qualified and elected still more legislative candidates that resulted in a total change of twenty-four Senate and House seats for the party. There were now three Republicans in the Senate: Ann Bedsole of Mobile, the first woman elected to the Alabama Legislature in 1978; Bill Cabaniss and Spencer Bachus from Jefferson County. Albert Lee Smith of Jefferson County lost one of the three remaining congressional seats to Democrat challenger Ben Erdreich.

Auburn University Professors Anne Permaloff and Carl Grafton analyzed the Wallace-Folmar race for the *Montgomery Advertiser*. They suggested that probably no Alabama gubernatorial race this century had been more heavily influenced by national trends, and that it had seriously affected Republicans in the governor's election. Nationally, Democrats were successful in linking Reagan and Republicans to unemployment, while playing down evidence of the economic recovery. It was vintage Democrat politics, and it helped defeat Folmar.

Permaloff and Grafton pointed to Folmar's weak appeal in the traditional Republican anchor counties of Jefferson and Montgomery. Folmar carried Montgomery, his home county, by a slim 174 votes. Wallace did not carry Montgomery County in 1970 or the 1982 Democrat primary runoff against McMillan.

It was true, Permaloff and Grafton explained, that Wallace had major negatives going into the election: cronyism, a poor industrial development record, his physical condition, and civil rights. Folmar slammed past Wallace administrations, but voters were suspicious that Folmar and the Republicans were no different than Democrats. Older Alabamians still had memories of living through the Great Depression under Republican President Herbert Hoover. Folmar had been correct about one issue in the campaign—the Wallace temperament had been a factor in keeping the industry from investing in Alabama.

The revelation that surprised voters most was how Wallace rolled up a huge majority of black votes. Not only did black Democrats vote solidly for him, but the high turnout was attributed to increased voter registration drives in African American communities. Wallace, who used a wheelchair, built a coalition of blacks, blue-collar workers, and the rural independent vote.

Folks chuckled about Wallace winning the black vote. Maybe . . . they saw the anointing of an old Southern racist by blacks as high political humor. The audacity of Wallace pleading with black leaders for their endorsement ranks up there with Big Jim Folsom admitting that he stole from the state, but he wanted the people to vote for him anyway.

The lone benefit of Wallace's final election was that Democrats—after having beaten, stomped, and cussed all things racial—were forced to address the more substantive economic and education issues facing the state—Emory Folmar's campaign themes.

CHAPTER TWELVE

Democrats self-destruct

The effects of the Carter recession lingered into the Reagan administration, but the economy eventually recovered, and the nation regained its economic strength by the 1984 presidential election. A nation sick with a malaise under Carter was back, and some Republicans referred to themselves as Reaganites, an endorsement of President Reagan's economic and public policies. Prime Minister Margaret Thatcher said that Reagan restored the faith of the American people in themselves. Alabamians were also experiencing the benefits of the economic recovery, riding the crest of reinvigorated American capitalism.

Again, referencing the Black brothers in *The Rise of Southern Republicans*, during the Reagan administration, the Alabama Republican Party benefited from what Earl and Merle Black termed as a major shift in voting trends. More conservatives identified their political and social philosophies with Republicans, specifically issues related to welfare, law and order, and economics. Reagan brought more Democrats and independents into the party by encouraging disaffected blue-collar voters to change their party affiliation, a radical departure from the business-education base of the GOP. That inclusion would vastly strengthen the conservative movement—considering the South is one-third of the nation's voting population.

The Republican Party expanded its growing middle-class base, and evangelicals found a home for their moral crusades. Following Carter's embarrassing and failed administration, white voters in Alabama and elsewhere in the South gradually identified as "conservative" to rid themselves of the wearisome mumblings of Democrats about racism. Further, Republicans strongly opposed the national agenda of liberal Democrats that tended to divide the nation with identity politics.

In 1986, Alabama Republicans wanted to protect the Senate seat won by Jeremiah Denton in 1980 and qualify a contender for governor, in that order. Wallace, who had kept Republicans at bay for over eighteen years, was leaving the governor's office to anyone capable of convincing voters to follow his legacy— a Democrat, of course. Wallace had hobbled Republican party-building ambitions, but his political dominance had also kept the state alienated from the America known as the greatest source of good in the world.

The other major races for Democrats focused on a single US Senate seat held by Howell Heflin and seven congressional seats, two by Republicans. Four Republicans qualified for Heflin's seat: Albert Lee Smith, Clint Walker, Doug Carter, and Joseph Keith. The two Republican-held congressional seats were challenged by strong Democrats. Alabama's political landscape was on the verge of change. The 1986 gubernatorial election served as the preface that reordered the state's ancient political system.

The governor's race that year was so controversial that it remains the hallmark for party intervention in a statewide election. Patrick Cotter and James Stovall authored a book, *After Wallace*, that detailed the intrigue of what eventually elevated the stagnant Alabama Republican Party to prominence. This chapter will reference that source, among others, to authenticate the maze of bad strategy and legal errors in that epic election.

We begin with Harold Guy Hunt, a perennial nice guy and reliable Republican activist, who won the GOP nomination for governor in 1986 by a shade over 29,000 votes. There was not much optimism that the Primitive Baptist preacher would eventually win. Hunt had run for governor in 1978 in a landslide loss to then-Democrat Fob James.

A vocational preacher of modest means and a North Alabama Hill Country farmer with a high school education, Hunt had proven his worth to the party by chairing the Alabama delegation to the 1976 Republican National Convention in Kansas City, where he lobbied unsuccessfully for Ronald Reagan's nomination for president. In 1980, Hunt again chaired the Reagan campaign and led the state's Republican delegation to the national convention, when Reagan won the nomination and went on to beat Carter. Hunt's reward was an appointment as state executive director for the Agriculture Stabilization and Conservation Service. Preparing for the 1986 gubernatorial campaign, Hunt resigned the federal position to pursue what most folks saw as another quixotic folly. On the way, Hunt easily defeated businessman Doug Carter for the nomination in the June 1986 Republican primary.

Republicans were overshadowed by the powerful Alabama Democratic Party primary, where veteran politicians customarily fought to face weak Republican opposition. As the election unfolded, the real excitement for the 1986 gubernatorial election rested with Democrats, not the less-relevant Republicans. The

Democrats would not disappoint, although in a surprisingly destructive way.

The Democrat lineup eager to succeed George Wallace looked like Murderers Row in the heyday of the New York Yankees. Former Lt. Governor George McMillan announced early in 1985 and began an aggressive media campaign. McMillan had reason to be optimistic. With the slanderous Wallace gang sidelined, he felt that he could pick up where he left off in 1982, when he gave Wallace a heart-stopping scare in the Democrat runoff despite smear tactics.

The other prominent Democrat was Fob James. James emphasized two major themes in the primary: government waste, and he wanted to finish the work he started during his term as governor from 1978–1982. But James did not resonate with voters, primarily because he did not prove himself as a capable state leader in his first term. When his campaign failed to attract substantial attention from voters and the media, it became obvious that Alabamians were not enthusiastic about granting James another term to do as he pleased.

Democrats were looking elsewhere. Wallace and his pals had already picked a successor; they were committed to Bill Baxley, the presumptive heir for governor. A dynamic speaker, Baxley led a colorful lifestyle as the youngest attorney general in state history. Handsome and charismatic, Baxley was a Las Vegas gambler, a lady's man while married to his wife, Lucy, and partied like a wealthy playboy. It was a career profile reminiscent of JFK in his prime, and the leading lights of the Democratic Party saw him as their kind of man—idealistic and liberal to a fault. Dutifully, Baxley played his role with the dash and aplomb of a rising Southern politician to the admiration of party elders.

McMillan, James, and Baxley, by themselves, could have created enough fireworks for a sensational election season and not have made any grievous mistakes that would do serious damage to the party, even with Wallace watching from his goat hill office. But Alabama Attorney General Charlie Graddick, a former Republican like Fob James, crashed the Alabama governor's race. Graddick brought a more conservative law-and-order dimension to the race, and an effective way of laying into Baxley that caught the attention of voters. With his Republican background, unlike charming Fob James, Graddick made no serious effort to rehabilitate himself to impress Democrat elites. He was the immoveable "stone face."

Graddick, a native of Mobile and educated in the private University Military School, achieved stardom as an exceptional all-around athlete. In 1963, he won a scholarship to the University of Alabama to play quarterback for Coach Paul Bryant. But his collegiate sports career lasted only a few days once Graddick found himself playing behind Joe Namath and another future All-American, Kenny Stabler. He opted for student life at the university and cheered for the Crimson Tide national championship football teams.

On graduating, he applied to Alabama's Law School and was turned down because there was no available room in the next class. Determined to earn a law degree, Graddick and his new wife, Corinne, drove up to Samford University in Birmingham, where he applied to the Cumberland Law School, which had moved from Lebanon, Tennessee, in 1961. Cumberland had room in its law school and accepted him immediately.

After law school and a brief private practice, Graddick was encouraged to run for district attorney in Mobile. In 1978, he ran in a crowded field of nine Democrats and won. At twenty-eight, he was one of the youngest DAs in the nation. His election was even more remarkable because he ran as a Republican, the family's political affiliation. When he decided to run for Alabama attorney general, he sought the wise counsel of Arthur Outlaw, who Graddick referred to as "Mr. Republican in Mobile." Outlaw advised Graddick to run as a Democrat because he didn't believe a Republican could win a statewide election. Outlaw, who served as state GOP chairman in 1989–'90, advised Graddick that Republican conventions at the time were so small that they could be held in a classroom.

Bill Baxley and Charlie Graddick came to Montgomery during the 1978 election cycle and both wanted to follow Wallace as governor. The 1986 governor's race served as the perfect setting for their ambitions, Baxley as the typical liberal with numerous endorsements: labor unions, the state teachers lobby, and the growing black vote now active in the Democratic Party. Graddick and Fob James were expected to split the modest conservative vote. In the mideighties, there were not enough Republicans in Alabama to form a competitive voting bloc.

Kendal Weaver, Associated Press, reported that early polls funded by the Alabama Farm Bureau showed a surprising shift in the governor's race. Graddick had moved into the lead over Baxley by 3 percentage points, with James trailing Baxley by 2 points. McMillan was in single digits. The Birmingham polling firm, Davis, Pebfield & Associates, had Baxley ahead of Graddick. Clearly, many Wallace voters were not supporting Baxley. "A lot of people assumed that Baxley would inherit the Wallace vote," Graddick said. "But we are getting many of them . . . the hardworking, God-fearing people."

There was a major reason for the sudden change. At the height of the campaign, revelations of an alleged affair involving Bill Baxley did serious damage to his already-suspect reputation. The *Birmingham News* reported in late March that Baxley's state car driven by a state trooper, had been used occasionally to ferry a reporter, Marie Prat, once employed by the Associated Press, back-and-forth to Baxley's Montgomery apartment. Baxley attempted to laugh it off with the comment that he had been giving rides to his friends. The subject came up again in a debate, and Baxley made stumbling remarks hinting of guilt. Graddick called him a liar for denying a romantic relationship with Prat. After that, the media camped out near Baxley's Montgomery quarters.

In the meantime, Lucy Baxley, Bill's long-suffering wife, held news conferences around the state in an attempt to temper the much-publicized infidelity of her husband. But Lucy's wifely pleadings only drew more attention to Bill's badly compromised character.

The polls were about right. Baxley polled 36 percent of the primary vote, but Graddick struck close behind him with 30 percent, forcing a runoff. Immediate controversy erupted in the runoff because state primary laws did not require party registration. This became a legal trap for Graddick, who had encouraged Republicans who voted in the GOP primary to cross over and vote for him in the Democrat runoff. Democrats had adopted a rule following Fob James's victory against crossover voting in party runoffs—but had not enforced it.

The Capstone Poll had Graddick slightly ahead in a race too close to call. Again, polling data was correct. Baxley jumped to an early lead in labor-stronghold Birmingham, but Graddick quickly made up ground with the Gulf Coast returns. Graddick overcame the 70,000-primary vote deficit and won the June 24 runoff by a very slim 8,756 vote margin, or 50.4 percent of the vote. He ran strong with conservatives, Republicans (it was estimated that between 10,000 and 20,000 Republicans voted Democrat), and independents. Hard-line Democrats were incensed by the prospects of a second Republican convert becoming governor, and party officials huddled to discuss their options. Graddick declared victory while Democrats squawked about illegal voting and met prematurely with some members of the Alabama Legislature to plan his administration.

Anticipating sure retribution for spoiling the Democrat primary, the day after the startling runoff victory, Graddick ordered the votes impounded. Mobile County Circuit Judge Braxton Kittrell issued the order for authorities statewide to impound all election materials and equipment. Graddick said that he was concerned that the Democrats might steal his narrow victory over Baxley. The move was the first legal defense Graddick would make. Subsequent events by Democrats intent on wresting the election from Graddick continued for over three months. Graddick's former affiliation with the Republican Party deeply angered heavily favored Democrats who plotted revenge.

Democrats persuaded a black couple in Huntsville to file suit in federal court, contesting Graddick's election, contending that Graddick had used his state office to diminish the black vote. The suit challenged Graddick's attorney general's opinion that Republicans should be allowed to vote in the Democrat runoff, claiming it violated the 1965 Voting Rights Act. On Montgomery television, Bob Ingram commented on Graddick's opinion when he questioned the legality of crossover voting. The suit went forward based on the Democrat crossover rule.

The decision of the three-judge 11th US Court of Appeals created the exact legal precedent that Baxley and the Democrats needed—a second shot at beating the upstart former Republican running as a Democrat. The panel ruled that Graddick violated the federal Voting Rights Act by encouraging Republicans to ignore party rules and vote in the Democrat primary. Graddick said the court decision insulted Alabama voters. That would be the top understatement of the entire voting controversy.

The ruling came with a risky double-edged option, however. The federal judges allowed Democrats to make an either/or decision: Either hold another runoff election or declare Baxley the winner of the Democrat runoff for governor. A five-member committee of Democrat officials, Baxley men at that, decided that another runoff was out of the question, fearing that Baxley would risk losing again. Democrats took the easy way out and awarded the nomination to party favorite Bill Baxley. (The committee was comprised of Democrat Chairman John Baker, Pat Lindsey, John Knight, Bill Blount, and Jack Boggan.)

The decision proved fatal, not only to Baxley, but it also further exaggerated the arrogance of Democrats. More importantly, the court decision did not bode well with the voting public. Alabamians were outraged that the losing candidate was awarded the nomination, knowing that Baxley was the party favorite. Baxley said publicly that the nomination should belong to him. (Cotter and Stovall created a three-page chronology of events during the July and August challenge.)

The most foolish miscalculation of all was the false assurance that voters had short memories and would forget by election time. It was premeditated senselessness for a party not known for character and ethics. Baxley and his Democrat allies would discover that their oft-spoken proverb about the short memory of voters did not justify a bad decision. Voters would remember with great clarity and take their revenge on the calculating Democrats.

Charles Graddick reacted to the ruling and the decision to remove him from the ballot by threatening to wage a write-in campaign, but he soon abandoned the idea. Now, only Guy Hunt and the profoundly overmatched and underfunded Republicans stood between the Democrats and their control of the state government. At that point, Democrats were vastly overconfident about winning the election, trying to convince themselves that the controversy would blow over before the November general election.

Elections are won and lost on tactical decisions. By pushing Graddick aside, Democrats committed a disordered political blunder that didn't square with regular folks. Further, Baxley and the Democrats had failed to recognize that their conservative opponent, Guy Hunt, seen as a political novelty, had greater ethical appeal among voters than the Democrats could overcome in the general election.

Democrats didn't fully understand the contempt that voters had toward their party. A reasonable assessment would have helped them realize that people had turned against them for violating the sense of fair play. Most Alabamians may have been unschooled in the rules of politics, but switching Graddick and Baxley was not the sporting thing to do, nor was the decision made with public involvement in a fair election. Alabamians passed judgment on heavy-handed Democrats, and many decided to vote Republican, even though they were only slightly familiar with the party and even less with Hunt.

Baxley made it worse. He insulted the simple Primitive Baptist preacher from Holly Pond and treated him with outright scorn. Democrats had extensive experience at loudmouthed jeering at political hacks, having practiced on Democrats like Ralph "Shorty" Price, the somewhat clownish rural character from Barbour County, who ran for governor four times. Baxley ridiculed Hunt as "unqualified" because he only had a high school education and worked as an Amway distributor and chicken farmer. It was downright snobbery.

But Hunt held firm. The sarcasms and criticisms did not sit well with ordinary people with a high school education and simple values. Baxley's insults, profaned by his own playboy reputation and the scandal with the reporter, further offended working families who attended fundamental Christian churches. The campaign had the appearance of an out-of-control catastrophe in slow motion. Baxley and the Democrats continually rubbed Hunt's nose in his lack of personal and professional success, a tactic that worked against them.

Many believed, with good reason, that Hunt's best asset was Republican strategist John Grenier, although Grenier had been late getting into the election. Previously, Hunt had managed his own campaigns as a family adventure, primarily a recreational vehicle loaded with friends and relatives. With a premier political drama playing out in their favor, Republicans rallied around their overwhelmed nominee.

Democrats turned the 1986 election into a political circus. Republican Party Chairman Emory Folmar and State Representative Spencer Bachus, who left the legislature to manage Hunt's campaign, gave Hunt experienced organizational support. Before the surprising election controversy, Republicans had shown little interest and provided few resources to the governor's race (Folmar didn't care for Hunt because he lacked a respectable profession); instead, the party focused on reelecting Senator Jeremiah Denton. This relegated Hunt to forgotten candidate status, understaffed and underfunded.

As the election controversy intensified, Folmar and Bachus quickly changed all of that. Though John Grenier only joined the campaign barely six weeks before the election, he made the best call of Hunt's campaign. He rightfully understood that Democrats had alienated voters, and Hunt would be elected governor if he kept a low profile. That strategy made Emory Folmar the public face of the GOP, and he backed Hunt with the full support of the party.

About that time, Hunt's campaign got a much-needed break from an unlikely source. Dr. Curtis Baker, a Clanton dentist, provided the means for Hunt, headquartered in Gardendale north of Birmingham, could mobilize a campaign team. GOP operative Bill Goolsby said that Baker provided Hunt with a large van and driver, a credit card for travel expenses, and a bodyguard. Hunt, Goolsby, and campaign staffers plastered *"Hunt for Governor"* signs on the van and launched a more visible campaign for Hunt.

Grenier and Folmar got busy raising money to keep the campaign afloat, but more importantly, the late-arriving Grenier kept a tight lid on the Republican nominee. He reminded Hunt that his silence would capitalize on public anger until frustrated voters cast their ballots in November. Hunt did just that. He made no comments to the media during the final days of the campaign, ignoring Democrat insults and furious public squabbling.

The strategy worked. On November 4, 1986, Alabamians elected Harold Guy Hunt as Alabama's first Republican governor since David P. Lewis in 1872. And it wasn't that close. Hunt polled 56 percent to Baxley's 44 percent—a powerful statement for Republicans.

Cotter and Stovall wrote in *After Wallace*, that a preelection Capstone Poll found that Hunt's initial support came from younger, more-educated, and higher-income voters. The final verdict of the electorate was just and well-deserved. The values of ordinary Alabamians formed a powerful voting bloc that demonstrated only the people should elect its leaders—not appoint them. This attitude reflected the belief that state elections were an unassailable populous tradition. John Grenier, who resurrected the Alabama Republican Party along with James Martin, served as Hunt's chief of staff.

In other statewide elections, Republicans held the two remaining congressional seats, reelecting Jack Edwards and Bill Dickinson. But disaster struck in Senator Jeremiah Denton's reelection. Denton, champion of the religious right in 1980, was challenged by Democrat Richard Shelby of Tuscaloosa. Shelby was the US Representative for the Seventh District. Early Capstone Polls had Denton comfortably ahead of Shelby 51-to-37, but Shelby was taking advantage of Denton's personal dislike for campaigning, opting to remain in Washington tending to his senatorial duties. Trying to serve in the Senate and campaign in Alabama had a wearing effect on Denton. Still, Senator Denton had a decided edge raising money.

Shelby cut into Denton's poll numbers as November loomed. He slammed Denton's voting record on Social Security, accused Denton of voting for four pay raises, and claimed unethical campaign practices. Shelby neutralized Denton's reelection campaign and further reduced his lead despite the high-profile furor in the raucous governor's race.

The Senate vote was close as Republicans were taking the

governor's office for the first time in modern history. Shelby won 609,360 votes and Denton's 602,537—less than 1 percent of the total vote. What should have been a solid Republican win in the Senate resulted in a 50.3-to-49.7 percent defeat. Shelby's victory saved Alabama Democrats from a total disaster.

Controversy over the 1986 election continued with accusations about unethical campaign practices. The tide had turned for Alabama Republicans, and significant change came from the controversy created solely by the reckless political arrogance of Democrats. Democrats looked on Republicans—exampled by Bill Baxley's criticisms of Guy Hunt—as lesser people undeserving of the opportunity to govern. Democrats further belittled Hunt by calling him an "accidental" governor. That would change too.

Governor Guy Hunt signs a proclamation

CHAPTER THIRTEEN

❦

Blessings and curses
for Guy Hunt

Guy Hunt was as much an anomaly in Montgomery as he was in his native Cullman County. Primitive Baptists are not exactly commonplace in the heart of the South's Bible Belt. Few people can speak of ever having known a Primitive Baptist. Churches are small and plain and concentrated primarily in the southern and western regions of the country. The denomination of less than a thousand congregations worldwide originated in Appalachia and observed the historic Old-School Christian theology, reminiscent of Swiss Reformed theologian John Calvin—undiluted. Primitive Baptist doctrine and church polity oppose theological education, Sunday schools, and missionaries at home and abroad.

Primitive Baptist theology is based on predestination, irresistible grace, and God's sovereign grace for salvation alone. The church practices foot washings for members and claimed the 1611 King James Version Bible as the only authoritative text. Also striking is the practice of not taking church offerings for preachers or the maintenance of church property.

Guy Hunt was born June 17, 1933, to a farm family in Holly Pond, a small rural community some twelve miles east of Cullman on State Highway 278. Originally a German wine colony, Cullman has a prominent Catholic presence—specifically, a medieval monastery founded by Benedictine monks in 1888; Catholic schools, tourist attraction Ava Maria Grotto, and the ornate Sacred Heart Church. The 400-acre Shrine of the Most Holy Sacrament and the monastery of the Poor Clares are located in nearby Hanceville. Cullman is also widely known for the annual celebration of Oktoberfest.

Hunt married Helen Chambers in 1951, and the couple had four children. He joined the army during the Korean War and served in both the 101st Airborne and the First Infantry divisions of the US Army. He was cited for outstanding performance of military duty and awarded the Distinguished Service Medal. Hunt returned to the family farm in Holly Pond following his military service. (William H. Stewart, *Encyclopedia of Alabama*)

Harold G. Hunt would eventually pastor two part-time congregations and mature into a thoughtful biblical scholar in the tradition of his denomination. He wrote articles for the church periodical, *Paths of Truth*, and published booklets on church doctrine and Christian living. His preaching and writing earned him a broad, respected reputation among Primitive Baptists. For that reason, Hunt kept a full calendar of church meetings.

With all that known, Guy Hunt's cultural background did not indicate an interest in politics. A Republican in a rural county and region dominated by Democrats, he understood the simple values and interests of the people. In January 1987, Guy and Helen Hunt moved into the Governor's Mansion on South Perry Street, so the first Republican governor since 1872 could devote himself to the heady routine of overseeing the affairs of state.

Hunt was not alone in that task. John Grenier remained by his side with sage advice, and conservative all-arounders like Jim

Martin provided immeasurable counsel. Democrats groused about Hunt's dumb luck, and members of the state news media patronized him as the "farmer from Holly Pond." Democrats harped that Republicans were more accustomed to country club meetings and had not paid their dues to compete in the higher forms of politics. *Au contraire*, John Grenier would say. (Chapter 2 records the long history of failed GOP elections.)

Of Gov. Hunt's more important cabinet appointments, James Martin's acceptance of Hunt's offer as commissioner of conservation and natural resources was one of the best. Hunt had witnessed Martin's leadership in resurrecting Alabama's languishing Republican Party. The job came with an urgent priority, according to Hunt. Alabama and the federal government were in a dispute over the state's three-mile limit for oil and natural gas exploration. It could have cost the state millions in royalties. Hunt wanted Martin to determine Alabama's rightful share of drilling permits for big oil companies, energy discoveries that were made in Fob James's first administration.

Martin justified the governor's confidence when he reestablished the correct offshore boundary in Alabama's favor. Jim Martin identified the original boundary after wading barefoot in the Gulf around the Sand Island lighthouse, where the state set its boundaries. Timing was critical. Hurricane Frederick had already altered the shoreline so radically that the state could have lost valuable drilling permits.

Martin's quick action retained the original state boundaries that increased oil and natural gas royalties for Alabama. It helped fill state coffers for the General Fund and the Education Trust Fund. The General Fund applied the windfall to essential public services—prisons, mental health programs, care for the elderly, and public safety. A Rainy-Day Account within the Trust Fund set aside money to shore up budget shortfalls.

John McMillan, Fob James's cabinet appointee as commissioner of conservation and natural resources, said that Fob James and Sonny Callahan deserved recognition for protecting Alabama's natural resources from plundering politicians. McMillan negotiated offshore lease sales that enabled the state to eventually create the Alabama Trust Fund to safeguard revenue from the leases. Otherwise, Democrats in the legislature could have, out of habit, sold the leases and spent the money harum-scarum on pet projects in their home districts. McMillan recalled that during that period, Louisiana's Democrat-controlled legislature sold their offshore oil and gas rights and quickly spent the money. "We were determined that that was not going to happen in Alabama," McMillan declared.

"Most noteworthy," McMillan explained, "was how we negotiated the leases—by acreage, bonus, and royalties. The first offer was $50 million, which we rejected. Alabama would eventually receive $180 million for the leases." Bob Ingram, commenting for a Montgomery television station, suggested that viewers call Fob James and thank him for rejecting the first offer and gave James's home phone in Gulf Shores.

Forever Wild

Just as importantly, a tenth of the annual revenue from the Alabama Trust Fund enabled Martin to establish another long-term natural resource for the state. Martin said most of Hunt's first term was spent working out the funding arrangements for Forever Wild. Starting in 1987, Martin set about to do what previous state environmentalists, like Nature Conservancy of Alabama, previously had been unable to establish: organize a state agency that would protect Alabama resources and natural beauty from the mountains in North Alabama to the shores of the Gulf of Mexico. "Our first efforts under Governor Hunt was getting the funding in place," Martin explained in reference to the commission's share of the revenue from the Alabama Trust Fund. "Once the legal aspects were satisfied, we had the money to begin preparing legislation for Forever Wild."

The preliminaries took time. But in 1991, Jim Martin convened a group of thirty-three conservationists and created the innovative conservation program for the state. Martin included everyone who had an interest in launching such an ambitious project: businessmen, hunters and anglers, representatives of the timber industry, ALFA farmers, environmentalists, even the Alabama Education Association . . . some Republicans, some Democrats.

By the next year, the state government under Martin's guidance established the Forever Wild program, the most significant piece of environmental legislation in Alabama history. Senator Ann Bedsole of Mobile and Senator Doug Ghee sponsored the Forever Wild amendment in the Senate. Alabama voters approved the statewide referendum creating the program with 84 percent of the vote, one of the highest margins ever recorded for similar environmental legislation in the nation. The vote proved people cared about the state.

A wildlife park in Gadsden and a wildlife management area near Skyline in Jackson County were named for Martin. In retrospect, Jim Martin recognized the historical significance of Forever Wild but insisted that his ultimate contribution to Alabama was leading the Alabama Republican Party out of a century of political failure: "That was a defining period for Alabama Republicans."

Hunt, with little results, attempted to develop a working relationship with legislators. His laid-back rural manner tempted people to underestimate him. Yet, Hunt and the Republicans remained connected to the business community, and their common goal focused on rehabilitating the reputation of the state and restoring confidence in Alabama's political system.

Alabamians were not at all sure what Republicans stood for beyond national elections as Republicans struggled to stake out a place of relevance in state government. This was a transformational period when conservative Democrats in greater numbers were moving their political affiliation to the Republican Party.

A pressing issue for the new conservative governor was reforming the Alabama court system generating runaway jury awards. By the time Hunt took office, civil awards had quadrupled over the past decade reaching unparalleled limits in the history of American justice. The Republican business base persuaded Gov. Hunt and Democrats in the Alabama Legislature to pass tort reform legislation. The laws were passed to help restrain the too-generous tendencies of Alabama juries. Alabama had earned the reputation as "tort hell."

The Alabama Legislature placed legal limits on jury verdicts in counties where Democrats controlled the majority vote. Black Belt counties, in particular, were running up dangerously excessive jury awards that threatened or closed numerous businesses. Tuskegee, in Macon County, was the epicenter of excessive jury awards. Encouraged by new legislation that reigned in disproportionate judgments, Hunt rented a billboard in New York City that declared Alabama *"Open for Business."* His confidence was short-lived, however. Plaintiff lawyers exacted their revenge by challenging the tort laws in the Democrat-dominated Alabama Supreme Court and continued winning more large settlements.

Hunt initiated yet another reform effort to restructure Alabama's revenue system to increase education funding. Yet, the Alabama Legislature, led by fierce opposition from the State Teachers Association (AEA), consistently turned down the governor's proposals. Hunt was responding to the need for education reform, but Democrats were determined that Republicans were not going to make changes on their watch. What Democrats were unable to accomplish at the ballot box, they pursued through the courts and the legislature.

Hunt further discovered that annual budgets were just another function controlled by Democrats. Democrats made no secret of their loathing for the governor and the smattering of Republicans in the legislature. This was most evident in the state budgets. By custom, governors had a major influence in developing budgets . . . until a Republican became governor. Hunt's budget was declared "dead" by Democrats in the legislature before it was even submitted to the Democrat chairman of the Ways and Means Committee.

One form of vindication for Hunt came from a lawsuit filed by fourteen poor Alabama counties charging that education appropriations were inadequate and inequitable. A Montgomery County circuit judge subsequently ordered the state to provide equitable education funding in all sixty-seven counties. The lawsuit affirmed Hunt's personal quest to improve Alabama's consistently low rankings and the much-maligned education system.

Yet, Hunt's interest in education was not reflected by his interest in the state board of education meetings. He missed more meetings than he attended. Board member John Tyson further revealed that Hunt made only one request from the board during his first term. Tyson said Gov. Hunt requested that the board ban hazardous chemicals in chemistry classes. The strained relationship with the state board of education convinced its members that the new governor was more interested in budgets than education.

As Democrats conspired to make trouble for the first Republican administration in over a century, Alabamians were pleased when *U.S. News and World Report* recognized Hunt as one of America's best governors. The chief reasons cited by the national magazine were Hunt's pursuit of new industry and attracting more tourism to the state. The editors further noted that Hunt was enthusiastically welcoming Democrats into the Republican Party.

Hunt further capitalized on Reagan's influence with the blue-collar voting bloc by encouraging growth in Alabama's conservative movement. The most active segment of the population inclined to switch parties were Protestants, Baptists, and Methodists, primarily in rural counties. They were among the last to change parties, mostly because of an inherited suspicion of Republicans. By trial and error through the electoral process, the rural religious population learned that the party Democrats despised represented their best interests.

Gov. Hunt's religious background could be attributed to many of his interests and personal style. He enjoyed meeting the people of Alabama the same as in church. In 1989, Gov. Hunt chose Birmingham businessman and past chairman of the Alabama Republican Party, Edgar Welden, to chair the **Alabama Reunions**, a statewide series of celebrations recognizing Alabama history and culture, reaching back to the early American exploration period.

Hunt and Welden caught the brunt of Democrat criticisms when the program was introduced.

Democrats grumbled and accused Hunt of using the Alabama Reunion organization as a thinly disguised public relations ploy for his 1990 reelection. Reunion organizers denied the accusations, explaining that the intent was a simple marketing campaign to promote tourism. Further, Welden raised three times more money from private sources than from the state. Still, Democrats continued to criticize Hunt and the program that promoted Alabama.

As it happened, Democrats more than Republicans were looking to the next election less than a year away. With a vengeance, they meant to take back the governor's office lost by default—squabbling among themselves to the point where it disabled the party.

Six contenders, including former Governor Fob James making his third run, qualified for the 1990 Democrat primary. Other candidates were: State Senator Charles Bishop; US Representative Ronnie Flippo; Paul Hubbert, executive secretary of the Alabama Education Association; Attorney General Don Siegelman; and Ed Daw. In an aggressive campaign move, Siegelman proposed a state lottery to help fund education. The lottery caught the attention of voters, and Siegelman finished second to Hubbert in the Democrat primary. Fob James, as a Democrat, failed to convince voters to give him another four-year term to finish his work.

Taking the governor's office was a natural objective of Paul Hubbert and AEA. After building the most formidable political organization in Alabama, taking the top office fit perfectly into their ambition of total domination of the state. Since 1969, the year the Alabama Education Association (AEA), led by Paul Hubbert, merged with the African American Alabama State Teachers Association (ASTA), led by Joe Reed—AEA had grown to over 100,00 members supported by a professional staff of a hundred. The headquarters lobbied from a modern three-story building on Dexter Avenue within sight of the capitol.

Tracing its roots as far back as 1856, AEA identified Paul Hubbert from the Hubbertville community in Fayette County as the most capable person to lead the state teacher's organization. A Florence State Teachers College graduate, Hubbert began a successful career as the superintendent of education for the city of Troy. That's what he was doing when the dormant and near-irrelevant Alabama Education Association hired Hubbert to lobby for them in the legislature. It was AEA's wisest decision.

Joe Reed led the small association of black educators prior to the merger with AEA. He had been an activist in Alabama's civil rights movement during the racially turbulent Patterson-Wallace era. An army veteran accustomed to integration in the military service, he helped stage sit-ins in Montgomery and was a strong advocate for black voter rights. His first job with Alabama State University paid twenty-five cents an hour. Reed eventually became chairman of the Alabama Democratic Conference (ADC), a black advocacy political organization that had a patronizing role in the Alabama Democratic Party. By the time Joe Reed joined AEA at the age of twenty-six, he had the reputation as a veteran activist for black political influence in Alabama. For the next forty years, Hubbert and Reed built the Alabama teachers union into an unparalleled political power. They helped improve the lot of the teaching profession in Alabama's poorly funded education system.

Paul Hubbert had a substantial 50,000-vote lead going into the 1990 runoff against Don Siegelman. Still, Siegelman stuck to his lottery proposal, stressing that Hubbert was a special interest insider who would raise taxes and that the union leader was more than a little responsible for Alabama's poor academic record because Hubbert opposed testing for teachers. Siegelman's campaign strategy, striking hard at Hubbert's record, failed to persuade voters, and Hubbert won the runoff by a 54-to-46 percent margin.

Paul Hubbert prepared for the general election heavily sustained by the multiple resources of the powerful AEA. However, more importantly, he was the nominee in a state where Democrats still controlled the courthouses and the majority of elected offices. By all indications, Hubbert was the most likely candidate to redeem the Democrat legacy and defeat the Republican incumbent. Despite Hunt's huge upset victory in 1986, Democrats were heavily favored to regain the governor's office.

Hunt, Republicans shock Democrats again

But it would be different this time. Gov. Guy Hunt and outmanned Republicans were more confident about a straight-up vote against Democrats. What they lacked in aggressive politics, they made up with the angry memories that cost the Democrats the 1986 election. Further, the Hunt team felt that the Republican's first incumbency had created significant advantages through the appointment process, and Hunt had improved the state's negative image made worse by Wallace. Best of all, Hunt and the GOP had installed Republicans in key state positions, the same as Democrats entrenched their political system.

Among Democrats, resentment in 1990 was so strong that the election turned into more mockery. Republicans weathered another season of hayseed insults, and union boss Hubbert flattered himself with the self-anointed claim that he was Alabama's "New South" political leader. Party hacks ridiculed Hunt like school yard bullies with cheap populous nonsense and bumper stickers that read—"*Goober, Gomer and Guy.*" Hunt did not back away from the association with characters from the highly popular *Andy Griffith Show.*

Emory Folmar, who chaired the Alabama Republican Party during most of Hunt's tenure, said the attempted rundown of Hunt backfired. Folmar recognized that the game could be played both ways and sported a shabby felt hat like native Alabamian George Lindsey wore in his role on the show as Goober.

The undetermined factor for Democrats was the extent of public bitterness, and if voter resentment was still strong enough, that would keep them from winning elections. While Democrats were concerned about voter sentiments from big cities down to Big Jim Folsom's "Yonder Boxes," Republicans ventured back out into the hustings with greater confidence. Both parties would soon know exactly what was on the mind of the people.

Republicans were thoroughly prepared to campaign this time around. They also realized that they had the attention of the state media weary of Democrats and the financial support of influential organizations. Money poured into the Hunt campaign, more money than the Republicans had ever seen in the party treasury.

The GOP was encouraged now that they had eight members in the Senate and twenty-two in the House—the beginning of a political resurgence in the legislature. Best of all, the people felt that the country boy from Cullman County had done a good job governing the state, a fact substantiated by one of America's most prestigious national political magazines.

A hint of trouble arose when a newspaper article in the capitol suggested something awry in the Hunt administration. In mid-September, the *Montgomery Advertiser* ran a story that raised ethical questions about Hunt and his finances. Shortly afterward, the paper withdrew the story, but the incident suggested improprieties in the governor's office.

With Hubbert leading in the polls, the retraction saved Hunt from a sudden disaster. Escaping certain scandal, Hunt's campaign team immediately attacked Hubbert and his union background, claiming that his relationship with the capital city crowd made him out-of-touch with regular Alabama voters.

The Hunt campaign did further damage with a commercial that set Hubbert and the Democrats back on their heels. A slick television commercial portrayed Hubbert as a card-carrying member of the highly controversial National Education Association. The ad reminded conservative voters that Hubbert did not share their same values.

The commercial hit union boss Paul Hubbert hard. Attempts were made to counter the ad, but Hubbert was unable to regain the advantage. Hunt and the Republicans, mostly unschooled in political brawling, won again. The result was a narrow but respectable 52-to-48 win over Montgomery's political establishment. Election surveys showed that Hunt's strongest support came from white, higher income, male voters, and independents in the more populous counties. Hubbert led in African American boxes and among female voters.

Hunt and the Republicans pulled off another unexpected victory at the top level of Alabama government, reminding Democrats and voters alike that conservatives had a well-deserved place in the business of the state.

Hunt and the Republicans strategically filled committees,

boards, and municipal offices that ended Democrat domination in state government. It was the beginning of conservative influence for the Republican Party in Alabama—and Democrats did it to themselves.

State planes and preaching trips

Immersed in the privileged circumstances of the governor's office, much as George Wallace did running for president, Gov. Hunt began scheduling state airplanes for far-flung preaching appointments. Wallace had the implied protection of fellow Democrats— Hunt did not. Further, Bobbi James, wife of Gov. Fob James, had used state planes to attend religious conferences, but she suffered little more than mild criticism from the media. When word began sifting through Montgomery's political haunts that the Republican governor was abusing the perks of his office, local wags and Democrat insiders reacted quickly to take down Hunt, something they had failed to do in two elections. Giving Wallace a pass for the misuse of state planes and personnel, and dismissive of Mrs. James's flights to religious conferences, it was not the nature of Democrats to accord a Republican the same consideration.

Hunt should have known to avoid the very appearance of wrongdoing in his use of state agencies for any reason, and his legal team should have advised strict caution. Even more perplexing was endangering his political career for the convenience of attending church meetings in such an impressive style. Hunt flew to Primitive Baptist meetings with the trappings of the governor's office and accepted money, "love offerings," wherever he preached.

Just as Hunt's first term had been marked by legislation that was either unfunded, obstructed, or struck down by Democrats in the courts, so would his second term be dominated by scandal, brazenly manipulated by Democrats out of their Montgomery stronghold. It was not as if Gov. Hunt was doing a bad job. Capstone Poll numbers showed that an overwhelming number of Alabamians, over 65 percent, saw him doing plausible work for the state.

The personal use of state planes, first reported by the Associated Press, launched a grand jury investigation into Hunt's personal finances that eventually led to his downfall. When the issue surfaced, Hunt agreed to forego the use of planes and refund the money he received for his preaching appointments. But the fix was in place when the Alabama Supreme Court ruled that taxpayers could sue Hunt for the use of state-owned planes. In addition to the ruling, Democrats overseeing the Alabama Ethics Commission recommended that Attorney General Jimmy Evans indict the governor. Evans, on the prowl for easy political scalps, moved quickly to charge Hunt with thirteen felony counts: one count of breaking state ethics laws; three conspiracy counts, six counts of theft, and three counts of receiving stolen property. Most of the charges would be dropped, but one fatal charge survived. Hunt was charged with taking $200,000 from his 1987 inaugural fund, money raised from private contributors, for his personal use. The issue, right or wrong, overwhelmed Gov. Hunt and his legal team.

Guy Hunt vigorously denied all the charges. "I've never stolen anything in my entire life," Hunt said, after being fingerprinted and photographed at the Montgomery police department. Jimmy Evans claimed that Hunt and three of his oldest political friends had systematically looted a nonprofit corporation that they had set up to pay for his inaugural activities and transition, diverting at least $200,000 of an estimated one million dollars for his personal use. Hunt's attorney, George Beck, insisted the financial transactions were complex but not illegal.

Circuit Judge Randall Thomas suggested that the attorneys settle the case among themselves. Hunt's legal team attempted to reach an agreement before the indictment came down that would allow the governor to plead guilty to a misdemeanor. Still, the Democrat attorney general was not about to let the Republican governor escape his grasp.

Less than six years away from the Baxley debacle, Democrats set a trap for the farmer from Holly Pond. Hunt went to trial on April 12, 1993, arguing that any money taken from the inaugural account was repayment for loans he made to his unsuccessful 1978 gubernatorial campaign. But the facts contradicted Hunt. His old campaign debt had long since been repaid. The trial took six days, mired mostly in technical testimony. Those observing the proceedings predicted that the jury would not convict the governor. They were wrong.

On April 22, 1993, after deliberating only two hours, the jury found Hunt guilty. Alabama law mandated his immediate removal from office, and Jim Folsom Jr., Democrat lieutenant governor, was sworn in. Guy and Helen Hunt had to gather their personal effects and leave the Governor's Mansion. During the sentencing phase on May 7, Judge Randall Thomas turned a deaf ear to vindictive Jimmy Evans, who wanted to send Hunt to prison, a move meant to humiliate the governor and embarrass Republicans.

Instead, Judge Thomas ordered Hunt to pay a $211,000 fine, do 1,000 hours of community service, and serve five years' probation. It was a heavy burden for Hunt, having never been financially secure, but he had escaped the clutches of avenging Democrats, especially Alabama's attorney general.

Democrats requited themselves with the legal retaking of the governor's office, another cutthroat version of Southern justice. For Hunt and his family in Holly Pond, they endured public humiliation. They stoically bore the notoriety of him being removed from the top job in the state, all at the hands of his political enemies. Hunt made arrangements to pay the huge fine in monthly installments of $100 out of the family's meager savings, income earned from preaching, and the farm that had gone fallow while the Hunts lived in the splendid Governor's Mansion down in the state capitol.

Hunt's legal dilemma continued into the next administration, when Fob James, running as a Republican this time, beat Jim Folsom Jr. in a close election. Hunt's first opportunity to settle the dispute came four years later in 1997 when the three-member (two appointed by Hunt) Alabama Board of Pardons and Paroles approved a rare pardon on the grounds of innocence. To officially validate the pardon, the signature of a judge or district attorney was required, but no such official agreed to sign the document. Bill Pryor, the new Republican attorney general refused, offering the weak explanation that his office did not have the right or power to approve Hunt's pardon. It was a crushing blow for the aggrieved Hunt family.

The matter worsened. In 1998, when Hunt applied for the termination of his probation four months early with the obvious intent to once again run for governor, Circuit Judge Sally Greenhaw extended Hunt's probation another five years, ruling that the ex-governor had paid only $4,200 of the fine and court costs in his case.

Ultimately, sympathetic Alabamians, Democrats and Republicans, in due time, settled Hunt's debt, and his probation was lifted after his attorney presented a check to the court for the balance of his debt. The Board of Pardons and Paroles immediately issued a second pardon on the grounds of innocence . . . no signature required.

Amazingly, the extent of political damage seemed lost on Hunt. The day after his official pardon, Guy Hunt drove down to Republican headquarters in Birmingham and paid the qualifying fee for yet another run for governor in the GOP primary. If Hunt had visions of a second miraculous election to redeem himself from scandal, voters were prepared to show him the current state of politics. In the March 31, 1998, GOP primary, Hunt ran a weak third behind Fob James and Winton Blount III, with only 8.15 percent of the total vote. It was an embarrassing failure from the robust and spectacular days of 1986 and 1990 that changed the fortunes of the Alabama Republican Party.

True, Hunt had been victimized by Democrats, but he had given them cause to question his honesty, and they turned an ill-advised matter into an outright scandal. Without question, the Alabama Republican Party had more qualified candidates, but Hunt was their man in 1986 when Democrats turned voters against their own party.

CHAPTER FOURTEEN

Sessions wins—
Shelby switches

G uy Hunt's removal from office did not offset Republican gains in the 1994 general election. And for a good reason. National Republicans took both Houses of Congress for the first time in forty years, driven by the anti-Washington, anti-incumbent Contract with America. Sonny Callahan, Terry Everette, and Spencer Bachus were among fifty-four new House members elected to Congress. Jim Folsom Jr. launched a campaign for governor, confident that Democrats had survived the 1986 debacle and once again dominated state politics.

Folsom had positioned himself as the top Democrat candidate for governor by virtue of his brief incumbency. Paul Hubbert and his AEA sidekicks made another run for governor, but the Folsom name still retained electoral power, particularly in the rural areas. Akin to his Senate race against Donald Stewart, Folsom had a significant advantage in name recognition.

He had made several key decisions during his brief tenure, with the intent of affirming the interests of Democrats. He had the Confederate flag atop the capitol removed, defiantly raised by enraged Democrats during the Civil Rights furor. The symbolic order placed him in good stead with African Americans, having realized full partnership in Alabama Democrats. Folsom also took a strong hand in an attempt to reform education.

He scored significant leadership points for his role in securing a major industrial development for Alabama. Mercedes-Benz shocked the business world by announcing plans to build a premier assembly plant near Tuscaloosa. Locating a global auto manufacturer comparable to Mercedes was a signal accomplishment for Alabama and Folsom.

In the 1994 Democrat primary, Hubbert still had not gained the confidence of voters to win the Democrat nominee for governor. Instead, Little Jim won the Democrat nomination with a 54 percent victory, the second loss that voters inflicted on the powerful teachers union and its influential leader.

The Republican primary was different in this election. Democrats, accustomed to the century-old practice of weak GOP nominees for governor, were surprised that six Republicans qualified for governor, which reflected a much-stronger conservative presence in Alabama. Fob James, a reconverted Republican, topped the list with Ann Bedsole, a sixteen-year veteran senator from Mobile, and wealthy Montgomery businessman Winton Blount III, son of Winton Blount Jr., rounded out the top three. Fob James held an edge for the simple reason that voters had seen his name on the ballot so many times.

The top candidates turned on one another uncharacteristically in their own season of political mudslinging. Bedsole ran on the routine platform of change and reform for education and government ethics, repeatedly criticizing James as a failed Democrat governor. Blount joined Bedsole in her criticism of James, mostly for having the gall to qualify as a Republican. Blount and James jumped in the race at the last minute, with Blount promising to keep control of state government away from James and Bedsole.

Perhaps trying to avoid the same reason for his father's failed Senate campaign in 1972, Blount sponsored a "Blount for Governor" sure-enough race car in the Touchstone Energy 300 at Talladega's huge NASCAR track. Indeed, it was a novel gimmick to enhance name recognition among auto racing fans . . . but the car lost, and so would Blount.

Fob James led the Republican primary with 39.5 percent of the vote; Ann Bedsole edged Blount for the other runoff spot. But James had a stronger record than Bedsole. He touted the creation of a trust fund for offshore drilling revenue, while Bedsole attempted to lay claim as the candidate for change and reform. In the end, James easily defeated Bedsole by a 62-to-38 percent margin, carrying fifty-seven counties, including Mobile, Bedsole's home county. Bedsole, deeply embittered by the loss, reacted in anger, claiming that Alabama was not ready to elect a woman governor. Of course, she meant a Republican female governor.

Entering the 1994 November general election, James and Folsom had numerous negatives. James had only middling success governing as a Democrat, and Folsom had ethics issues reminiscent of his rollicking heavy-drinking father. Little Jim had accepted money for plum legislative committee assignments, arranged to get his wife on the state payroll, and benefited from free labor and materials for his home. If those were not enough ethical issues, press stories surfaced about the Folsom family taking a vacation in an airplane owned by someone associated with an Alabama casino. Folsom was also implicated in a pork-barrel project in Morgan County.

But that didn't seem to matter. Folsom held a surprising lead in the polls, 10 to 12 points, throughout the campaign until the final week in October. Then public sentiment shifted, and James pulled ahead only days before the general election. At least some of the late surge could be attributed to Bobbi James and her relationship with Alabama's fundamental religious organizations. Mrs. James also had strong connections to several national religious leaders, including Billy Graham.

In what may have been Fob James's political salvation, campaign workers distributed over a million brochures written by James to churches across the state unbeknownst to the Folsom camp or wiseacre pollsters, for that matter. Fob James won a second term as governor, the first man to pull off the feat as a Democrat *and* Republican. His razor-thin margin of 50.3 percent was slightly more than 10,000 out of 1.2 million votes cast.

The James family was not seen necessarily as loyal party people, perhaps a little Libertarian, but were mostly for themselves and ran in whatever way that made them electable. Bradley Byrne, who worked in Fob's first campaign, said, "Fob was indifferent to most of the duties of the office." The James family had casually declined to live in the Governor's Mansion as Democrats. Don Siegelman beat Republican nominee Charles Graddick for lieutenant governor, which surprised many folks. Siegelman would use the office to bedevil Fob James and Republicans for four years and position himself for the next election.

The growing strength of the Republican Party was seen in other races, one in particular. Republicans were still incensed over Democrat Attorney General Jimmy Evans, for his overzealous prosecution of Guy Hunt on near-fictional charges. Only a sense of fair play by the trial judge kept Hunt from going to prison. Evans was tagged the "Rat Attorney General."

With the objective of electing a fair-minded attorney general, Republicans made overtures to Jeff Sessions, the US Attorney from South Alabama. Republicans eventually persuaded Sessions to run against Evans, convinced that Evans was vulnerable because of his hostile behavior toward the party.

Jeff Sessions had a very respectable legal reputation. A native of the small town of Hybart in Wilcox County, where his family owned a country store, he had served as US Attorney from 1981–1993, carefully building a distinguished record for a future judicial career. In 1986, President Ronald Reagan did just that, nominating Sessions for a federal judgeship in District Court for South Alabama. But his Senate confirmation stalled on NAACP accusations of racism. Sessions had prosecuted African American civil rights activists for voter fraud. Ted Kennedy said that Sessions would be a "throwback to a shameful era." In league with liberals during Senate confirmation hearings, Alabama Senator Howell Heflin cast the deciding vote against Sessions. Sessions later admitted that the Senate vote was "heartbreaking."

There were larger issues in the attorney general election, Sessions said in an interview. "People were very dissatisfied with the politics and corruption in Alabama, and I felt that I could offer leadership that would improve conditions in our state." His message resonated with voters. After soundly defeating incumbent Jimmy Evans in the 1994 general election, Sessions served as Alabama's attorney general with an eye on the US Senate.

The 1994 general election included another long drawn out election challenge by a Democrat. The controversy erupted when the incumbent chief justice of the Alabama Supreme Court Earnest "Sonny" Hornsby refused to leave office after losing a controversial election to Republican Perry O. Hooper Sr. Hornsby was bitter toward Democrat Secretary of State Jim Bennett, who tossed out some 2,000 unwitnessed absentee ballots contested by Republicans. Bennett's decision, upheld by the courts, cost Hornsby the chief justice position.

Hooper's courage stirred another period of expansion for Republicans. The state supreme court, long dominated by Democrats, had been extremely hostile to the Hunt administration. Hooper was elected probate judge in Montgomery County in the 1964 conservative sweep, and he had been elected circuit judge before running for the chief justice position in 1994 at age sixty-nine. He beat Hornsby by a startling 262 votes, making absentee ballots a critical factor in the election. It would be eleven months before Hooper was allowed to take the oath of office. In subsequent state judicial elections, Hornsby's mulishness contributed to a loss of support for Democrats. In quick succession, all nine seats on the Alabama Supreme Court and all ten state appellate court positions were won by Republican judges.

Alabama's political landscape became more conservative in the 1996 general election. Republican Attorney General Jeff Sessions qualified for retiring Howell Heflin's open Senate seat. Democrats nominated State Senator Roger Bedford, a perpetually loudmouthed liberal. Bedford attempted to convince voters that he was conservative, but like Folsom, he had nagging ethical issues. Bedford ran a high-dollar media campaign, but money did Bedford no good. Sessions stuck to his policy of not debating opponents, and he went on to poll 52.45 percent (786,436) of the total vote to win the general election.

The election of Sessions to the US Senate, replacing Howell Heflin, the man who had agreed to false accusations of racism and rejected his federal judicial appointment, was a matter of political justice. Sessions's ascendancy as a solid conservative signaled the growing strength of Alabama Republicans. The election prompted Richard Shelby to switch parties, giving Alabama two Republican senators. Shelby won reelection in 1992 as a Democrat, yet, the day after the 1994 elections, when Republicans took control of both Houses of Congress, Shelby changed his party affiliation. The Sessions-Shelby party alignment instilled even greater strength in the development of the GOP in Alabama.

Earl and Merle Black, tracking conservative growth and the rise of the Republican Party in the South, said college-educated white Protestants became the most important source of political power in the South. The Black brothers wrote in *Divided America* that this group was "the heart of the region's new urbanized middle and upper classes, the social group most strongly attracted to the Republican Party."

The GOP Contract with America complemented the Reagan realignment in the South. The emerging Republican Party could be seen in the eleven states of the Old Confederacy: Alabama, Georgia, Mississippi, Louisiana, Florida, Texas, Arkansas, North Carolina, South Carolina, and Tennessee. GOP victories in upper Southern states enabled Republicans to win elections where liberal Democrats had once dominated.

The same observations could be seen in the realignment of Alabama's congressional delegation that started in 1964 with the Goldwater election—two Republican senators and six Republican congressmen. A second wave of congressmen represented Alabama: Sonny Callahan, businessman, 1985–2003; Bud Cramer, lawyer, 1991–2009; and Terry Everette, newspaperman, 1993–2009. In 1980, Reagan urged the South to redefine itself as more than the party of The Great Depression. Reagan promoted traditional American values that helped establish conservatism in the South, according to the Black brothers. At the same time, voters were also reminded that Democrats were the party of slavery, hostile to civil rights and racial conflict.

CHAPTER FIFTEEN

Fob James the Second

$\mathbf{A}$bsent from public office for more than a decade, Fob James sat in the gallery and watched Wallace, Hunt, and Folsom govern Alabama before making a fourth run for the top office. The Republican movement in Alabama was showing signs of life but still needed development. Alabamians were not exactly overwhelmed by the conservative style of government. Guy Hunt's accidental political career had ended in a bad way, and Fob James's first term as Republican-turned-Democrat governor had controversial overtones (and undertones), at best.

In a sign of normalcy, James believed that he had wasted his first administration. Both parties would agree with that. Still, James felt that he had a significant appeal with the voting public. Failing to retake the Democrat nomination for governor in 1986 and 1990, James unapologetically reclaimed his original membership with Republicans. The decision was seen as an indication of the growing populous strength in Alabama and the Deep South.

Commendably, during his first term, Fob James made a sharp contrast between himself and the Democrats' strict racial policies. James did not hesitate to appoint African Americans to state agencies and cabinet positions. The one appointment that signaled his intention to name blacks came with the selection of Oscar Adams to the Alabama Supreme Court. Adams went on to win statewide elections until his retirement in 1993.

James also appointed Gary Cooper from Mobile to head the Department of Pensions and Security. Cooper was a Notre Dame graduate, decorated marine, and state legislator. No one should have been surprised, considering that James declared in his first inaugural address that his administration would be "free from racism and discrimination." Those were indeed strong words in Alabama, especially people with a critical Democrat mind-set. Picking Adams and Cooper set a new standard for fairness and equality for both of James's administrations.

But that was not all. As a Republican governor, Gov. James appointed Aubrey Miller, African American, to head the Alabama Tourism Department. James's inclusive, evenhanded attitude was founded in what he called "fundamental American values." With high-profile appointments, Republicans still had limited success with minorities. As early as the 1960s, blacks in Alabama were aligning themselves with Democrats despite a history of racial bigotry and violence. Ignoring antislavery Republicans, African Americans reaffirmed that the Democratic Party had appeal in black churches and communities and that included the growing black political class.

Soon after his second inauguration, Fob James mired himself and the state, once again, in controversy, federal and religious. Gerald Johnson, professor of political science at Auburn University, observed, "His initiatives to thwart federal judiciary power and to assert Christian symbols in public life attracted national attention. And he promised more combat in his second term." More combat meant Judge Roy Moore's fight to keep the Ten Commandments in the Alabama Judiciary Building down the street from the state capitol. James quickly sued the American Civil Liberties Union after the ACLU sued Judge Moore.

In the 1998 general election, Republicans made another effort to take control of the Alabama Legislature. At this point in Southern politics, Alabama had not been successful at winning control of the legislature the way other Southern states had. The threefold reasons were simple: The influence of rural politics (fifty-four of Alabama's sixty-seven counties have rural profiles), and the cash-rich Alabama Education Association (AEA) led by Paul Hubbert and Joe Reed. A third reason also contributed to the weakness of Alabama Republicans. The hard-to-break tendency of some conservatives, who often voted Republican in national elections and Democrat in local races, because there were few competitive GOP candidates on the ballot.

With the Republican Party unable to field electable candidates in local and state races, more often than not, Republicans cooperated with Democrats to have a role in government. Not until the Reagan era did the GOP become more successful at nominating candidates in local races with any hope of winning. Dual loyalty became a relic of the past once Ronald Reagan welcomed conservatives into the Republican Party. As late as the nineties, the affinity to cling to old voting tendencies remained strong among Republicans.

Republicans could not expect to change the state government without the financial resources to invest in House and Senate candidates. Furthermore, Paul Hubbert exploited the dual voting trends by working both sides of the aisle, bankrolling Democrat *and* Republican candidates willing to accept campaign contributions from AEA. Hubbert's strategy had kept Alabama Republicans in a minority role in the legislature, although Republicans were winning some statewide races primarily on the strength of Republican presidential elections.

Worth noting in 1998, Republicans confidently vetted a long list of candidates, although the party had few resources to fund campaigns. It was a classic power struggle. Republicans qualified 100 candidates for the House compared to 118 Democrats. In the Senate, Republicans placed forty-five candidates on ballots opposing Democrats. The plurality of Republican candidates failed to win the legislature, but it did close the numerical gap. Democrats retained their majority by electing sixty-nine representatives to offset forty-five Republicans. The same pattern was evident in the Senate. Republicans fell short there also, winning twelve seats compared to twenty-three for Democrats. Still, the 1998 elections represented significant changes for Republicans in the legislature.

Trying to divine a clear understanding of both Fob James's administrations can be a puzzling undertaking. Historians saw James as distracted and eccentric, but the same could be said of Wallace during his four terms. Perhaps voters felt that James could afford quirky behavior, considering his business success enabled him to win two elections as governor without special interests, big-money lobbyists, and traditional party leadership. As it was with Big Jim Folsom and John Patterson, Fob James believed his first obligation was to the people.

Right or wrong in his governance, both political parties watched James closely, and newspapers noted his inexperienced style of management. He had problems in organizing the legislature and often found himself outwitted in both Houses—as a

Democrat and a Republican. Of particular remembrance was a package of anticrime bills in 1982 passed during a special session that James had called. The bills did not become law because the governor's office did not send them to the secretary of state within ten days. (William Stewart provides other James miscues in the *Encyclopedia of Alabama.*)

Added to his confusing attempts at leadership, James attempted to push too many new programs through the legislature at the same time. He seriously riled the legislature when he insisted on un-earmarking state funds mandated by voters that were sacred to AEA. Even worse, James suggested decentralizing the state government when he asked the legislature to grant home rule to counties. Gov. James prorated state budgets as required by the state constitution when the Alabama economy slowed due to a downturn in national economics.

Sandra Baxley Taylor chronicled both James's administrations as the sometimes clumsy, the politically unsanctified Democrat-Republican businessman that he was, stubborn and untraditional. But a definite strain of conservatism influenced a man more accustomed to running a successful business.

Remembered as a serious engineering student at Auburn, James earned money at several enterprises (Fob once sold Sewell suits to fellow athletes). He also romanced Bobbi, his future wife, as a star halfback. James attempted to preside over budget hearings with a legal pad.

One history of the state written at the time reduced Fob James's historical legacy to a single paragraph, suggesting that his administrations were marked by "disorganization and indecision." *Alabama: The History of a Deep South State*, whose chief contributor, Wayne Flynt, belittled James, among others, with scorn.

The lengthy history (700-plus pages) focused much too often on racial harping (a Democrat trait) rather than actual historical objectivity.

Criticisms aside, Guy Hunt and Fob James broke with the Wallace-Democrat tendencies of appointing party hacks, good ole boys, and very few females. More interested in equality and respect of women and minorities, Hunt and James moved beyond the typical twists and turns against blacks and poor whites. Both Republican governors offered those outside the political power structure an open door that ultimately created more opportunities for women and minorities. That, within itself, was a generational change that helped improve Alabama's backward image.

Agreed, Fob James did have an impact on state government, primarily in his oversight of state agencies. The State Highway Department, a major funding drain on the annual budget, had its staffing reduced from 5,838 employees to 3,621 by the end of James's second term. Vehicle use, work schedules, expenditures, and business practices were closely monitored by the governor to help make the state government more cost-efficient.

Reminiscent of Big Jim Folsom's farm-to-market paving projects, in his first term, James completed several unfinished interstate highway projects, delivering on his promise that $270 million in projects would be under some phase of construction before the next governor took office. Every county benefited from road work (Sandra Baxley Taylor's biography provided a detailed record of road, highway, and bridge projects). James modestly refused to allow his staff to publicize his role in the projects.

Yet, by the conclusion of Fob James's second administration, James was regarded as controversial as ever. Newspapers reported on funding disputes for education, chain gangs, school prayer, and James's ongoing battle with federal courts. He was criticized when he "seceded" from the National Governor's Conference, the only governor to do so.

Fob James combined legacy as a Democrat and Republican, concluded with the summary that, despite all his progressive ideals and modest accomplishments, James may have been a successful businessman, but he rarely developed beyond mediocrity as a state leader. Ironically, many of his battles were the same as Wallace's—the federal judiciary and big government.

A major change for Fob and Bobbi James was that they did live in the Alabama Governor's Mansion during his term as a Republican governor. The Jameses had been heavily criticized for buying a house in Montgomery rather than living in the Governor's Mansion during his first term as Democrat governor.

CHAPTER SIXTEEN

Fob fumbles away the governor's office

Once serving as a Republican governor, Fob James ceded the state government to the Democrats. It was not entirely unexpected. In doing so, he broke a short run of Republican victories starting with Guy Hunt's 1986 spectacular upset over Bill Baxley. Elected as a probusiness governor, business leaders lost patience with James's bewildering management style.

Recognizing that James was losing support among Alabama's business community, Lieutenant Governor Don Siegelman grasped the opportunity to compromise Republicans and began meeting with key business leaders as the second man in the capitol. Siegelman and the Democrats exploited James's manifest weaknesses and did it at the time when Republicans were making inroads in state and local elections.

By comparison, Siegelman had developed political skills that Fob James had never shown in both terms as governor. Siegelman had steadily built his organization, starting as executive director of the State Democrat Executive Committee, then secretary of state and attorney general. In 1990, his string of successes stopped with his failed run for governor against then Democrat Fob James and

AEA's Paul Hubbert. Underfunded, he lost the Democrat runoff bid against Hubbert with empty pockets in Hunt's 1990 reelection.

By 1994, Siegelman had identified another niche in state government; he ran for lieutenant governor, defeating Republican nominee Charles Graddick employing Hubbert's campaign strategy. As the top Democrat, Siegelman immediately positioned himself as Fob James's chief antagonist, effectively creating an interim base for another shot at governor. The second most powerful position in state government gave him the authority to appoint legislative committees, name committee chairs, and regulate the flow of bills through the Senate.

Siegelman made himself the bully Democrat in the state capitol by crippling or killing outright Republican legislation that business leaders needed to recruit new industry and create jobs. Siegelman's obstruction endeared him to special interests—labor unions, AEA, trial lawyers, and civil rights organizations, the liberal core of Alabama Democrats. Business leaders soon regretted their many chummy, off-the-record meetings with him.

Fob James's 1998 reelection campaign differed little from his personal issues as governor: freedom of religious expression and defiance of big government. Democrats did not have to develop a different election strategy due to James's reliance on his favorite political and social interests. Even worse, Republicans were needlessly compromised because no one could persuade James to change his message, frustrating GOP campaign advisers.

Further, with Fob James heading the Republican ticket, the campaign became a critical matter for Christian conservatives in churches and religious organizations that backed James in his battle with the federal government over school prayer and the Ten Commandments. Allied with the future of the religious right,

Christian groups were in a survival mode to keep James in office. It would be a hard sell to voters, even those who agreed with the fundamental issues of the conservative movement.

At the same time Fob James was lambasting the feds, Don Siegelman and the Democrats were gaining ground with voters who recognized that James was also wasting his second term. The more James talked, the more voters remembered his shortcomings.

James was not alone in the 1998 campaign. Sen. Richard Shelby, Congressmen Sonny Callahan, Terry Everette, Bob Riley, Robert Aderholt, Bud Cramer, and Spencer Bachus were on the GOP ticket. If that failed to create sufficient interest among Republican voters, a Religious Freedom Amendment that "prohibited the burden of the free exercise of religion" excited the emotional fervor of the state's religious communities. Bill Pryor stood for election as attorney general, and Jim Bennett led the race for secretary of state. All of that should have created enough interest to stoke the election fires for the sitting Republican governor.

Instead, serious controversy erupted in the lieutenant governor's race. Steve Windom, a two-term Democrat senator from Mobile, switched parties in 1997 to run for lieutenant governor. Windom brought a very plausible record as a conservative and had been recognized for his outstanding legislative work by the Alabama Wildlife Federation, the National Federation of Independent Business, and Independent Insurance Agents. Regardless of Windom's legislative achievements, Democrats tried to cripple him with dirty tricks because they wanted to take the two top positions in state government and felt that they already had the edge over the controversial Republican governor. Dewayne Freeman, Jasper trial lawyer, won the Democrat primary for lieutenant governor.

Democrats immediately attacked Windom in an attempt to create a devastating career-ending scandal. False charges were made that Windom had frequented a high-dollar prostitute, and in 1991, he had roughed up the woman, breaking her arm. Democrat operatives blanketed the media market with the hoax about the prostitute.

Remarkably, Windom was able to fight his way through the salacious attacks. Garve Ivey was eventually convicted of witness tampering and criminal defamation for conspiring with a private investigator, Wes Chappell, to frame Windom. The former call girl, Melissa Myers Bush, who had been paid to make false allegations against Windom, later recanted her testimony. Cleared of the nonscandal, Windom went on to defeat Dewayne Freeman, Senate president pro tempore, for lieutenant governor.

Anne Permaloff, professor of political science at Auburn-Montgomery, correctly called the entire sordid affair as just another dirty trick: "The rumor-mill process of developing false stories has been a part of Alabama politics for at least the last 60 years."

Fob James repeatedly stumbled because he had governed to his personal agenda, often ignoring the good of the people. With Republicans intent on taking the Alabama Legislature, James should have led the ticket for the GOP. Instead, his culture war over religion and personal politics neutralized the impact of Christian conservatives, and the Alabama business community that believed James was scaring away business investments. Business leaders, who had cringed at James's attacks on the Washington establishment, did not believe that the state could afford yet another divisive governor.

James ran first in the Republican primary and faced

Montgomery businessman Winton Blount III in the runoff. Harsh words flew from both camps. Blount attempted to portray James as an old-style Southern politician who was hurting business. James called Blount a monkey, and his wife, Bobbie, said he was a "big, fat sissy." The bad news for Republicans was that the polls showed James and Blount losing to Siegelman in the general election.

Fob James beat Blount in a rough-and-tumble runoff 55.9-to-44.1 percent, an easy win for James. Every major newspaper in the state endorsed Blount. (Blount chaired the Alabama Republican Party from 1999 to 2001.) Even more damning, the James strategy of mixing state's rights with his fundamental faith was grating on the nerves of Alabama voters. James's confrontational style reminded people of the George Wallace self-serving drama.

Extensive polling showed James behind Siegelman in the general election. Wayne Flynt, an Auburn historian, said prior to the general election that there might have been enough hard-core Democrats and swing voters to elect another Democrat governor. But that was not necessary according to one Republican strategist, who observed that James seemed indifferent to his reelection. Some Republicans said they didn't see any "fight" in his campaign.

Commendably, Siegelman did not hint of anything racial in his campaign, a traditional Democrat campaign issue. Sidestepping James's religious activism, instead, he championed a Georgia-style education lottery. The message had appeal among voters who needed financial assistance to educate their children. At the same time, Windom, supportive of the religious right, promised voters he would block legislation creating a state lottery.

Don Siegelman won a convincing landslide victory, 57.9

percent to 42.1 percent over a halfhearted Fob James to take back the governor's office. Like Paul Hubbert, Democrat-leaning newspapers attempted to label Siegelman as Alabama's first "New South" governor. A worthy ideal by the political class to improve the state's image, but Siegelman would prove that he did not have the integrity to lead Alabama through an evolution of business and education.

CHAPTER SEVENTEEN

꧁≈≈≈≈≈꧂

Siegelman's final folly

It took all of three months for Governor Don Siegelman and his allies in the Senate to neutralize Lieutenant Governor Steve Windom. Democrats were especially spiteful to Windom, the first Republican lieutenant governor since Alexander McKinstry of Mobile during Reconstruction. (Republicans created the office in 1868; Democrats abolished it in 1875 and restored it in the 1901 Constitution.) Windom's political legacy comes with an odd sort of remembrance. During the first session of the Alabama Legislature under Siegelman, Windom was surrounded by hostile Democrats led by Lowell Barron, the seven-term senator from Jackson County.

Barron had initially agreed to join an eighteen-member conservative bloc in the Senate, but he double-crossed Republicans after meeting with Siegelman and being elected president pro tempore of the Senate by the Democrat majority. Windom said that Barron didn't keep his word and betrayed the conservative voting bloc.

Democrats systematically removed many of the critical powers of the lieutenant governor and gave them to Barron. So bold and aggressive was the threat against Windom that he could not risk leaving Senate chambers for a bathroom break for fear of losing the rest of his authority as presiding officer. He resorted to relieving himself in a glass jug behind the podium, a not-so-discreet necessity that made national news.

Windom's laughable juggling act in Senate chambers was a bizarre and questionable episode. Soon afterward, Democrats went on to rewrite Senate rules to their advantage, yet Windom claimed that the negative publicity was worth the ridicule. He took a victory lap around the state by plane, displaying his prize Senate gavel at each stop. Windom said the jug became such a symbol of public notoriety that the state archives asked to display it as a piece of history. Windom was not flattered by the request and destroyed the jug.

The biggest obstacle for Republicans was competing with the affluence of the Alabama Education Association (AEA). The teachers union had built itself into an unrivaled political machine early in Wallace's long tenure—and had steadily grown in power as a lobbying force that reigned supreme on both Houses of the legislature. Republicans were winning statewide races, but without the financial resources to invest in House and Senate elections, they were limited at dismantling AEA's legislative stronghold.

Add to these formidable factors the self-defeating voting tendencies of many Republicans, and that is an accurate measure of why the party could not change the legislature. Reiterating once again, many Republicans voted Republican nationally and Democrat locally. This quirk in Republican politics evolved, by necessity, because Republicans were rarely competitive at the local level. It was a strange but logical voting practice until the 1980s when Ronald Reagan understood the frustration of conservatives in the South and invited them into the party. Once a New Deal Democrat and union member himself, Reagan's commonsense conservatism helped Alabama to escape Democrat control eventually.

The Siegelman era requires a more critical assessment. The most obvious reason is that Siegelman and the Democrats manifested all that was wrong with the state government. Hence, their greed and bungling created an unstable political crisis that would return Republicans to power. And they did it in a single four-year term. Siegelman generated extraordinary public attention into the affairs of the state government through widespread graft and corruption. *Toujours*, John Grenier would say.

The Siegelman saga is so much recent history that public humiliation, legal recriminations, and mistrust lingered for years that chronicled Don Siegelman's embarrassing fall from grace. Eddie Curran's definitive book, ***The Governor of Goat Hill***, describes extensive details of Siegelman's political career that led to convictions of fraud and corruption. News outlets reported a succession of ethical failures that compromised the Siegelman administration. At a steady pace, he led his party off the cliff.

Given his due, Don Siegelman took the top constitutional offices in Alabama: secretary of state, attorney general, lieutenant governor, and governor. His political success stands as an unparalleled accomplishment in state history. Comparatively, in following Siegelman's career, he did things that convinced people, like the Clintons, that some politicians are a crooked, shoddy lot. Siegelman's leftward tendencies once again severely weakened Alabama Democrats—much the same way that Baxley's misjudgments angered voters in 1986. The lesson: do not offend or ignore voters.

Siegelman came from tradition-rich Mobile, an Old South city with a French influence. He attended the University of Alabama, where he immersed himself in campus politics and won election as president of the Student Government Association. He studied law at Georgetown University in Washington, D.C., and attended Oxford University in London studying international law. Siegelman's education suggested ambitions beyond Southern politics. That may explain why he never hung out a shingle and practiced lawyer-style legal work.

Although steeped in top-drawer legal education, Siegelman fit the profile of an ambulance chaser, a referral lawyer who sent cases to other attorneys for a standard contingency fee of 25 percent. He collected handsome paychecks for writing letters and making phone calls on behalf of his clients. Still, he prospered, once taking a million-dollar payout in a Big Tobacco case involving a state hospital.

The quest for money, *lots* of money, led to Siegelman's downfall. Caught shorthanded in the 1990 governor's race against Paul Hubbert had been a sobering lesson. Outspent by Hubbert, Siegelman lost the runoff hampered by the costly mistake of having precious little cash in the bank. He determined that it would not happen again.

Siegelman went into the political wilderness following the 1990 Democrat primary, and political insiders thought that his public career was over. But Siegelman had suffered a severe political loss because he had been unable to coax sizeable campaign donations from major donors. As governor, he was transformed from asking for money to *demanding* it from his friends, other Democrats, and companies doing business with the state.

Following up on his campaign promise, Siegelman quickly launched the legislative process to get a lottery amendment on the November 1999 ballot, the only statewide issue before the people. The education lottery had popular appeal, especially for low-income families needing financial help to educate their children—$150 million for college scholarships, a prekindergarten program, and computers. But the lottery campaign came with high risks.

Siegelman hit the money trail once again to promote passage of the lottery bill. Specifically, he solicited funds from companies with an eye on state business. One of those business interests was HealthSouth CEO Richard Scrushy in Birmingham. Siegelman and Scrushy casually brokered a deal for a seat on the state hospital board in exchange for a $500,000 contribution to help fund the lottery campaign.

Eddie Curran's *Goat Hill* story tracked these and other Siegelman missteps all the way to federal prison. Curran researched and wrote articles for the *Mobile Press-Register* exposing Siegelman's real estate deals, motorcycles, questionable fund-raising tactics, and scurrilous attempts to shift blame for his numerous misdeeds to Republicans.

The lottery started out deceptively quiet but soon ramped up into a church-and-state battle spearheaded primarily by rural Baptist churches. Early polls indicated that Alabamians were willing to vote for an education lottery, but that changed once the religious community raised the ethical issue about gambling. Voters did not trust politicians or their relationship with Alabama's gambling empire with managing lottery proceeds, and they were not that sure Alabama education would benefit from the income as much as the gamblers.

The lottery collapsed, another example of the influence of Alabama's religious community (similar to Denton's first Senate race), especially in rural areas where independent voters heavily influenced elections. That was where fundamental congregations helped finance a critical television ad showing politicians sitting at a table smoking cigars and pushing piles of money around. It was the antithesis of pro-family, good-government politics. Casting the religious convictions of people aside, Siegelman thoughtlessly encouraged church folks to ignore the principles of their faith and vote for the lottery anyway.

But independent-minded Christians did not heed Siegelman's advice. Even though his lottery foundation outspent rivals 3-to-1, the opposition won by 54-to-46 percent. Afterward, a disappointed Siegelman said that he did not have another tax plan.

With the lottery on the bottom of the muddy Alabama River, in 2002, Republicans whetted their swords for the next gubernatorial campaign. The GOP felt that the rising trend of the Republican Party would be a factor in winning back the governor's office, knowing that voters were still angry and eager to remove the Siegelman crowd from the state capitol for making embarrassing legislative decisions.

The November 2000 midterm elections had been an accurate indication of just how out-of-sorts people were with Democrats; Republicans won the majority of the state court of appeals and congressional races. Lucy Baxley, destined for the distinction of being the last Democrat to hold a statewide office, illustrated the world of changing political trends during her generation when she admitted that growing up in Alabama, she did not know a single Republican.

Controversy and endless revelations of fraud generated grist for stories in big-city newspapers in Mobile, Montgomery, Birmingham, and Huntsville—completely engulfing Siegelman and putting Democrats at odds with the expectations of ordinary citizens. He continued pulling in six-figure legal fees from court cases, using free office space and the secretarial services at the Alabama Sheriff's Association.

For Republicans, however, the excesses of the Siegelman administration was the absolute perfect background for change. Voters were deeply embarrassed and more than a little disgusted by an unbroken list of absurdities in the governor's office. People were ready to send Siegelman to his next challenge—a federal court in Birmingham.

CHAPTER EIGHTEEN

❦

The Riley doctrine: fundamental change, reform

Republicans, more than Democrats, knew how to solve the manifest problems in the governor's office in 2002 and unhorse Don Siegelman. Democrats were somewhat limited to what they could do with an incumbent governor in their own party. Furthermore, the voting public would agree to everything known and unknown about the Siegelman crowd.

In the Democrat primary, Siegelman easily defended himself against lightweight challenger Charles Bishop from Jasper. A former coal miner, Bishop became wealthy developing a mining equipment business and tractor dealership. He brought that tough coal mine mentality to state politics, serving in the Alabama Senate, state agriculture commissioner, and commissioner of labor. Bishop later earned national notoriety by slugging abrasive Democrat Lowell Barron in the Senate chambers, caught on tape by an Alabama Public Television camera. He claimed that Barron defamed his dear mother by calling him a son-of-a-bitch. In the 2002 Democrat primary, Alabamians didn't like what they saw or heard from the roughhewn ex-coal miner and backed Siegelman for the nomination with 76 percent of the vote.

The Republican nomination was far more competitive. Qualifying for governor: Tim James, the handsome, athletic son of two-time governor Fob James; Lieutenant Governor Steve Windom; and vaguely known Bob Riley, three-term Third District congressman. Windom and Riley were given an equal chance of winning the GOP nomination, with James fading in the primary. Also factored into the Republican primary was the considerable influence of Judge Roy Moore, the famed Ten Commandments judge from Gadsden, who had built a substantial following with his unrelenting stance for the public display of Judeo-Christian symbols in government buildings. James and Windom courted Moore in the primary for the simple reason of cozying up to his supporters. Windom made good use of Moore's blessings, mailing and passing out campaign literature with a photo of himself and Moore—all smiles.

Riley kicked off his campaign for governor on Independence Day, 2001, with a massive rally that filled Ashland's courthouse square, where the Riley brothers once worked in the family grocery store. But tragedy struck quickly. In August, Jenice Riley, the Rileys' oldest daughter and chief fund-raiser, died at age thirty-three after a long battle with cancer. Afterward, the still-grieving family decided, with resolve, that the campaign would continue. It was a deeply personal and wise decision. The campaign would be a proper tribute to Jenice and two years of planning and preparation for her father's run for governor.

Bob Riley easily rolled through the Republican primary, winning the nomination with a sensational 73 percent vote. Tim James polled a weak 9 percent, but more surprising, Lieutenant Governor Steve Windom came in second with a poor showing of 18 percent. Windom immediately threw his support to Riley and helped him raise money. Republicans believed that they had a strong, well-financed candidate to retake the governor's office.

The election would be another historic gubernatorial race for the Republicans. Term limiting himself in Congress, during his six-year tenure in the US House, Riley earned a reputation as a staunch conservative who could attract the two most important elements of political success: people and money. The Siegelman campaign tagged him "Honest Bob," attempting to make sport of Riley's reputation for honesty. Riley's considerable best character would haunt Democrats throughout the election.

Around the time the 2002 governor's race got underway, Siegelman found himself embroiled in yet another controversial scandal. The talk around Montgomery concerned Group One, a web technology company that had been awarded a contract by the Department of Economic and Community Affairs (ADECA) to design and maintain a web page for the astronomical cost of $798,000. What attracted attention was that simple websites at the time, even for government functions, could be designed for only several thousand dollars. Investigative reporter Eddie Curran of the *Mobile Press-Register* began receiving anonymous letters and emails about Group One, and Siegelman became the target of yet another Democrat scandal. Soon, the Associated Press also received similar not-so-secret information.

Montgomery-based Group One, owned by two Siegelman supporters, didn't have as much as a telephone listing, and eventually scrapped the worthless website. It was further revealed that the governor had personally approved the Group One contract. When the US Housing and Urban Development (HUD) learned about the questionable website, the agency demanded an accounting of the $800,000 undocumented grant. Riley pointed out that this was another example of why the state government was in a financial crisis.

The Group One story was but one of many that the state media reported during the campaign. Unfettered by any semblance of ethical restraints, Siegelman's white-collar conceit allowed him to do as he pleased for money. Scandal-by-scandal, Siegelman's frantic grasp for money became a dog show of corruption. He was running for reelection while under joint state and federal investigations into his personal finances. Alabama's state government had seen many hucksters and cheats—but Siegelman topped them all!

Laying aside Siegelman's assorted political accomplishments, Bob Riley hammered away at Siegelman's penchant for ethical compromise and scandal, promising "honest change" in state government. On television, during debates and personal appearances, voters felt that Riley could be trusted, reminding people that the Siegelman administration had tarnished the already-negative image of the state with compromise and fraud. A wealth of negative news reports underscored the core message of the Riley campaign.

There was no middle ground in the 2002 elections—nationally or in Alabama. The nation was still grieving over the 9/11 terrorists' attacks, and the war on terrorism had become routine in the daily life of the American people. Midterm elections that year broke the customary pattern of the incumbent party losing congressional elections. Contrary to that tendency, congressional Republicans gained two Senate seats and eight seats in the House. The prevailing national mood of patriotism, shown by President George W. Bush, no doubt had an equally compelling influence among Alabama conservatives.

None of that mattered to Siegelman. Public ridicule did little to embarrass the governor or the Democrats. Instead, Siegelman attempted to turn the tables on Riley by demanding that he identify his $50,000 contributors in President Bush's fund-raiser that generated a record $4.02 million. Siegelman, goaded by his resentment of the congressman's ability to keep a supply of money streaming into his campaign, demanded to know the source of Riley's big donors. The money was raised during President George W. Bush's July 15 visit to Birmingham on Riley's behalf. In his remarks, Bush reminded the audience that he was familiar with Alabama because he worked on Winton Blount Jr.'s 1972 Senate campaign. Siegelman had reason to worry. Riley was banking campaign money at breakneck speed.

At first, the Riley campaign ignored calls to identify its large donors, but Riley, prodded by the press, eventually shifted the request to the National Republican Party to release the donor list. In a midsummer television debate, Riley promised that the contributors would be listed on the forty-five-day report. Yet, when the report was made public, the lone identifiable $50,000 donor was Auburn trustee Bobby Lowder, a staunch Democrat and ally of Siegelman. Neither did the list provided by the National Republican Party satisfy Siegelman, nor the media, because the sheer volume of the report made it all but impossible to identify most donors.

Just as fund-raising became a strategic battle for both candidates, polling showed an almost equal balance of voter strength between Siegelman and Riley. Early in the campaign, Siegelman held a decided edge, but in the final days of the campaign, a sudden change in polling indicated that Riley had closed the gap and had a slight lead.

Democrats were the first to notice. John Anzalone, Siegelman's campaign consultant, said that the race was within the margin of error. But it was Gerald Johnson polling for AEA, who informed the *Montgomery Advertiser* that "as of the last couple of nights, Riley is leading." Energized by the shift in their favor, during the final weekend, the Riley camp took advantage of their growing support by contacting undecided voters.

Siegelman, on the other hand, went on visiting tours of black churches with a final seven-stop fly-around on Monday. Riley greeted large crowds at each stop of his five-city fly-around. "We're this close to absolutely turning this state around once and for all. We're going to make the kind of changes we could have only dreamed about just a few years ago."

Ultimately, an estimated record of $24 million was raised and invested in the November 5 general election. Siegelman was paranoid about Riley's near-legendary fund-raising, and rightly so. According to reports, Riley spent heavier than Siegelman and was primarily funded by business groups and insurance companies. Organized labor and the Alabama Education Association (AEA) backed Siegelman. Both candidates received contributions from their respective national parties and political action committees (PACs).

Newspaper endorsements followed the same trend. The NRA, *The Montgomery Advertiser, The Anniston Star*, and *The Tuscaloosa News* endorsed Siegelman. Riley received endorsements from *The Mobile Press-Register*, *The Birmingham News*, the Business Council of Alabama (BCA), and numerous business organizations.

Almost out of character at the time, Donald Watkins, influential Birmingham attorney, led a group of African American

Republicans for Riley. Siegelman turned Riley's modest black support into accusations that "Honest Bob" was cutting deals with blacks behind closed doors, the only incident when the racial issue was raised during the campaign.

All the same, Riley courted black Democrats. He greeted voters in a tent outside Birmingham's Legion Field, the site of the annual Magic City Classic between Alabama State University and Alabama A&M. Riley also campaigned in Alabama's famed Black Belt, making good use of African American Representative Alvin Holmes's tarring of Siegelman for abusing the state's no-bid contracts. Riley said that he always got a good reception from people in the black community, the way he did back home in Ashland.

Otherwise, Siegelman had the near-exclusive support of Alabama's Democrat-leaning African Americans. By then, race was not a battleground issue in Alabama politics. Democrats could no longer use racial division as a weapon because of their alliance with blacks, and Republicans did not have a history of racial tactics.

On Election Day, Bob and Patsy Riley drove back to Ashland to vote on Tuesday, November 5, and to join the huge celebration downtown. "Our people are ready to vote," Riley told his friends and neighbors filling the town square, where he and his brother David once peddled parched peanuts for a nickel a bag. That night, the campaign shifted to the Talladega Super Speedway, where the Riley organization gathered for election returns.

The Riley campaign was not surprised when the voting returns matched their polling data in a tight race. Riley ran strong with Siegelman close behind as the election progressed through the night. Libertarian John Sophocleus was receiving modest support. The election, however, was on the verge of a statewide controversy.

Something amiss in Magnolia Springs

Controversy, Florida-style, immediately created an unneeded distraction for Riley. Initial media reports had Siegelman winning by a narrow margin, and Siegelman made his victory speech, thanking everyone who had a role in his reelection and calling for Riley to concede. Wednesday's *Montgomery Advertiser* erroneously headlined a Siegelman victory—without reporting on the precinct controversy that contradicted their story. A reporting problem which the Siegelman team knew favored them surfaced in Baldwin County. Election officials quickly discovered the tabulation error and conducted a recount after midnight after the Democrats had gone home to celebrate four more years of wide-open chicanery.

Some 6,334 votes first credited to Siegelman were adjusted from his total to Riley, changing the statewide results in Riley's favor by a 3,117-vote margin. Siegelman had the right numbers that showed him losing, but he challenged the correction and announced that he had won a second term. Again, Siegelman ignored the facts and celebrated.

The confusion was easily explained. A downloading error caused a computer to misread a data pack (cassette) from the Magnolia Springs precinct, where Siegelman received 342 of the 1,294 votes. When the data pack was taken to the Baldwin County Sheriff's office with the others and inserted into the computer, the computer garbled the Magnolia Springs numbers.

Rob Riley, in conversation with campaign operatives in Baldwin

County, emerged from a back room at the Talladega Speedway around 1:30 a.m. Wednesday morning with good news for his father. There had been a change in the final vote. He had won the election! Riley had 672,325 or 49.2 percent of the vote, with Siegelman receiving 669,105 or 49.0 percent. Sophocleus received 23,272 for 1.7 percent. Later that day, Baldwin County officials certified the election, and Riley claimed a legitimate victory.

Correcting the technology glitch infuriated Siegelman. He made baseless accusations of voter fraud—declaring himself both victim and winner. Siegelman had reason to be upset, but he insisted wrongly that the vote correction had been a Republican conspiracy. Blame went to all corners in the matter—county election officials, AP wire services for reporting the wrong numbers, and Riley operatives monitoring the Baldwin County elections. However, Siegelman would discover over the next few days that his options were futile at reversing the vote and overturning the election on any grounds other than the correct vote. (*Birmingham News*)

From Wednesday, November 6, until Monday, November 18, the governor's election was discussed, questioned, and explained endlessly, but never to Don Siegelman's satisfaction. To make matters worse, his demand for a statewide recount was rejected outright, and dread spread across the state at the possibility of another long-drawn-out election controversy by Democrats, reminiscent of the protracted 1994 Hooper-Hornsby election for the Alabama Supreme Court. Riley told the press that Siegelman knew he had lost the election, and he wanted to get his hands on the ballots. The following Saturday, Attorney General Bill Pryor refused to open the ballots, accepting the Baldwin County official certification. (*Montgomery Advertiser*)

But for Siegelman, there was too much at stake, and he was not about to quit. He had the ultimate body politic to change the outcome of the election—the Alabama Legislature. State law provided a more authoritative method of settling election disputes. The legislature could, according to previsions in the law, hear the merits of the case and make a final decision about the election. Siegelman attorney Joe Espy said that the governor was considering calling a special session of the legislature and let the Democrats decide the outcome of the election.

Siegelman's confidence in his allies in the legislature was ill-placed, although the profile of the Alabama Legislature should have been a sure bet for him. Democrats held sixty-four of 105 seats in the House and a 25-to-10 majority in the Senate. But both parties were equally weary (and wary) of Siegelman's grasp for power and money.

Demetrius Newton, the first African American speaker pro tempore of the Alabama House and a Democrat civil rights attorney from Birmingham, opposed asking the legislature to decide: "It would be disastrous." Following a caucus meeting with fellow Democrats, Newton further said, "It would be totally divisive to come before the legislative body." Neither party in the legislature was interested in deciding the election controversy, according to Newton.

Seth Hammett, Speaker of the House, agreed with Newton. "A legislative contest would hurt some of our members, particularly those from rural areas, and white Democrats more than blacks." Siegelman's perceived solid support in the legislature during his scandal-ridden tenure had been reduced to a few reliable friends. In the end, the 2002 governor's election was the closest in the history of the state, and it had not been stolen.

Democrats talked among themselves about how voters took revenge on the party following the 1986 election that saw Guy Hunt become governor, and how Republicans gradually took control of the Alabama Supreme Court following the 1994 Supreme Court controversy. Siegelman's legal team made a token petition to the Alabama Supreme Court, but even that failed to develop on the day his legal team was prepared to argue the case. It was useless. Eight of the nine justices were Republican.

Siegelman would neither acknowledge defeat nor concede the election. Unable to find a way out of the impasse by Monday, November 18, Siegelman realized the futility of a recount and came to grips with his election loss. The drama came to a peaceful end late that afternoon in Rob Riley's Birmingham law office, where his father and a small group of campaign insiders lingered around a long conference table with a speakerphone in the middle. Siegelman's communications office in Montgomery notified Riley to expect a call from the governor later that day.

Bob Riley said the phone finally rang at 5:30 p.m., and an uncustomary humble Don Siegelman called from the governor's office to formally concede the election. Riley described the conversation as "gracious" and said Siegelman promised a professional transition. When the conversation ended, the room erupted in a roar of laughter and a backslapping celebration for the Riley people.

The Riley campaign quickly called a press conference at their Jefferson County headquarters near the Galleria in Hoover, where Governor-elect Bob Riley made his victory speech. At the same time down at the state capitol in Montgomery, reporters observed that Siegelman was noticeably nervous and uncomfortable in a televised press conference as he struggled through his rambling concession statement. The election was over. Alabama had a new Republican governor.

Riley had already named Bill Cabaniss of Birmingham to chair his transition team and lead in the selection of an administrative staff. Riley said that his platform would include the revision of the old constitution and election reform. With official confirmation, within hours, President George W. Bush called Riley to congratulate him and made lighthearted conversation about Florida and his own election controversy.

Bob Riley was the first congressman elected governor of Alabama since 1894, when Democrat William C. Oates, the seven-term congressman from Abbeville in Henry County, beat Populist candidate Rueben F. Kolb, to become Alabama's twenty-ninth governor.

CHAPTER NINETEEN

◦◦◦◦◦

A different kind of state leader

Ronald Reagan was known to joke: "Status Quo was Latin for the mess we're in." Bob Riley knew exactly what a fine mess the Democrats had made when his transition team began assembling a twenty-five-member cabinet: three key staff members and the heads of twenty-two state departments. Chief of Staff Dave Stewart, Communications Director Jeff Emerson, and Legal Advisor Ken Wallis served as Riley's confidants. Riley made his choices carefully. He chose experienced professionals to lead state agencies and picked from the ranks of successful CEOs, although some he didn't meet until the first cabinet meeting. Riley would govern by the tenets of the Republican Party—easy on regulations, tough on crime, education reform, and industrial recruitment. Increasing revenue for education reform would be the rare exception.

When the initial list was released to the media, the *Birmingham News* pointed out the composition of the initial chief advisors: fourteen white men, two black men, two white women, and one black woman. Racial equality within the state's leadership positions was an issue with Riley, and he wanted African Americans and women on state boards, commissions, and authorities. Blacks made up 15 percent of the positions. But the administration did reflect, as did Fob James in his two terms, that the new Republican governor had carefully chosen minorities and women to serve the people of Alabama.

The Riley organization planned a three-day inauguration. Mike Hubbard, chairing the event, reported that $1.3 million had been raised to underwrite the inaugural celebration leading up to the swearing-in ceremony and the black-tie ball at the Garrett Coliseum. Some eighty-nine corporations and lobbying organizations gave generously. AEA chipped in $15,000.

Saturday afternoon prior to the inauguration, Ashland residents gathered for a Hill Country street party on the town square, string bands and all. The Rileys, absent Jenice, greeted their neighbors, and Bob spoke proudly of Ashland and Clay County. As the cold darkness descended, a long caravan of friends and family trailed behind the Rileys to Montgomery. The Sunday-morning edition of the *Montgomery Advertiser* headlined: *"Riley's party hits town,"* and published the schedule of inaugural events beginning with a prayer breakfast.

On January 20, 2003, the morning of the inauguration, the Riley family attended worship services at the Dexter Avenue King Memorial Baptist Church, a tribute to Martin Luther King and generations of African Americans who suffered under the mean hand of racial repression and hatred. Riley stood in the pulpit and spoke about his personal faith. Back at the capitol prior to swearing-in, Bob and Patsy Riley made their way through the capitol corridors to a portrait of Confederate General Robert E. Lee. Riley saluted the portrait, and the small crowd observed a moment of silence. The new governor placed a wreath beneath the portrait, and some in the crowd sang "Dixie" to whoops and cheers. (*Birmingham News*)

The inauguration followed the precise schedule of the Riley planning team. Supreme Court Chief Justice Roy Moore administered the oath of office to Riley, Lieutenant Governor Lucy Baxley, the first female to hold the office in Alabama, and eleven other state officials. The Riley family acknowledged the grievous loss of their oldest daughter, Jenice, with an empty chair on the podium and a single white rose. Bob Riley wore the western boots that she had given him. The new governor took the oath of office with two Bibles; the ceremonial state Bible and his personal study Bible.

Gov. Riley gave the speech that daughter Minda Riley Campbell helped draft. He spoke in simple language about his faith and vision for Alabama, connecting his religious convictions to his political beliefs, so that people knew his decisions would be based on the principles of his faith and business experience. Riley had thoroughly prepared for the moment. The Riley agenda had been published during the campaign, a ninety-page booklet proposing a new vision for Alabama—from ethics and education, to constitutional reform, to study groups for a myriad of issues that needed attention.

Addressing the people of Alabama, Riley called for "fundamental change and reform," but he did not dwell on the state's perpetually low rankings of the public education as other governors had. He made a sweeping pledge to fix the state's more pressing problems, pledging action rather more promises. The *Birmingham News* reported that Riley mentioned God ten times and did not use his new bully pulpit to take cheap shots at the previous administration that he had so harshly criticized throughout the campaign.

He spoke with the viewpoint of ordinary people that he lived among—that they were more interested in good government than political ideology. He affirmed the simple beliefs of the people in the tradition of the Christian faith. Reporters observed that Riley's speech was the most forward-thinking of any governor in recent history, showing people what was possible.

Commendably, Riley sought to rekindle the state's unique spirit that he said had inspired civil rights pioneers, successful sports programs, Mike Spann, the first casualty in the war on terrorism, and Condoleezza Rice, the Birmingham native serving as President George W. Bush's national security advisor. The speech lauded a diverse group of Alabama notables from Helen Keller in Tuscumbia to Harper Lee in Monroeville.

He spoke with feeling and conviction about his concerns for the state and called for racial unity. Gov. Riley said he wanted to change the tax code that "continues to unfairly prey on the poorest among us." Tax equity was an important issue of the Riley doctrine (his opposition to gambling was based on the same conviction). He wanted to move beyond the archaic issues that had burdened the people since statehood in 1819. The state media gave Riley high marks for his vision and agenda.

Riley introduced special recognition for citizens who had contributed to progress in Alabama. First recipients of the "Spirit of Alabama Award": war hero Mike Spann; Johnnie Carr, Montgomery Civil Rights leader; Hal Moore, US Army general and Viet Nam survivor who wrote the book, *We Were Soldiers Once. . . and Young*, and Alabama, the famed country singing group from Fort Payne.

The Riley celebration signaled a new era for Alabama. The inaugural parade was held under unusually good weather for January, and Riley's horse, "Sandman," that he had ridden in campaign commercials, brought up the rear. That night, over 7,000

Republicans celebrated at the Inaugural Ball, far exceeding the 4,000 tickets allotted for the event.

Alabama's fifty-second governor, only the third Republican since Reconstruction, faced the task of improving Alabama's badly marred reputation and repairing the state government after four years of Siegelman ruination. It would not be easy. The problems were as old and worn as the Alabama Democratic Party.

Bob Riley caught the imagination of progressive visionaries. Bailey Thompson, journalist, educator, and advocate of constitutional reform, was one of them. Thompson pleaded for the fair treatment of the poor and had often written about Alabama's unfulfilled potential.

Soon after the election, Thompson penned an editorial that ran in major newspapers throughout the state in which he said that Alabama yearned for the inspiration of a "New South" governor who would confront the state's "ancient enemy," quoting Lister Hill, "those who oppose progress."

Thompson further said that "Riley has all but wrapped himself in the mantle of New South governance," having thoroughly studied Riley's campaign for constitution reform, the immoral tax system, more flexibility in how Alabama spends its tax dollars, and increased oversight of wasteful spending. Thompson was prophetic. The Riley administration would evolve as an exact mirror of his campaign—open, honest, and visionary—the kind of change needed to lift the state out of the mire of political greed and backwardness that had held Alabama back for over a century. Bob Riley intended to be a different kind of governor, and Bailey Thompson and others were counting on him to do exactly that.

Growing up on the courthouse square

Bob Riley grew up on Ashland's courthouse square. God-fearing parents and a rugged work ethic prepared Robert Renfroe Riley for a life of opportunity and success. He was born on October 3, 1944, in Eustace and Elizabeth Riley's family home in Ashland, Clay County, Alabama. The Rileys lived within sight of the home place of the county's most famous citizen, Supreme Court Justice Hugo Black. County residents were justifiably proud when Black represented Alabama in the United States Senate, especially in 1937, when President Franklin D. Roosevelt nominated Black for a seat on the US Supreme Court. Too young to remember Justice Black, the most prominent public personality that Riley met on the town square, was Pete Matthews, a well-known local attorney who represented Clay County in the Alabama Legislature, House and Senate.

The Rileys lived three blocks off the town square, where Eustace operated a small grocery store purchased with money he saved during World War II. Eustace Riley was following the family tradition. The history of Clay County tells about seven generations of Rileys, beginning with Patrick Riley, who migrated from Ireland to Charleston, S.C., in 1740. Patrick's business was selling flour and gunpowder to the South Carolina militia during the American Revolution. He eventually moved to Alabama, and at times, the Riley name appeared on one or more buildings on Ashland's business district.

Early on, David and Bob Riley worked in their parents' grocery store, one of five around the square. Bob said he and his brother were "schooled in the country store business," helping customers and running errands for their parents. As youngsters, the Riley boys peddled parched peanuts from a small wagon on Saturday, a nickel a bag.

On Saturday, the town and the dirt streets surrounding the courthouse were filled with people in farm wagons and automobiles, a ready-made audience for street preachers and handshaking politicians. Regular customers brought their grocery lists to Riley's Store and returned to pick them up as late as midnight. Around nine, Riley remembered, Elizabeth Riley put the boys to bed on a pallet in the back room of the store.

Eustace and Elizabeth Riley were more than good to their two sons. They provided a proper home environment, taught them the value of honest work, and provided for their education. David, eighteen months older than Bob, was a more serious student, and Bob made respectable but not scholarly marks. Friends say that he was more interested in fun and frolic. David may have been the best student, but Bob had the size and skills to play high school sports for the Ashland Panthers—forward in basketball, end in football. He was elected president of the student body his senior year and captained the basketball team. In a class of forty-one, he was voted "Best Looking."

Store keeping in a small rural town helped prepare Bob Riley for a broad understanding of Southern people, and from that, he drew on skills that he learned meeting people around town. More importantly, it was how he learned to appreciate the viewpoint of others. Ashland and its simple goodness provided Riley with a good life and an education that would serve him well.

The boys were in high school when Eustace Riley expanded into the chicken business. His two sons provided the operating labor—feeding, catching, and cleaning out the chicken houses for the next batch. During the Great Depression, chickens replaced

cotton as the chief source of income for Clay County farmers after boll weevils came in swarms from the west and destroyed the
local cotton crops. David and Bob never really warmed to their
father's chicken business and felt that one day they would leave it
all behind. They were wrong.

Then, there was romance. Bob Riley was a junior in high
school when he began dating Patsy Adams, a perky ninth-grader
versatile enough to march as a majorette in the school band and
lead cheers for the Panthers. Like the Rileys, the Adams were
successful small-town merchants. Patsy's father, John Q. Adams,
owned Adams Drug Store across the square from Riley's Store.
Her mother, Verna, helped with the family business. Friends say
that Patsy inherited her mother's spirited personality. David enrolled at the University of Alabama, and on weekends, Bob visited him for the excitement of university life. It was a given that
one day he would attend the University of Alabama and marry the
Adams girl.

Higher education for the Riley boys with an understanding.
Eustace Riley spelled out his terms: go to school, but when they
were not in school, they would work with the chickens. That was
enough incentive that kept Bob in class year-around. He briefly
played basketball on Alabama's freshman team at the invitation
of the coach until he realized that college basketball was more demanding than Clay County sports. He majored in business administration, graduating in 1965 at age twenty, amid the civil rights
turmoil that gripped the South and the nation. He would witness
history in the making.

Raging anger against racial integration was not an issue for
Riley. He remained apart from the controversy, claiming that he

was nonpolitical at the time. He didn't find anything useful in Gov. George Wallace's attempt to block the integration of the university. Riley said that for several days prior to the state-federal confrontation, tensions had been building on campus. State troopers patrolled the streets of Tuscaloosa, and Klansman Robert Shelton and the media kept a keen eye out for the feds.

By the time Wallace made his defiant stand against integration at the university, Bob Riley had a bird's-eye view of the event. On June 11, 1963, Bob and David hurried over to Foster Auditorium, climbed the stairs, and watched from open windows on the second floor with a sweeping view of the historic confrontation playing out below. The Riley brothers had a front-row seat for the Wallace media circus.

They watched as assistant US Attorney General Nicholas Katzenbach, a hulk of a man in a rumpled gray suit, led a contingent of federal marshals and Alabama National Guard to the auditorium where students were registering for summer classes. Waiting at the front door of the auditorium behind a small lectern stood the sullen-faced, diminutive governor of Alabama. David and Bob overheard the conversation when Katzenbach asked Wallace to step aside. Wallace refused and began reading from his prepared speech denouncing the intrusion of the federal government.

Wallace complained that the government was infringing on the rights of the sovereign state of Alabama, citing the Tenth Amendment establishing the state's authority. After speaking, Wallace planted himself squarely in the doorway and refused to move. It was pure political theater. The university had arranged a different agreement with the Justice Department. Winton Blount Jr., the university trustee, had arranged with Attorney General

Bobby Kennedy that Wallace would make a statement—all for show.

The conflict received national news coverage, providing Wallace with material for his campaign speeches. In the end, Wallace's self-importance came to no good. Standing in the schoolhouse door marked the beginning of integration in Alabama. By September 1963, two schools in the rocket city of Huntsville integrated over Wallace's political opposition.

Bob Riley knew that Wallace was delivering on his promise of "segregation forever" in his inaugural address in January. Riley said that the campus was rampant with wild rumors. Klan leader Robert Shelton cruised the streets of Tuscaloosa in a big black car with two conspicuously long antennas. Later, the Riley brothers learned that two black students, Vivian Malone and James Hood, had enrolled at the university despite Wallace's grandstanding and were attending classes. Vivian Malone graduated with Bob Riley in 1965.

Back home in Clay County

Bob Riley and Patsy Adams married on December 27, 1964, in the First United Methodist Church of Ashland, the Adams' family church, shortly before Bob graduated from Alabama. Unlike many new graduates anticipating professional careers, Bob and Patsy Riley knew they were expected back home in Ashland to start their own family. Bob had a job waiting for him in the chicken business, the only work he knew as a university graduate.

They did just that. The Riley brothers never gave a second thought to living or working elsewhere other than Clay County. In an age of conformity, they felt that they had deep roots in the community of fewer than two thousand people and never entertained leaving. Bob and David Riley started their business careers selling eggs door-to-door. Yet, the scope of the Riley brothers' business sense quickly eclipsed weekly egg routes.

At first, they sold eggs out of a Dodge van with the cartoon character Snuffy Smith painted on the side and a sign that read *"Uncle Bob's Eggs."* Their business education enabled them to expand into the more lucrative poultry industry, which they developed into one of the largest in the southeast. Ironically, Eustace Riley's original investment in chickens served as the pivotal business opportunity that launched the Riley brothers' entrepreneurial career.

Eventually, Bob Riley developed other business enterprises: drugstore, automobile and truck dealership, grocery store, and a real estate firm to go along with his large cattle farm. And of all things, an airport. In less than two decades of investing in his home county, he had created his own version of a successful rural conglomerate. He had also attained a place among the financial elite, exceeding the million-dollar mark in assets and income.

During the time Riley was developing his business career, he was encouraged to get into local politics in a very unusual way. When the Rileys' home burned while they were attending an Alabama-Tennessee football game, there was no way to extinguish the blaze because the city didn't have reliable fire protection. The Riley brothers, with a group of friends, organized a volunteer fire department. In 1972, at age twenty-eight, his firefighting buddies insisted that he run for the Ashland City Council. He did and won. That led to a run for mayor in 1976, also backed by the same group, and Riley lost his only political race—and badly. The failed race completely dampened his enthusiasm for politics.

All of that changed when the Reagan revolution swept through America, and Bob Riley self-identified with Reaganism. He had experienced the negative effects of how bad government affected business and recognized that change was needed. By the time the last Riley child left home, Bob and Patsy were trying to reimagine their future together. Needing time to consider his options, Bob took a long motorcycle trip down to Key West, Florida, to relax and come to a decision. When he wasn't scuba diving, he spent days alone, in thought and prayer, contemplating entirely new directions for his family.

Back home, Riley called the family together to announce his decision. Before he could speak, Patsy blurted out that Bob was going into the ministry, a logical conclusion for the churchgoing Rileys. On the contrary, he explained to his startled wife that he was going into politics, and he was going to run for Congress. He said Patsy didn't speak to him for two weeks.

Riley explained that two factors changed the direction of his life. His brother David died suddenly at age forty-nine after returning home from a deacons' meeting at Ashland's First Baptist Church. Bob idealized his older brother and business partner, calling him the best man he has ever known. Equally important to the Rileys was the birth of their first grandchild. Riley said he realized that he wanted to get involved in public service as an expression of his personal faith. "I was the most nonpolitical person in the county until our children were grown. It was all business with me during that time."

He got the same skeptical reaction when he discussed his plans with John Adams, Patsy's father. Mr. Adams told him flat-out, "There is no way in hell that you can get elected in Clay County as a Republican." Once the shock wore off, Patsy and her father understood the decision to serve people that he knew in his personal and business life, particularly their skepticism about running as a Republican. The next big step in Riley's political career was actually becoming a Republican. He attended his first party meeting in the offices of Wellborn Cabinet in Ashland at the invitation of Paul Wellborn. He said there were about six men there the night he announced that he was running for Congress. They were surprised too.

Divining a new life direction

Riley sensed, correctly, that the timing was right for a Republican to represent the East Alabama Third Congressional District. The mostly rural Deep South district had voted for George Bush as president and Guy Hunt in 1986, anchored by two universities: Jacksonville State University in Calhoun County to the north, and Auburn University in Lee County to the south. In the 1989 congressional election, Johnny Ford, African American mayor of Tuskegee, attempted to attract the white vote by running as a conservative. Riley was reading all the political signs correctly. The potential of a Republican victory was better than ever, especially for a successful businessman with money to invest in an aggressive campaign.

The incumbent congressman, Glen Browder, had attempted to straddle the political fence for three terms as a "Blue Dog Democrat." Recognizing Riley as a threat to his reelection, Browder opted to run for the US Senate, which Jeff Sessions ultimately won for the GOP. After generations of Rileys voting Democrat, the opportunity to work in the national government had Riley's full attention. He qualified at Republican Party headquarters in Birmingham to run for Congress, inspired by the conservative ideals of Ronald Reagan.

Bob Riley put his conservative principles into a broad-based campaign and invested heavily in the race against Democrat Ted Little from Auburn. Riley's deep pockets financed media advertising in the Montgomery, Birmingham, and Columbus, Georgia, markets—introducing himself to voters in east-central Alabama. Riley said that he purchased eight-hour blocks of time on Alabama Public Television, running a continuous loop of fifteen-minute commercials (the state party offered no advice about how to run a congressional campaign). Riley said one of the most effective campaign innovations was a tractor-trailer painted white with big red letters—"*Riley for Congress.*" He said the big rig drew a lot of attention and was driven throughout the district. In large cities, the rig was moved from place to place each day.

Bob Ingram, who had seen politicians come and go for decades, recognized something special in Riley. "Riley has a lot going for him," Ingram wrote about the campaign. "He is a small-town boy made good, and he will come across on television as well as any candidate."

Riley opposed abortion rights, gun control, and racial quotas while supporting school prayer, tax cuts, and a balanced budget. Conservative positions and traditional values earned Riley a 50-to-47 percent victory over Ted Little that helped Republicans to retain control of the US House in the 1996 national elections.

In Congress, Riley positioned himself as a staunch conservative willing to take the lead on critical issues. He said that Newt Gingrich's "Contract with America," like Reaganomics, made sense to him as a businessman. He expressed satisfaction that Republicans had forced President Bill Clinton to accept a balanced budget and welfare reform despite repeated vetoes. He served on the Banking and Financial Security Committee and the influential Armed Services Subcommittee on Military Readiness, a key position in his district for military installations in Montgomery and Anniston. Promising to limit himself to three terms, Riley worked in the national government while keeping Alabama politics in sharp focus. At some point in his first term, Riley said that he began entertaining the idea of running for governor.

By the next congressional election in 1998, Riley had another strong challenger in Joe Turnham, a Democrat with excellent name recognition. Pete Turnham, Joe's father, served in the Alabama Legislature for forty years and had been recognized as the "Dean of the Alabama Legislature." The Turnhams double-teamed Riley up and down East Alabama, but Riley's conservative voting record and high-energy campaign style gave him the edge. He beat young Turnham by a 58-to-42 percent margin to fend off another liberal Democrat challenge. Riley saw the election as yet another rejection of Alabama's failed Democrat leadership.

Congressman Bob Riley had watched Don Siegelman shame the governor's office and drag the state through the gutter with high-profile scandals and corruption not seen in over a century. Riley decided, after extensive spiritual thought and talks with his family, to do something highly improbable for a sitting congressman. He was going to run for governor.

CHAPTER TWENTY

Atticus Finch loses his big case

"The Siegelman administration cleared out of the capitol on Friday, Jan. 17. That night, three of the younger members returned. Though never publicly identified, they were seen by security cameras erasing data and programs on more than half of the office's 50 computers."

Eddie Curran, The Governor of Goat Hill

The first day of work for Gov. Riley and his staff held a major surprise. They discovered that the communications system in the governor's office had been sabotaged. Many of the office computers were useless, incapable of even sending simple messages. Taking the high road of civility, Riley's people kept quiet about the late-night technology raid until someone leaked about what the Siegelman crowd had done. Restoring the communications system required two months and some $100,000 to repair or replace computers in the governor's office. Riley did not turn the incident into another media brawl. Instead, he chose to move on from what happened the previous Friday night. Riley spokesman David Azbell put the matter into more lighthearted terms: "Our computers had a full-frontal lobotomy."

Computer mischief by the Siegelman lads was more than a fraternity prank and could have been a dark omen for the new administration. Eager to get on with their work, disabled computers were little more than a minor distraction compared to the problems that needed immediate attention. Anticipating controversy, Gov. Riley understood that the most pressing problem for Alabama was fixing a major budget shortfall—*$675 million*. And Riley would have to identify funding by the end of the fiscal year. Furthermore, Riley would need to do it with a hostile legislature looking over his shoulder, where AEA's Paul Hubbert sat in the gallery, flashing hand signals to legislators about how they should vote. He also knew that Hubbert and his AEA coalition only supported legislation that benefited their members.

The task of finding additional revenue fell to Dwight Carlisle, the revenue commissioner with a CEO background in top management. Carlisle had helped guide Alabama-based Russell Corporation to manufacturing and marketing success in the textile and sportswear industry. Riley and Carlisle knew that it would be a stretch coming up with $675 million.

Riley immediately eliminated $40 million for pork projects passed by Democrats before Siegelman left office. Then he appointed a commission to study the effects of earmarking tax revenue and identifying new ways of funding through the state constitution. "We couldn't prioritize the funds we had and direct them where they were needed," Riley explained in frustration. "We needed flexibility to meet the state's financial obligations and write budgets. Earmarking is an obstacle to an efficient government."

The new governor got his answer about un-earmarking by the legislature . . . quick and to the point. Paul Hubbert, executive secretary of the Alabama Education Association (AEA), flatly stated, "I'm agin' it."

Gov. Riley was not exactly shocked by Hubbert's response. Some 87.2 percent of all state money was earmarked, either by the Alabama Constitution or by state law. State income tax receipts were earmarked for education in 1947 by a statewide vote. State sales taxes, another major funding source, was also earmarked for education. The majority of state revenue sources followed a similar pattern. "We've nailed everything down in Alabama to the point that we cannot move," said William Stewart, professor of political science at the University of Alabama. Stewart served on Riley's task force for constitutional reform, which recommended that the state refrain from earmarking new tax dollars.

There was a reason for the extremely high percentage of designated funds. Voters did not trust Montgomery politicians to invest tax revenue wisely—even though Alabama had the lowest tax rates in the nation. By comparison, Georgia earmarked only 5.7 percent of its tax revenue. Further, the National Conference of State Legislatures suggested minimal earmarking is one of the hallmarks of a sound state revenue system.

But that was not all the new governor wanted. At the same time Riley was struggling to make sense of numerous inefficient fiscal policies, he was preparing to ask voters to approve an amendment that would raise taxes annually by $1.2 billion. Both moves had much the same shock effect: earmarking on Democrats in the legislature and higher taxes for the people. Siegelman had tried and failed to pass a state lottery to balance the budget.

Riley had not been secretive about his intentions. In his inaugural address, he noted that money might have been short, but he had no plans to force the poor to pay a disproportionate share of the tax burden. Instead, he wanted those who could afford taxes—people in higher income brackets and corporations that owned vast expanses of property and timberland—to pay more taxes. Riley's vision extended beyond the budget. He needed additional resources to reform the state education system and improve the tax base for a world-class education system. He also knew that doing so would require partnering with Paul Hubbert, the dominant power in the Alabama Legislature.

What Riley and his legislative team designed for the tax amendment was complex and would eventually be misunderstood by voters and distorted by critics. The radical new proposal would transform state finances. He called for spending cuts and, at the same time, raising state and local taxes by $1.2 billion. The daringness of Riley's tax plan seemed to enrage everyone except Hubbert and AEA. Education would be the primary beneficiary of the controversial tax amendment. That factor alone infuriated conservatives in the governor's own party.

Riley was right about the most virulent opposition to the tax amendment. Republicans turned on him in open revolt. His plan violated one of the first principles of the Republican Party by raising, not lowering, taxes. Republicans felt betrayed after supporting Riley's no-tax campaign promise. It was not the conservative way of problem-solving. Even Siegelman had refused to raise taxes. (Georgia ramped up its tax system in the 1960s.)

In the mind of many voters, the fact that Hubbert was promoting the amendment indicated that the plan was a tangle of hazards. Opposed to removing earmarks, the teachers union readily agreed with the new governor because Riley made two major concessions: maintain teacher pay at present levels and invest tax revenue in an AEA-controlled Alabama Excellence Initiative.

With that, AEA got on board funding radio and television ads that endorsed Amendment One, recommending that voters fix education—"once and for all."

Riley said that he got the education tax concept from North Carolina, which had increased education investments in the 1960s that resulted in much-higher test scores in schools. He understood that to improve Alabama's education system required extensive funding. The plan had merit and promise, but it was not workable. Alabamians wanted a better education system, but they were dead set against paying more taxes for schools. As in the past, property owners were unwilling to send more money to Montgomery for Democrats to squander. Yet, Republicans had no such intentions. Gov. Bob Riley wanted to lift the education system out of the bottom ranking, and he needed more than thirteen cents on the dollar to do it.

A major factor in the amendment was financial accountability from state agencies. Language in Amendment One restricted legislators (ostensibly Democrats) from the age-old practice of directing how state agencies funded specific projects in their home districts. With most of the revenue assigned to particular functions, Riley wanted to invest money where it was needed, the way he did with his numerous businesses. "We literally didn't have the flexibility to spend money where the need is most critical," Riley explained.

More than anything, Riley was motivated by his faith. He wanted to remove some of the tax burdens on Alabama's poor. "When I read the New Testament, there are three things we're asked to do: That's love God, love each other, and take care of the least among us." Riley said concern for the poor was one of the great moral decisions of his life.

Paul Hubbert's blessings also signaled the support of the Alabama Democratic Party, a startling alliance for a Republican governor. Not surprisingly, the billion-dollar-plus tax amendment turned loyal Republicans against Riley. Two cabinet members resigned. Charles Bishop, the combative commissioner of labor, left in anger. The Alabama Republican Executive Committee passed a resolution 122–100 opposing Amendment One and recommended a "no" vote. The rift between Riley and Republicans went deep. State GOP director Marty Connors said it would take a year to get the governor's office back to par.

A record number of voters went to the polls on September 9, 2003, and soundly defeated Riley's controversial but well-intentioned Amendment One tax referendum. The huge turnout came close to eclipsing the previous November general election. Voters turned thumbs-down on the new tax program. The vote was not even close: 67-to-33 percent. The amendment was approved in only thirteen counties in the Black Belt and lost by more than 3-to-1 in conservative North Alabama. Democrats approved, and Republicans disapproved.

Atticus Finch lost his big case. Riley had staked his political future on transforming Alabama's tax system to reform education, only to have it defeated to the point of embarrassment. The loss staggered Riley, but it did not fell him. Ever since he had been president of his senior class in Ashland, Riley had been successful at getting what he wanted. But raising taxes in Alabama was different. When asked about his "Plan B" after the big loss, the governor quickly responded, "Amendment One *was* my Plan B."

Antitax groups came down hard on Riley the same as Alabama Republicans. Low-income and minority voters, the very people who stood to benefit most from the amendment, voted against it, even though they would have paid lower taxes. More importantly, Riley had staked out the high moral ground and won the ideological battle for progress in Alabama.

But shades of *schadenfreude!* Grover Norquist, president of Americans for Tax Reform, blasted Riley before the vote. "I want the whole Republican Party to watch this guy fall on his face," Norquist said in scorn. "He lied to the voters. He's been a disaster. He'll never be elected to anything again in his life." Political analyst Stuart Rothenberg said that "Riley has a better chance of winning *American Idol* than getting reelected."

The loss was enormous and reverberated throughout Alabama. Polls taken by the *Mobile Register/University of South Alabama* two months after the big defeat found that only one in four adults rated the governor's job performance as good or excellent. At the same time, 68 percent described Riley as fair to poor. Worst still, in a hypothetical primary, Riley trailed Supreme Court Justice Roy Moore by 17 points, and he was down 8 points against Don Siegelman under federal indictment, who he had defeated a year earlier.

All of that meant that Riley would not have the opportunity to transform the tax structure and reform the education system. Instead, for several weeks, he huddled with Dwight Carlisle and department heads to cut $675 million out of the state budget. With that done, Gov. Riley sent the budget down the hill across South Union Street to the Alabama Legislature.

Wayne Flynt, a historian at Auburn University, noted for his biting criticisms of Republicans, applauded Riley's courage in fighting for substantive change. "No opportunistic politician concerned about his own reelection would have done this. He's one of the few governors in recent generations to try to exercise leadership."

Kathryn Tucker Windham, author and storyteller from Thomasville, was inducted into the Alabama Academy of Honor with Riley in 2003. A self-professed "Yellow Dog Democrat," Mrs. Windham praised Riley's daring vision. She said that Riley "attempted to lift Alabama from the bottom and put us on the road to progress and make us a leader and give us pride again." Mrs. Windham further lamented, "He failed. And we failed. And it still hurts."

Bob Riley got much the same reaction from the national media. Mitch Frank, writing for *Time* magazine, agreed with Flynt and Windham. "Alabama's Republican Governor Bob Riley is either politically suicidal or the bravest chief executive in the country." No one, enemy or friend, doubted Riley's determination to improve Alabama education. As for the reduced state operating budget that he sent to the legislature after the defeat of the amendment, not a single Democrat rose to object to the budget cuts. "No one, not even the Democrats, criticized the new budget," Riley explained. "The Alabama Legislature voted to accept the budget as proposed by the governor's office."

Lauded by some for his effort to change Alabama but rebuked by the majority for the same reason, Bob Riley absorbed his losses, learned his lessons, and went on with the immediate management of the state. Seen as a failed governor, it soon became apparent that he was nothing of the sort.

In the months ahead, Riley methodically adjusted some taxes and fees and increased taxes on the state's oil and gas severance. The largest increase came from a decision by the Alabama Revenue Department. The department changed the decades-old practice of assessing property from a quadrennial basis to annual appraisals. In all, the collective revenue adjustments enabled the state to end 2004 with $150 million surplus and 100,000 new jobs—an astonishing reversal from Siegelman's staggering budget deficit!

Improving state revenue allowed Riley to implement selected portions of the tax referendum. He reduced taxes on lower- and middle-income families, gave state employees a 5 percent raise, increased pensions for retired state employees, and improved budgets on a broad range of state services. Riley also realized a personal objective by raising the threshold that working families paid state income tax, thus, lowering their annual tax obligation.

Again, prodded by his faith principles, Riley corrected many old racial wrongs. He signed the Rosa Parks Act that allowed African Americans convicted by all-white Democrat Jim Crow juries to apply for a pardon. Further, in Riley's proclamation designating April as Confederate Historical Heritage Month, the Associate Press informed him that the final version of the proclamation had dropped a paragraph that acknowledged slavery as the cause of the Civil War. Riley quickly reissued the corrected proclamation and posted it on his website.

Redemption from tax failure

Riley's political redemption, many people believed, came in the form of a destructive storm. Hurricane Katrina wreaked havoc across the Gulf States, devastating Alabama beach property and the fishing industry. Riley mobilized state resources and took a personal role as the hurricane roared into Alabama. He declared a state of emergency and requested President George Bush to issue an "expedited major disaster declaration" for six counties in south

Alabama. What had been a PR disaster for President Bush became a turning point for Riley. He also appeared with the president in a press conference in Mobile.

He went further, providing emergency services to help storm victims by opening military bases to house evacuees, most of them from neighboring Mississippi. Riley's preparation for disaster complemented the courage he had displayed in the failed tax amendment and earned him recognition from state and federal agencies for his leadership.

Riley, the businessman, applied himself with the same level of energy recruiting business and industry that he did with education reform. The Riley administration job numbers went up, and the state economy experienced unprecedented growth. Unemployment gradually declined to 3.1 percent by the end of his first term. This was the lowest unemployment recorded in Alabama since statistics began being tracked in 1976.

Not missing a step, Riley continued pursuing his goal of education reform. The Alabama Reading Initiative (ARI) and the Alabama Math, Science, and Technology Initiative (AMSTI) were at the front of Gov. Riley's reform objectives, and school funding increased by $2 billion. During his first term, the reading initiative was expanded to every kindergarten through third grade. Not surprisingly, the effects of the reforms had Alabama's fourth-graders leading the nation in reading improvement according to the "Nation's Report Card." A new Pre-K program was introduced to help develop early childhood education.

The Alabama Math, Science, and Technology Initiative systematically expanded from some forty schools to almost 700 by the end of his first term. Further, in 2005, Riley spearheaded a new education program that increased distance learning for rural schools. ACCESS Distance Learning used videoconferencing and the internet so students could take advanced-level courses previously unavailable at their schools.

Continuing to govern by Christian principles, Bob Riley established the Black Belt Action Committee (BBAC) to implement new methods to help the most economically depressed regions of the state—former homes to some of Alabama's largest plantations. Democrat Rep. Artur Davis, who later switched to the Republican Party, chaired the effort. The Black Belt was the region that sent African Americans to the state capitol when the Alabama Republican Party organized in 1867. Under Democrat rule, blacks had become perennially impoverished, with most families living on government assistance.

Emerging from the near-disastrous tax referendum, Bob Riley fought his way back with the sound management of state resources. The measure of success would be seen in the next election when he went back to the people seeking a second term. His poll numbers had risen, but the reelection campaign would be a hard sell to people who did not see the need to pay taxes and were deeply suspicious of the government.

The first lady and the Governor's Mansion

During the time Gov. Bob Riley was leading Alabama through change, First Lady Patsy Riley initiated an ambitious program to renovate the executive mansion. The 1907 Neo-Classical Revival residence had fallen into disrepair and had been off-limits to the public for a decade. Disappointed by the appearance of the historic state property, Mrs. Riley recognized the need for an extensive renovation so Alabamians could once again enjoy its original beauty and historic appeal. Returning the residence to its original glory was one thing, paying for it another. Persuading her governor-husband to put the renovation in the state budget was out of the question. Mrs. Riley would have to finance the project with private funds.

Alabama has had only two governors' residences. The first was the Beaux Arts brownstone that the state purchased in 1911 for $46,500. Prior to that, Alabama governors resided in private homes, hotels, or taverns. The brownstone served the state for forty years.

Big Jim Folsom wanted a stately residence for governors. He authorized the purchase of the Ligon mansion from the original family in 1950 for $100,000 and spent another $130,000 renovating and furnishing the home. It was seen at the time as an extravagant expenditure. The house had 8,500 square feet of living space on two levels. Governor Folsom and his family lived there during his second term in 1954–'58.

By 1993, Governor Jim Folsom Jr. had spent over $511,000 updating the residence; yet, less than a decade later, the place had taken on the worn and shabby appearance of an overused historical relic. Style-conscious First Lady Patsy Riley immediately grasped the opportunity to complement her husband's tenure as governor. The need for extensive improvement was glaring to those who walked through the place after the Siegelmans moved out—worn carpet, frayed upholstery, rotting wood, cracked molding, missing plaster. And the plumbing and electrical systems needed extensive work. The 1907 home was nearing the century mark and needed a complete makeover to solve the problem of age and neglect.

Forming a nonprofit, "Friends of the Mansion," Patsy Riley,

sold tickets to two fund-raising events, 800 tickets at $100 each. The "Somewhere in Time" fund-raisers featured tours of the mansion led by ladies in 1907 costumes, and a marketplace of carefully selected vendors. Guests were invited back to a party in November to enjoy the improvements.

Still, the sold-out events did not cover the cost of the renovations, forcing the First Lady to improvise. Turning to the nearby state prison where prisoners with specialized skills languished behind bars, Mrs. Riley soon had a working list of over fifty inmates assigned to specialized projects inside and outside the mansion— for free.

When removing the old asbestos became a health concern during renovations, there were no state prisoners experienced in asbestos removal to offset the $50,000 cost. Mrs. Riley solved the problem by requesting prison officials to send three prisoners to specialized training. The men professionally gutted the asbestos in the old building, and they had a new work skill when they eventually returned to the outside world.

To fund-raising and free labor, Patsy Riley added a third element. She and her staff researched and assembled a book about Alabama's first families who had lived in the current residence, titled, *Alabama's First Ladies and Their Governors*. The venture generated additional income for the mansion, and the books were sold in a new gift shop operated by volunteers across the street from the mansion. Mrs. Riley followed up with another book, *When the Dinner Bell Rings at the Governor's Mansion*, sold at the gift shop for the continuing maintenance of the mansion.

The freshly groomed, renovated, and landscaped Governor's Mansion opened to the public in the fall of 2003, an impressive venue for state entertaining, special occasions, holiday events, school, and garden tours. It was a signal achievement for First Lady Patsy Riley, volunteers, and the administration.

Next door to the governor's residence, Mrs. Riley and the group of renovation activists turned their attention to the state-owned Farley-Hill House, another century-old mansion used for official dinners and events. The nonprofit "Friends of the Alabama Governor's Mansion" purchased the Georgian revival house in 2000 for $350,000. Mrs. Riley initiated a second fund-raiser to restore that residence also. The two homes comprise the mansion complex, complete with a bungalow (that Fob James used as an office) and a pool in the shape of the state. The Montgomery Master Gardeners organization maintains the landscape and keeps it immaculate and healthy the year-round.

Turning her attention to the capitol, Mrs. Riley initiated the "Capitol Grounds Improvement Project," adding new plantings of camellias, azaleas, and roses to improve the appearance of the capitol grounds. Her efforts won an award for landscape design and improvements in 2008.

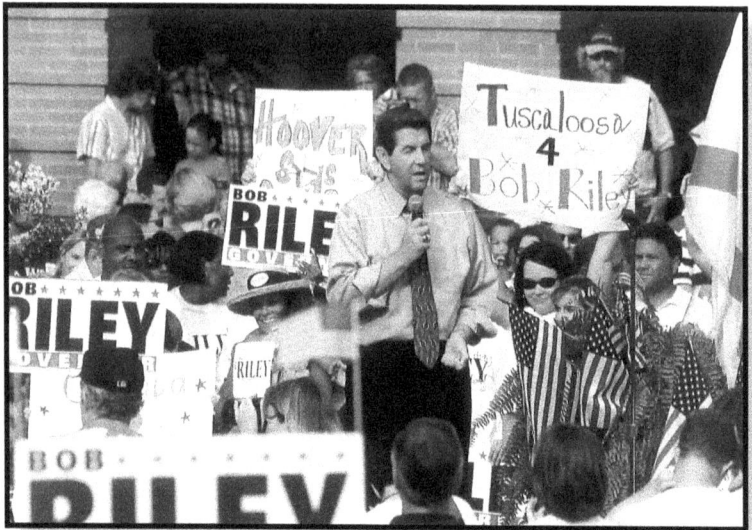

Bob Riley kicks off his campaign for governor

(Stephen Gross, The Anniston Star)

CHAPTER TWENTY-ONE

*I waited all my life for a New South Democrat
governor, and when Alabama finally
elected one—he was a Republican.*

H. Brandt Ayers, publisher, *The Anniston Star*

Bob Riley accepted the New South tribute with modesty. Don Siegelman and Paul Hubbert attempted to lay claim as visionary leaders, an achievement that did not fit their liberal agenda. Accolades came to Riley from many sources, from the left and the right, which noted his courage in the Amendment One defeat and the many positive changes made during his first term as governor. Thorough preparation during Hurricane Katrina stood as the high-water mark of his first term, Riley resolved numerous contentious issues while battling stubborn-as-mules Democrats, predisposed to their own style of break-the-bank government and wished failure on the conservative governor and Republicans.

Riley's rise from political penance changed the downward trend of his poll numbers and positioned him in the lead for a second term. When the *Mobile Press-Register* conducted a poll in 2005, Roy Moore had a substantial lead over Riley. By the next spring, the numbers had been reversed, and Riley had a comfortable lead for another impressive win in the Republican primary. No scandals or awkward incidents tainted the Riley administration due to his leadership style and the careful selection of cabinet members.

The economy had improved, and Alabama had a healthy

budget surplus. The state enjoyed a period of record low employment and strong economic growth that enabled the governor to push a modest tax cut through the legislature. It was clear that the people of Alabama were finding Riley's leadership more favorable. (*Birmingham News*)

Alabama's political climate also favored Republicans due to widespread corruption and scandals by Democrats on two fronts: almost daily media revelations about out-of-control corruption in the community college system, and Siegelman's trial in a Birmingham federal court that stretched into the fifth week leading up to the June 6 primary. Democrats were hard-pressed to remain loyal to their own party that was immersed in compromises and scandals.

Chief Justice Roy Moore had shown a sharp competitive edge after the Amendment One failure. But in the interim, Moore had been removed from office for refusing to comply with a federal court order. A specially appointed Supreme Court (ex-Governor John Patterson served as chief justice) heard arguments for violating federal Judge Myron Thompson's order and upheld Moore's removal. The issue was that Moore had a Ten Commandments monument carved into a huge 5,280-pound block of granite and installed in the foyer of the Alabama Judicial Building. The monument had been surreptitiously moved into the building in the dead of night, without consulting members of the court. Judge Thompson appreciated neither the esthetics nor the symbolism of the monument and ordered it removed. Moore refused.

Theatrics aside, the polls were on the money. Riley beat Moore decisively by a 2-to-1 margin to claim the Republican nomination for governor in 2006. Moore conceded the election in his hometown, Gadsden, before half of the votes were counted—then refused to endorse Riley because he claimed the governor accepted PAC money.

John Davis, a *Montgomery Advertiser* reporter, examined the influence of religion in the Riley-Moore campaigns. Even though a ban on gay marriage passed statewide by 81 percent, Moore fell short of attracting the majority vote of evangelical Christians. The Christian Coalition did not endorse either candidate, which seriously hampered Moore's ability to attract religious voters. John Giles, president of the Christian Coalition in Alabama, which distributed fliers around the state on Sunday prior to the election, said some voters were confused by the lack of an endorsement—as was Moore.

Riley's victory disproved the theory that the Moore campaign was a Christian movement. (Fob James supported Moore's Ten Commandments crusade.) The loss went deeper for Moore because other candidates running on his judicial philosophy also lost. In the end, Moore, ever the courageous defender of Christian values, was seen as a sore loser. In the mind of voters, there were no questions about Riley's faith principles. Starting with his congressional career, Riley had a perfect voting record with the Christian Coalition.

In the 2006 Democrat primary, Don Siegelman, under indictment for federal racketeering and conspiracy charges, and Lieutenant Gov. Lucy Baxley led a field of seven candidates. Polling had Baxley leading Siegelman, but not by much. Yet, Baxley went on to soundly trounce Siegelman, 59-to-36 percent in basically a two-person race. The lackluster lineup of candidates in the Democrat primary was an accurate measurement of the party's weakened voting strength, similar to Republicans in the past. (*Birmingham News*)

Democrat Secretary of State Nancy Worley took an obstructionist position as the election neared with her noncompliance with a new federal requirement creating a computerized, statewide voter list. Worley ignored the January 1 deadline, and in May, the Justice Department sued the state prior to the June primaries, the second time that year, for not complying with the "Help America Vote Act of 2002." The secretary of state did not coordinate the database with drivers' license records and federal Social Security records—although the government had given Alabama $41 million to update voter records.

Unwilling to allow Democrats to sabotage the election, the Bush Justice Department took responsibility for compiling the database from Worley and gave it to Riley. Democrats cried foul at the lost opportunity to compromise state elections clearly trending Republicans.

Baxley flailed away at Gov. Riley the last week of the campaign without doing any real harm. She resurrected an old Siegelman accusation that Riley had not paid some taxes, which he promptly labeled as "recycled garbage." Knowing that she trailed in the polls, Baxley made an obviously wrong-headed accusation for a Democrat. In a fumbling attempt to counter Riley's claim of a scandal-free administration, Baxley said that corruption in the two-year college system had occurred on his watch.

The ridiculously false accusations allowed Riley to turn the charge against Baxley and the Democrats. Riley revealed in a press conference that AEA had given Baxley $1.2 million in the final days of the campaign for television ads. Even still, William Stewart, a political scientist for the University of Alabama, said Lucy Baxley was the decided underdog due to a lack of financial backing. Democrats had a dreadful fear of Riley because he could find the money. Paul Hubbert was known to call him a "fundraising fool."

Democrats were not successful at putting the slightest dent in the Riley administration. In the November general election, Bob Riley rebounded again with the goodwill and affirmation of the people for his competent leadership—beating Baxley convincingly 57-to-41 percent. It was total vindication after the rough beginning in the first term.

To Riley's early missteps with the GOP, former party chairman Marty Connors said people had expended their anger when they voted down the failed tax amendment. "He had his trip to the woodshed," Connors explained. Democrats were as baffled by Riley's re-election as they were by Guy Hunt's 1990 reelection. They thought the people would help them regain the governor's office, although conservative Democrats were rapidly switching parties.

Riley: Alabama Legislature must change

Burdened by history as an unsuccessful political party, Gov. Bob Riley's second term set the tone for the eventual political domination by Alabama Republicans. The 2006 election may have been Bob Riley's redemption, but the Alabama Legislature remained under the unbending control of Democrats and the domineering AEA led by Hubbert and Reed. In the Senate, Republicans picked up two more seats to raise their total to twelve. In the House, forty-three Republicans were outmaneuvered by sixty-two Democrats. Six conservative Democrats, disgusted by Senator Lowell Barron's harsh tactics, moved quickly after the election to form a coalition with the twelve Republicans. It was a good strategy, but Democrats beat back that effort too.

Any hopes of the GOP gaining strength in the legislature from the top down with Riley's impressive win had been dashed. Joe Turnham, state Democrat chairman, defiantly predicted that the Alabama Democratic Party was "here to stay." Going into the 2006 general election, Democrats were not at all concerned by the threat of a Republican takeover. Two reasons explained why: AEA's overpowering financial advantage kept Democrats in control of the legislature, and Democrats had helped their cause after the 2000 US Census, by gerrymandering select Senate and House districts to ensure liberal control.

Facing the inevitable loss of power, Riley said Democrats were determined not to allow Republicans to leverage a conservative legislative agenda without a fight. "They were focused on retaining control of the legislature because they were dominating the state from the House and Senate," Riley explained. "We had to change the legislature so that the state could move forward." (The 1901 Constitution vested control of the state in the Alabama Legislature.)

Breaking down the Democrats' formidable power structure in the Alabama Legislature topped the list of objectives for Riley's second term. Recruiting business on a global basis created jobs and strengthened the state economy, but Republicans were unable to fully exercise their probusiness, proeducation principles with Democrats blocking change.

The scandalous community college system

An out-of-control crisis in the two-year college system gave Riley valid reasons to act decisively on two fronts. Community colleges and technical schools had created continuing public embarrassment due to incompetence and corruption. Chancellor Roy Johnson had mismanaged the system that had been politicized from the year George Wallace organized it. The schools were exploited more for their political assets than serving as educational institutions. Major newspapers in Birmingham, Mobile, Huntsville, and Montgomery were turning out articles about how the midlevel education institutions were seriously off-course. Gov. Riley was determined to stop the embarrassment to the state.

As a first step, Riley sought to draft Sen. Bradley Byrne from Fairhope (Baldwin) as chancellor of Alabama's two-year college system. Byrne had served two terms on the Alabama Board of Education, which gave him added insights into the state education system. But it would not be easy for the governor to take Byrne away from his family and a prosperous practice as a business attorney.

Byrne recalled how it all began when Gov. Riley called one Saturday morning in early May 2007. "When he told me what he wanted me to do, I immediately turned him down because of Rebecca and the kids and my law practice. I knew about the two-year college situation, and I knew it was out of control. But I agreed to meet with him in Montgomery the next week to talk about it—with the intention of not taking the chancellor's job."

Riley wouldn't take no for an answer. He explained to a reluctant Byrne that the system was getting worse every day that he wasn't chancellor. Byrne finally relented. When he left home that morning for the drive to Montgomery, he told Rebecca that he was not accepting the chancellor's job. Then again, the Byrnes had not reckoned with Bob Riley—country salesman.

Bradley Byrne, like Riley, was of Irish descent from tradition-rich Mobile. His grandfather had been elected sheriff of Baldwin County as a reform-minded Republican in a Democrat county. A graduate of Duke University and the University of Alabama School of Law, for over twenty-five years, Byrne had built a successful law practice. Furthermore, he had a reputation for being fearless as a senator and as a member of the state school board. Riley knew that Byrne was a tough-minded conservative and wanted him to rein in corruption that had thoroughly compromised Alabama's education system. Interim chancellor Renee Culverhouse resigned suddenly for health reasons, and the state Board of Education was looking for the fourth chancellor in a year.

The two-year college system was far more corrupt than Byrne had known; mismanagement of funds, nepotism, abuse of scholarships, fake grants, and outright fraud pervaded the system. He also discovered that the same systemic corruption existed in the chancellor's office. Even more daunting, Democrats and AEA stood ready to defend the community college system with an added vengeance. The schools served as a source of high-paying, no-work jobs for themselves, family members, and friends.

For Democrat legislators, the system was extraordinarily generous. Some legislators were hired for virtually nonexistent jobs, just to have a legislator on the school payroll. Community colleges employed fourteen legislators (thirteen Democrats and one Republican) by the time Byrne took control of the chancellor's office. Riley said he counted forty-five legislators with vested interests in the system. "Every one of them was a lobbyist for Democrats and voted in their own self-interest, including pay raises," Riley explained to the press.

Community colleges had become a royal road strewn with taxpayer dollars for the Alabama Democratic Party—a distinct George Wallace brainchild. By 2007, the number of institutions in the two-year system had expanded to thirty-five community colleges, technical schools, and their branches. The system had taken on the character of its founder and was perpetually influenced by political appointments brazenly manipulated by Democrats. The previous chancellor, Roy Johnson, had been the tough-as-nails Democrat Speaker of the House. Johnson was so overbearing and heavy-handed in the legislature that he had been mentioned as the eventual successor to AEA chief, Paul Hubbert.

Riley's sense of urgency was justified. A month before Byrne became chancellor, Brett Blackledge, a journalist for the *Birmingham News*, earned a Pulitzer Prize for investigative reporting on corruption in the two-year college system. Blackledge articles read like Tammany Hall schemes: the family of the Fire College president was being paid more than $560,000 annually; Chancellor Roy Johnson benefited from hefty budget increases from his pals in the legislature, no-bid software contracts worth millions were being awarded, and contractors were providing free work on Johnson's million-dollar home in Opelika. It was all that and more, just as Gov. Riley had described in his initial conversation with Byrne. Johnson could control and bully legislators, but he could not intimidate the state press.

Byrne met the media in a press conference to explain that his priority was transparency: "We need to face our problems . . . in a way that we can come up with solutions." He said that he would research the system before making a recommendation to the board about Riley's proposed policies to keep two-year employees from holding "no-work jobs," while simultaneously serving an elected office.

The bubble finally burst when the state board of education fired Johnson, following a grand jury report confirming Brett Blackledge's revelations that the chancellor's family had been given high-paying jobs. Democrats essentially handed Johnson the chancellor position not long after his appointment as president of Opelika Technical School and Southern Union College—somewhat dignified by a dandied-up honorary doctorate.

The breadth and scope of lawmakers' easy access to community college jobs was stunning. Blackledge, in the *Birmingham News*, reported that about one-third of House and Senate members had varying financial ties to the system, with legislators, their relatives, or businesses receiving money since 2002, the year Johnson became chancellor. Blackledge could have won the Pulitzer on *that* revelation alone. He revealed even more in an October 8, 2006, explosive headline: *"Alabama's two-year college system has paid more than three dozen state lawmakers or their relatives in recent years, including several legislators who received paychecks from two different colleges."*

The situation was made worse by how Johnson found jobs for top-level state officials. Newspapers reported that four members of the state school board had relatives working in the system. Yet, another strange twist surfaced when Alabama Attorney General Troy King had to step aside from the investigation after the press reported that King had asked Johnson to hire the mother of a staff member at the same time the attorney general's office was investigating the two-year college system. Johnson found her a job.

First strike for ethics in state government

Starting with an internal housecleaning, Bradley Byrne said about half of the community colleges required intervention. Bishop State Community College in Mobile topped the list of schools plagued by financial and academic issues. In a joint investigation with state and federal authorities, Byrne was successful at recovering some state funds squandered indiscriminately at community colleges throughout the state.

But it was Roy Johnson who brought the ethical schemes and shady deals of the Democrat Legislature to the chancellor's office. Starting in 2002, during the time Riley and Republicans in the legislature were focusing on improving education and helping the poor, Democrats were constructing a system of self-serving jobs and easy money, often originating with the chancellor. Following four years of carte blanche budgets from the Democrat-controlled legislature, federal authorities charged Johnson in a multiplicity of bribery, conspiracy, obstruction of justice, money laundering, and kickback schemes.

Especially damning for the chancellor was the testimony of Robert Higgins, a maintenance worker at Southern Union Community College. Johnson hired Higgins as his driver and aide, bumping up his modest blue-collar salary from $32,000 to $54,000. Higgins and the chancellor created bogus businesses that submitted false invoices and collected kickbacks from vendors, which were turned over to Johnson. In court, Higgins and some vendors admitted to illegal plots that exposed the corrupt system and the chancellor.

Ultimately, a long list of defendants was convicted or pleaded guilty in the federal probe of corruption in the two-year college system. As punishment, the court ordered stiff restitution, fines, and forfeitures. William Langston, Fire College chief, drew a hefty $1,689,417 forfeiture, but prosecutors hit Roy Johnson the hardest, forcing him to forfeit an astounding $18,206,485 and his lavish million-dollar home in Opelika. On November 18, 2010, Roy Johnson was sentenced to six-and-half years in prison. (*Birmingham News*)

Former Southern Union President Joanne Jordan pled guilty to receiving free services from a contractor who she hired for work at the college. Jordan admitted giving a fictitious contract to the former chancellor's son-in-law and authorized spending college funds on Johnson's girlfriend. Newspaper accounts reported how Johnson and Langston had made a deal to hire each other's children at outrageously high salaries with virtually little work and no responsibilities. The scandal took down legislators, chancellors, businessmen, grandmothers, fathers, sons, and daughters—an embarrassing lineup of Democrats guilty of plundering the state treasury.

Purging the community college system was not the only legal challenge during Bradley Byrne's tenure as chancellor. Gov. Riley recognized a special windfall for some well-placed legislators. Riley learned about the practice of double-dipping when newspapers reported that some legislators were drawing more than one state salary. During the federal fraud trial of Rep. Sue Schmitz, Riley pointed out why double-dipping—holding two state jobs—should be banned.

"It proved that Montgomery insiders turned the two-year college system into a no-work jobs program for legislators," Riley stated. "It proved that taxpayer dollars intended for educating students were, instead, used to bankroll a job for a well-connected legislator, a job for which she never showed up for work." The Feds tried, convicted, and sent Schmitz to prison.

Byrne said that the state board agreed with the governor and voted 6–1 to ban double-dipping in community colleges, a critical blow to Democrats. "Once the board had the authority to correct the problem, we never wavered. The board had the legal power to prohibit holding two public jobs, and we moved to change the practice," Byrne said. He said that the ban effectively reduced from fourteen to five the number of legislators holding dual jobs.

Gov. Riley explained that other states had taken the same legal action against drawing two state salaries. When he raised the subject to some Democrat legislators, they agreed that the practice was wrong. "But Paul said no." Paul Hubbert was dead set against any change in the two-year system that effected his influence over the state legislature.

Hubbert and AEA were determined to have the last word in the dispute. They immediately filed suit to stop the implementation of the ban, and Riley and Byrne fought the issue all the way to the Alabama Supreme Court, which upheld the decision of the state board of education. Failing at that, Paul Hubbert and AEA attempted to push through the legislature an outrageous bill removing the community college system from the state board of education and giving complete control to the Democrat-controlled legislature. Republicans helped defeat that power grab too. (*Montgomery Advertiser*)

Throughout the two-year college crisis and the fight to ensure that education was the priority of state learning institutions, Bob Riley and Bradley Byrne were tormented by the AEA in the media and Democrats in the legislature.

AEA saw both men as threats to their freewheeling kingdom, some four decades in the making. Democrats complained about investigative newspaper reporting, claiming that Republicans were behind the legal attacks. They were right about that. Riley and Byrne were acting on behalf of the people of Alabama!

CHAPTER TWENTY-TWO

The big agenda: win the legislature

Soon after the 2006 elections, but prior to his second inauguration, Bob Riley met with Representative Mike Hubbard (Auburn) and asked a favor, a huge favor. Hubbard had successfully won his House seat at Riley's urging and chaired the committee for Riley's first inauguration. This time, Riley had an even more demanding request—chairing the state party. "Had I known what awaited me at the time, I might have declined the invitation and gone into hiding," Hubbard said about the 2010 legislative elections in *Storming the State House*.

Twinkle Andress Cavanaugh, chair of the Alabama Republican Party, agreed to serve in Riley's cabinet, and the governor wanted ethical leadership at the top level of the party. After all, the state executive committee recommended a "No" vote on Amendment One. Like Byrne, Hubbard turned down Riley for the same reasons—family and business. On cue, like Byrne, Hubbard left the meeting doing exactly what Riley wanted. Now, he had to go home and tell his wife about his humdinger of a new job. He also realized how Riley became a successful businessman and won tough elections. He was an excellent country salesman.

Hubbard agreed to seek the chairman position of the Republican Party as the first major step toward changing the Alabama Legislature. Riley made a rare appearance at the February 10, 2007, executive committee meeting in Montgomery in full campaign mode. "This is a young man I encouraged to get into politics a few years ago," Riley commented to reporters about his endorsement of Hubbard. Hubbard won the GOP top office unopposed, and Gov. Riley had a reliable leader to help develop his ambitious second-term agenda of beating the Democrats at their own game.

Initially, Hubbard speculated that Republicans would win special elections for seats vacated by legislators convicted in the two-year college scandal. But those elections were only moderately successful for the GOP and did not create the level of change that Riley anticipated. Radical change had reached critical mass for Democrats. The two-year college scandals had generated sensational news stories under Chancellor Bradley Byrne at the same time federal authorities were prosecuting Don Siegelman.

Riley knew what he wanted. During his second term, Republicans would mount a concerted challenge for control of the legislature. The planning, strategy, fund-raising, and recruitment of candidates fell primarily on the shoulders of Bob Riley, Del Marsh, and Mike Hubbard. The men named their plan, *Campaign 2010*. Minda Campbell, Riley's daughter, came up with the "136 Years" tag line. The last time Republicans controlled the Alabama Legislature was 1874. David Lewis was the governor, and Reconstruction was ending in Alabama.

The challenge of electing a Republican Legislature was further conceptualized by Hubbard during his campaign to chair the Republican state party. He proposed the idea in a letter to the GOP state executive committee, explaining to members about his plan to raise funds and assemble the resources to elect a probusiness, proeducation Republican majority in the Alabama Legislature. During Hubbard's two terms chairing the Alabama Republican Party, changing the legislature was the primary objective of the party.

The third member of the 2010 team was equally important. Hubbard had asked Sen. Del Marsh of Anniston in Calhoun County to serve as the party's finance chairman. An Auburn graduate (wife, Ginger, was a cheerleader) and successful businessman, Marsh had served in the Senate in 1998 during the Siegelman days. Also, like Riley and Hubbard, Marsh was new to politics, reinforcing the party's business-education profile.

It is important to note that not one of the three men came through the ranks of the mostly ineffective Republican political hierarchy. They were not bound by the party's old clubbish ways of choosing candidates that lacked a credible sense of competitive politics and lost elections much too often. They fit the profile of James D. Martin of Gadsden, who, along with John Grenier, had resurrected the modern-day Alabama Republican Party in the sixties. The three professional businessmen brought real-world experience to the party, and each knew how to generate capital and identify winning candidates, necessary factors in changing Alabama's deeply flawed political culture.

The Riley-Hubbard relationship began when Riley ran for Congress in 1996. In his book, *Storming the Statehouse*, Hubbard described how Bob Riley called from Washington to tell him that Pete Turnham, the Democrat representative from Auburn, was not going to stand for election again. The two men became acquainted the previous year, and Hubbard had attended the swearing-in ceremony for Riley in Washington, D.C. Eager to bring the enterprising Hubbard into state politics, Riley encouraged him to run for the open seat. At the time, Hubbard was actively building a media and advertising business and raising a young family. Hubbard further understood that winning was a long shot because Republicans had been backbenchers in the Democrat district for over a century.

Congressman Riley convinced Hubbard that he could overcome the odds and promised to make important contacts and raise money for his campaign. Once again, Riley had an accurate sense of the shifting political trends in Alabama, having won his congressional seat due to growing conservatism in East Alabama. Hubbard recalled how after qualifying at state headquarters in Birmingham late on the final day, the GOP left him (like Riley) to his own devices about how to organize and fund a campaign. That experience taught Mike Hubbard one of his first political lessons . . . that conservative candidates would need substantial financial resources and professional advice about their district if the party were going to qualify competitive candidates and meet Democrats in tough elections.

The premier race for the GOP in 2008 was Sen. Jeff Sessions's third term, a solid win over Democrat Vivian Figures. Otherwise, Alabama was back to 1964 levels of congressional representation with four Republicans: Jo Bonner, Mike Rogers, Robert Aderholt, and Spencer Bachus. Further, political campaigns had changed from barbecues, fish fries, and country music to new technology—television, mail pieces, and social media, with only a smattering of newspaper ads. Now, candidates and parties could have an immediate impact on elections.

Still, a major factor had restrained Republicans from becoming

Alabama's majority party. Democrats seemed to have had eternal control over the Alabama Legislature, beginning with statehood and formalized by the 1901 Constitution. Essentially, Democrats established resistance to change that crushed the poor—black and white—while fixing the state's tax burden on the victims. This century-old system permitted Democrats to dominate Alabama for the long term. Riley's legislative team meant to attack those entrenched Democrat institutions.

Wallace had further defined Alabama Democrats with his tirades of racism and antifederalism in campaigns that dominated the political temperament of voters. Though Wallace had died a decade earlier, Paul Hubbert's firm grip on AEA had campaign cash and plenty of it. More than anything, money generated through monthly membership dues made it possible for the union to buy influence in the legislature. Other state constitutional offices and judicial seats may have gone the way of the GOP, but once Wallace left the state political scene, Hubbert kept the legislature on a short leash by underwriting legislative campaigns, including a few Republicans. Easy money from AEA reinforced one of the reasons that Republicans had remained the minority party in the all-powerful Alabama Legislature.

In the mind of Gov. Riley and Mike Hubbard, the legislature was the critical element in turning Alabama into a conservative, probusiness, education-driven state. As they prepared for the next two elections, they saw that polling revealed that most voters thought that the legislature was already Republican. Hubbard and the Republicans set about to fix that perception before 2010.

But first, Hubbard assembled a top-notch staff and went to work making good on his campaign promise. John Ross, who had worked with Hubbard coordinating Riley's first inauguration, became the executive director. At that point, Hubbard's strategy for staff personnel veered in another direction. He hired two fund-raisers, a first for the party. Kate Anderson and Sidney Rue would help guide the GOP's strategy to identify and generate financial resources far exceeding anything the party had raised in the past. Philip Bryan, a journalist entirely new to politics, was brought in to coordinate communications. There were others, but Ross, Bryan, Anderson, and Rue formed the nucleus of the initial headquarters staff.

Mike Hubbard also got a big break, or an edge—perhaps both. Only days after his election as party chairman, he received a book in the mail that became important in developing the GOP's election strategy. A close friend sent Hubbard a copy of Rahm Emanuel's book detailing how he masterminded the takeover of the US House in 2006. The book, *The Thumpin': How Rahm Emanuel and the Democrats Learned to Be Ruthless and Ended the Republican Revolution*, written by Naftali Bendavid. A journalist with the *Chicago Tribune*, Bendavid was given access to Emanuel and the Democrat Congressional Campaign Committee (DCCC) by Nancy Pelosi to document the Democrats' four-year plan to take over the US House. Pelosi had designs on becoming the first woman Speaker of the House, and she needed Emanuel to help end twelve years of GOP electoral control.

Hubbard ignored Emanuel's abrasive foul mouth (continually effing about something), but he identified a critical factor that was ready-made for his own plans. Emanuel focused on candidate recruitment as the pivotal strategy, often handpicking the right person himself. The logic was as simple as it was profound—raise money to finance campaigns and recruit candidates with conservative values. That dual concept provided Mike Hubbard and the Republicans with a winning strategy.

Hubbard was prepared to make a serious run at taking the legislature. A classic political battle was brewing for both parties, unions duking it out with business. Considering all that it would require to dismantle the Democrat machine—Hubbard's objectives were bold, historic, and impressive.

Siegelman's second grand hoax

Just as the Hubbard plan was taking root prior to the 2008 election, Gov. Bob Riley was forced to endure yet another round of senseless accusations from Don Siegelman under federal indictment and his allies in the media. Siegelman's lack of personal guilt and public shame seemed boundless. In 2006, he would sit through his federal trial during the day, and once court adjourned, a car waited to chauffeur him around to Democrat hot spots until the late hours.

Although embroiled in his legal troubles, some Democrats continued to stand with Siegelman, and he won 36 percent of the vote in the Democrat primary, an indication of brazen ambition and misplaced loyalty. Democrats were spared further embarrassment when Lucy Baxley won the nomination for governor with 60 percent of the vote.

Eddie Curran, in his book, *The Governor of Goat Hill*, characterized the media game that persecuted those who prosecuted Siegelman as, "The Hoax That Suckered Some of the Top Names in Journalism." It was vintage gutter politics accurately labeled. The reaction among the liberal media erupted like a failed afterthought when they were charged by liberal activists that they had not been diligent in their defense of Siegelman.

Converting Siegelman's proven guilt into political persecution was directed at the highest level of the GOP, allowing Siegelman the opportunity to recast himself as an innocent man. Lacking ethics and a moral conscience, Democrats and the liberal media pounced on respectable judicial professionals who had delivered the facts and advanced the case against Siegelman with evidence that judge-and-jury found plausible.

It was another trifling lineup of false accusers in the uplands of the North, condemning Southerners for having the temerity to bring a fellow Democrat to the bar of justice. Furthermore, Riley and Republicans were accused of being advised by Carl Rove. Dana Jill Simpson, a self-described Republican attorney from Rainsville, Alabama, signed a sworn statement that five years earlier, she had heard that Carl Rove was preparing to neutralize Siegelman politically with an investigation headed by the US Justice Department. Simpson, broke and burdened with a multiplicity of state and federal tax liens filed against her, admitted that another Siegelman supporter helped her with the affidavit. In a weak attempt to legitimize the hoax, Simpson explained that she felt morally obligated to speak out.

Not surprisingly, Siegelman's latest ruse was nothing more than a reimagined bit of prejudice. Siegelman defenders, cued to phony outrage, spoke with new anger and called for investigations. They were obliged with a witch hunt by the Democrat majority of the US House Judiciary Committee. Curran labeled it a "scandal" by its own creation.

Among the chief talebearers was Scott Horton, a journalist for the venerable *Harper's* magazine. During a meeting with a liberal group in Huntsville, Horton announced the premise for his accusations: "I'm convinced that the local press fell down on its responsibility to properly report the Siegelman case and at this point, the national media is stepping in." Horton creatively authored more than 130 online columns for Harper's about how Siegelman had been wronged, and similar articles for *American Lawyer*, fictionalizing facts about dark conspiracies in the Deep South.

False accusations did not cause Riley to miss a step when Siegelman's left-wing apologists attacked him. His stewardship of the state government did not slacken amid the rolling turmoil surrounding Siegelman. Instead, the governor remained fixed on recruiting businesses that created jobs and identifying funding for education. He knew that he didn't have much time to address many of the state's legendary shortcomings.

Bob Riley at work for the people

In his second term, Gov. Bob Riley followed the conservative-business blueprint with exacting measures. The plan called for more funding for schools, including construction projects and repairs, and the continued expansion of the state's reading, math, and distance-learning programs. Riley continued to lead his education agenda forward by expanding the prekindergarten program, which is rated the best in the nation by the *National Institute for Early Education Research*.

Economic Development took huge blocks of Gov. Riley's time, and the results were historic. The opening of an aeronautical engineering facility in Mobile by the parent company of Airbus meant more high-paying jobs for working families. Falling unemployment rates affirmed Riley's probusiness agenda, as new and expanded industry contributed to Alabama's steady growth among the highest in the South.

Alabama, under Riley, was recognized as the "State of the

Year" by *Southern Business and Development* magazine four years running, among other awards for job creation and economic development.

Worldwide Interactive Network named Alabama's Office of Workforce Development the No. 1 US employee development agency. *Expansion Management* magazine also ranked Alabama Industrial Development Training No.1 among workforce training programs. Democrats were silenced when Gov. Riley announced a major economic coup in 2007. ThyssenKrupp would construct a $4.2 billion state-of-the-art steel mill north of Mobile, the most significant economic announcement in state history, and the largest corporate project in US history. Over 2,700 top-wage scale jobs were created.

During Gov. Riley's industry recruiting trips for the state, he recognized an innovation other states were using to promote their people and opportunities—state encyclopedias. Riley was intrigued by the concept and wanted Alabama to create one, as well. "I felt that it would help promote the state to people we were trying to recruit for business and industry," Riley explained. He was involved with the initial organization and funding for the *Encyclopedia of Alabama*, a free online reference service that provides information on Alabama history, culture, geography, and natural environment. The Alabama Humanities Foundation developed the *Encyclopedia of Alabama* with offices at Auburn University. Some forty institutions support the information-sharing service.

The most remarkable gain for Gov. Riley was that the education funding increased by $2 billion, and test scores rose statewide as the result of the *Alabama Reading Initiative*—climbing from the near bottom to twenty-fourth in reading, a record for Alabama's schoolchildren.

Reading proficiency became Riley's momentous challenge. His goal was to have reading instructions taught in every school to achieve 100 percent literacy. "This program is doing things we would have only dreamed of a few years ago," Riley said at an assembly of teachers.

With the intent to harm, Democrats in the legislature refused to act on most of the tax proposals to fix the state's education system. Still, Riley got increased funding for the Alabama Reading Initiative and the creation of ACCESS—*Alabama Connecting Classrooms, Education and Students Statewide* distance learning to every high school in the state.

The education reforms justified increased funding and investments to train some 27,000 teachers to mentor the reading programs. The success demonstrated that Alabama's much-maligned school population had the innate ability to learn—black, white, Hispanic, and Indian. Leading as a champion of education reform complemented the same vision that Gov. Riley displayed in his Amendment One tax proposal.

All the while, Riley battled Democrats in the Alabama Legislature led by Paul Hubbert and AEA. Exposing serial corruption and political bribery became routine for the administration, and Riley showed no fear in risking his reputation and political career in reshaping a state government that seemed hopelessly lost to century-old corruption. As late as the Patterson administration in 1958–'62, business and industry organizations opposed legislation that funded Alabama schools and social services for the poor.

Monthly expenditures of the Governor's Contingency Fund and quarterly flight logs for all state airplanes were posted on the governor's website in an effort to avoid some of the misdeeds of past governors. No-bid contracts, a Siegelman largess, were eliminated.

At long last, the poor get a tax break

Democrats, more than any other state organization, had preyed on the poor. The disputed state constitution had defeated opposition to the Alabama Democratic Party, and much of the tax burden had been placed on the poor and uneducated. To Bob Riley, growing up with the working poor, it was unconscionable for the government to penalize the least defended segment of the population, people that he knew in Clay County.

In his first inaugural address, Riley boldly announced that it was his Christian duty to change the tax burden on the poor. (Roosevelt was convinced that he "was his brother's keeper," which drove his New Deal economic policies.) A two-parent family of four had the highest state income tax rate in the nation, with an exceptionally low tax threshold of $4,600. During Guy Hunt's administration, the few Republicans in the legislature attempted to raise the low threshold, but Democrats repeatedly defeated legislation for tax equity.

The unfairness of Alabama's tax system was fully exposed in 1990 when the *Birmingham News* published a series of eight articles urging tax reform. Research for the articles began with the corrupt 1901 Alabama Constitution, detailing how state law gave generous tax breaks to large timber and property holdings, while unfairly taxing the poor.

Each editorial pointed out that the inequities had been noticed but had gone unchallenged for decades by Democrats in the legislature. *Birmingham News* writers Harold Jackson, Ron

Casey, and Joey Kennedy won a Pulitzer Prize in 1991 for tax fairness.

In 2006, at Riley's urging, the Alabama Legislature reluctantly provided the first tax relief for the poor, raising the threshold to $12,600 for a family of four. Riley, who had called Alabama's tax system "immoral," lobbied for a higher threshold of $15,000. Riley said Paul Hubbert attempted to kill the legislation. For a touch of irony when announcing tax relief for the poor, Riley gathered black lawmakers in the original capitol House chambers for the media announcement—where the Confederacy organized in 1861, and the Alabama Republican Party did the same in 1867.

The issue of tax fairness continued to be a point of interest in the press. In 2008, the *Montgomery Advertiser* renewed public interest with a front-page headline, *"Study: State taxes on poor highest."* The study by the "Center on Budget and Political Priorities" in Washington, D.C., reported that Alabama had the second-lowest threshold for paying state income tax. Only Hawaii was lower. Gov. Riley made another attempt to persuade the legislature to raise the threshold again, only to have it defeated by Democrats in the Senate by a single vote.

Democrats did Republicans a huge favor late in Riley's second term; they gave themselves a 62 percent pay raise. Riley vetoed the unusually large raise, only to have Democrats override the veto along party lines with protesters marching outside the state House.

Indifferent to ordinary citizens, Democrats predicted that people had short memories and would forget about the pay raise by the next election. Not surprisingly, voters had excellent memories, and the big pay raise came back to haunt Democrats in the break-through 2010 campaign.

Yet another major expansion of conservatism spread across the nation, like the Carter and Clinton administrations. The election of President Barack Hussein Obama, a liberal with a vague background as a community organizer, brought more disaffected Democrats into the Republican Party. Obama would make his mark as the most racially divisive president ever.

CHAPTER TWENTY-THREE

Unprecedented
Republican victory

President Obama's election in 2008 did not slacken GOP plans to take control of the Alabama Legislature, nor did it alter Republican intentions of changing Alabama politics. With attention focused on the presidential election, Democrats and the national media were immersed in a heady thrall. Barack Obama, the Democrat nominee from Chicago's crime-ridden inner city, carried the banner for liberals, and for the first time in American history, Obama represented the hopes and dreams of historically repressed African Americans.

The national media stumbled all over itself in praise of the moment when Democrat Obama beat Republican John McCain to become the forty-fourth president of the United States. Alabama voted in record numbers, according to Beth Chapman, Alabama secretary of state. Alabama voter rolls approached three million by the time of the November general election, and more than two million people voted. McCain won Alabama by 60-to-38 percent.

Macon County, in the heart of the fabled Black Belt, had one of the highest voting percentages in the nation—almost 87 percent voted Democrat. "This is the promised land," African Americans exclaimed after the election. Representative Artur Davis said the election proved that a black candidate could win in Alabama, which he disproved in the next election.

Republicans had other problems. The nation was overwhelmed by the financial crisis in the final months of President George Bush's second term. Wall Street stocks shot up 300 points, and correspondingly, so did gun sales. In Congress, Democrats controlled the House and Senate as well as the White House—the ultimate for Democrats and the mainstream media. The Alabama Republican Party lost Congressional District 2 for the first time in forty-four years, reducing the GOP to four representatives.

Obama claimed his election was a "defining moment" in American history. The *Montgomery Advertiser* proclaimed that the Obamas were the coming of "a new Camelot," comparing them to the Kennedys. The paper further supposed that his election would undoubtedly influence Chicago's bid for the 2016 Olympics. Much to their disappointment, it did not.

The faltering state economy did not hinder Gov. Bob Riley from winning passage of another amendment (there were thirty-five on the ballot) voters approved that invested $248 million in the state's Rainy-Day Account. The reserve fund had been created to stabilize state finances when tax revenues fluctuated to maintain state education budgets should there be another round of constitutional proration. (*Birmingham News*)

Mike Hubbard's plan to take over the legislature did not show immediate promise and for good reason. With only random special legislative elections, Hubbard did not have an accurate measurement of GOP strength leading up to the 2010 elections. In addition to his carefully planned strategy and the growing campaign account to bankroll elections, Hubbard had the unforgettable pay raise that Democrats gave themselves—a whopping 62 percenter. Republicans would not let voters forget the greed factor of the Democrats.

The beginning of the end for Democrats

Riley, Marsh, and Hubbard had prepared for the ultimate clash with Democrats. During a time of growing tension in the Alabama Legislature, some members said that Democrat insults toward Republicans approached evil in hostility and defiance. With the threat of Republican dominance, Democrats were in a surly mood.

Money had steadily accumulated for the GOP. Hubbard and Marsh had crisscrossed the state, meeting with party loyalists and business leaders who agreed to contribute $10,000 a year for four years. Some gave more. The Governor's Circle would finance the party's legislative campaign, apart from the expense of operating Republican headquarters in Birmingham. Even with that, Hubbard and Marsh needed more money to compete with the Democrats and AEA's big money accounts replenished monthly with membership dues. That's when they looked beyond Alabama for another revenue source for the campaign.

The search began when Mike Hubbard attended the Republican national leadership conference in 2006, and the national GOP helped fund an election campaign in Alabama, Hubbard explained in a *New York Times* article, "I remained involved with them, going to fund-raising meetings around the country. When I became GOP chairman in 2007 and was a member of the RNC, I became even more involved." That relationship connected Hubbard and Marsh to sources at the national level willing to donate to the Alabama GOP. The relationship paid off. Hubbard began moving money into Alabama's Campaign 2010 PAC. The money came from several out-of-state sources, all legal under state election laws.

Alabama Republicans were benefiting from what was described by the *New York Times* as a "sophisticated political apparatus designed to channel money from around the country into states where conditions were ripe for Republican takeover." With the Obama administration beginning to run roughshod over American values, Alabama was one of nineteen states poised for change. Hubbard and Marsh worked with moneyed conservative activists, who invested over a million dollars with the Alabama GOP through the two campaign committees. Marsh said, "The conservative investors looked at our plan to take over the legislature and our candidates and believed in our strategy."

The previous best effort to influence change in the legislature had been led by Republican Party Chairman John Grenier in 1964–1966 (see page 59). Grenier recruited some 250 candidates but was unable to overcome the popular appeal of George Wallace, nor did Republicans have the money to challenge Democrats dollar-for-dollar. Mike Hubbard understood that a lack of money had hobbled Alabama Republicans for decades.

For the first time, Republicans were raising more money than Democrats, but that became a liability for Gov. Riley. Democrats retaliated with a vengeance once they realized that Republicans were deep into a legislative takeover bid. Joe Turnham, Democratic Party chairman, said Riley's fund-raising strategy may have been successful, "but it cost him three years of good legislation." (*Montgomery Advertiser*)

The campaign indeed had the persuasive attention of fund-raiser-in-chief Bob Riley. Decades of business success and six years in Congress had earned Riley a reputation for finding money.

The construction of a new Clay County High School in his home county is an example of his financial resourcefulness. He helped raise over $28 million to build a state-of-the-art campus that resembles a community college. There were calls to name it Bob Riley High School, but he refused. Instead, Clay County named the road leading to the school Bob Riley Drive. David Proctor, a newspaper publisher in Lineville and Ashland, said, "We couldn't have built the school without Governor Riley's personal help. It was too big of a project."

The Campaign 2010 PAC eventually generated over $5 million, essential for funding Republican campaigns. In the meantime, Hubbard and Blaine Galliher (Southside, Etowah County) traveled over to Georgia. They met with Republican legislative leaders to learn from their experience in taking over the Georgia Assembly. It was time well spent. Hubbard and Galliher were also shown how the GOP caucus developed a dues plan that funded legislative races, a system that Alabama Republicans adopted to create a continuous financial source for future elections.

Mr. Peepers drubs Hubbert, AEA

Tragedy prematurely interrupted the takeover plan. On October 26, 2009, District 40 Democrat Rep. Lea Fite died suddenly of an apparent heart attack at his home in Jacksonville. Fite's district had been targeted as a potential win for Republicans, and Hubbard had already settled on a candidate prior to Fite's passing. Rep. Randy Wood (Anniston) had introduced Hubbard to K. L. Brown, owner of funeral homes in Jacksonville and Anniston, as the strongest Republican candidate capable of beating Fite.

Fite barely survived the 2006 election against former Democrat

State Rep. Tom Shelton by a very thin margin of some 400 votes. The district had trended conservative during Fite's tenure and was ready for change. Brown, a successful and respected businessman, resembled Wally Cox, who played Mr. Peepers in a 1960s television show. Confident of his favorability ratings, the party waited out the results of the five-person Republican district primary for Brown's official nomination for the vacant seat.

As expected, K. L. Brown won the Republican special election primary and was saved from a runoff by second-place contender, Jacksonville businessman Jay Dill. Dill bowed out of the runoff to give Brown and the GOP a clear field to take on the Democrat nominee Ricky Whaley. Dill's gesture saved the state some $50,000 in election costs.

In the normal course of Democrat politics, Whaley would not have been more than a second-rate candidate, but he had the blessings of Paul Hubbert and AEA's financial support, which appeared virtually unlimited. Whaley had also ingratiated himself to Gerald Willis, former Democrat state representative, who become wealthy in the lumber and timber business. Willis ran for president in the 1980s, styling himself after President Andrew Jackson. He built an exact replica of "The Hermitage" for his family home in rural Nances Creek near Piedmont. Whaley often accompanied Willis to the Alabama Legislature and sought his endorsement to keep the district Democrat. Willis did that, and more.

AEA was fighting to retain its political power in District 40. Republicans and Democrats alike understood that a Brown victory in the Democrat stronghold, a sure win for Democrats since Reconstruction, would be the bellwether race for the 2010 legislative elections. Knowing that, Democrats threw the book at the soft-spoken Brown, making scurrilous accusations and false claims about his squeaky-clean personal and business reputation. Brown was mystified by the charges and shaken by the viciousness of the attacks by the AEA and local teachers. It was the lowest gutter politics that AEA could construct and included attacks on Brown's family.

Desperate AEA operatives, aware that they were losing their electoral grasp, went as far as to threaten to boycott local business owners who displayed Brown's campaign posters in their store windows. Some area schoolteachers working for Whaley stooped to the salacious mischaracterization of Republicans as a "bunch of rednecks."

Gov. Riley attended a huge rally for Brown at Jacksonville State University's Merrill Hall, with Mike Hubbard, Del Marsh, and the entire staff from party headquarters in Birmingham. Democrats complained to JSU officials about Republicans holding a political event on campus, but with Riley chairing the state board of education, their whining was ignored. Republican Party Director John Ross and communications director Philip Bryan set up a war room at a local hotel. They worked with county GOP officials making phone calls and coordinating a door-knocking campaign. Both parties knew what was at stake: an election that would either save the Democratic Party from defeat or usher in a new era of government.

K. L. Brown won the election by almost 15 points, a landslide by Alabama standards. Polling data had been favorable throughout the campaign, but Republicans needed confirmation that the party had strong conservative appeal with voters. The big win gave the party a solid measurement by beating AEA without exhausting its modest $100,000 campaign budget. Hubbard had an accurate reading of voter hostility toward Democrats, all the way to the

White House. Republicans sensed that the party was on the verge of a great tidal wave of voter backlash. Conservative voters were incensed by the corrupt Alabama Democratic Party and the liberal policies of President Obama and the national Democratic Party.

Riding the wave of popular appeal

On Tuesday, November 2, 2010, angry voters took revenge on the Democratic Party in Alabama, sending it to the political grave-yard. The GOP was given the opportunity to govern in all consti-tutional offices, the court system, congressional and Senate seats, open positions on the Public Service Commission, and control of the all-powerful Alabama Legislature. Further, the ripple effect helped the party win judicial seats, governing boards, councils, and commissions in county and city government throughout the state. It was the beginning of a new political era.

"I think a lot of it had to do with the national mood," said Sen. "Jabo" Waggoner, Vestavia Hills. He blamed national Democrats and their big-government ambitions. "I think it trickled down from Washington to Montgomery." The Democrat state execu-tive director agreed that national trends had impacted Alabama's election.

"It's a big deal," explained Brad Moody, a political scientist at Auburn-Montgomery. He said that Alabama was late joining other Southeastern states in having at least one chamber of the legislature controlled by Republicans. "Republicans," Moody added, "are going to discover it's harder to govern than to be in opposition."

Conservatives were benefiting from the liberal national party. "The Obama-Pelosi Democratic party just does not sell with many white Southerners," explained Merle Black of Emory University. "No longer could white Democrats, whether conservative or moderate, win elections by disassociating themselves from the national party." Black said that in the Deep South, the Democratic Party had been reduced to African Americans and liberal whites.

Alabama Republicans were thoroughly prepared to grasp the opportunity of the historical change, now holding sixty-two seats in the House and twenty-two in the Senate. The election set off another round of party switching that increased the House total to sixty-six Republicans, a supermajority. At the same time, county Republicans began assimilating elected Democrat officials into the party.

In closed-door caucus meetings, the Republican House chose Mike Hubbard as Speaker of the House, and the Senate elected Del Marsh as president pro tempore of the Senate. Both men were the face of the party that had engineered the takeover and were given leadership positions in the legislature for the diligent work they did for four years to change the way Alabama governs its people. Hubbard, Riley, and Marsh were recognized as the chief architects of the legislative takeover.

.

All signs pointed to a Republican sweep in the legislature. Del Marsh said on the night of the election, he closely monitored Gerald Dial's (Lineville) District 13 Senate race in East Alabama to determine if the Republican takeover was on course. "Gerald had lost the previous election and was running on the Republican ticket this time," Marsh explained. "I felt that if he won, then we would have a chance for a supermajority." Marsh got his answer when Dial edged Democrat Greg Varner with 51 percent of the vote.

"Lowell Barron gave Varner $1.2 million to try to keep the district Democrat," Dial explained. "I spent over $600,000, half the amount." Dial said it was the most money spent by a losing candidate in a legislative race in the state. At the same time Dial was winning his race, Lowell Barron (Fyffe) lost his own Senate seat in a major upset to Shadrack McGill.

Marsh said he sensed a strong anti-incumbency attitude among voters. "The demand for change was so great that there were some races where a Republican could have won without spending any money." He also believed that the Republican campaign peaked during the last week of October. On the night of the election when the numbers started falling in place for the GOP, Marsh said that Gov. Riley called and expressed surprise by the overwhelming success.

"The governor was shocked by the record vote we were getting," Marsh explained. "But Mike and I were watching the House and Senate races very closely, so we were not surprised by the results." Marsh, who had managed the PAC that financed the landmark win, said Republicans invested the entire five million-plus dollars in the classic 2010 political election.

Democrats were responsible for their own political ruin. Decades of corrupt politics and reckless decisions had finally taken a fatal toll—reaching as far as Folsom's rural "Yonder Boxes." Republicans had outworked and outspent Democrats, employing a proven strategy designed by national Democrats to take control of the US House.

More importantly, the hands-on work had been managed by a successful probusiness, proeducation governor, his hand-picked state party chairman, and finance chairman. Republicans had ridden the wave of popular appeal to unparalleled victory.

Furthermore, Bob Riley's two terms and the successful take-over of the Alabama Legislature marked the final struggle of the unproductive and controversial Wallace era—something that Guy Hunt and Fob James had failed to do. Republicans were now responsible for their own history.

CHAPTER TWENTY-FOUR

The passing of a political dinosaur

M**ontgomery** . . . The epicenter of Alabama politics was rocked by the election night drama unaccustomed to the minority party winning in such resounding fashion. The *Montgomery Advertiser* headlined its banner story in 72-point type: *"Historic GOP Sweep,"* rightly attributing the win to anti-Democrat sentiments. The election bombshell cited voter anger stemming from the still-active community college scandal, the federal investigation into vote-buying for passage of favorable gambling legislation, and corruption in the Jefferson County sewer system that resulted in twenty-one convictions or guilty pleas.

That same night, Steve Flowers, a Troy State University professor and former Democrat member of the House, offered his usual political commentary for Montgomery CBS affiliate, WAKA. At the approach of midnight, when it became apparent that Alabama Democrats had been wrecked, Flowers gave a proper requiem: "They can turn out the lights and leave the keys on the mantle. The Democratic Party is dead in Alabama." Two years later, in the 2012 election, when Obama won a second term, Flowers affirmed his previous assessment and said he was convinced that he had been correct in 2010. Flowers added that "history will record that Barack Obama drove the final nail in the Democratic coffin in Alabama."

The 2010 election accelerated the movement of conservatives and independents into the Republican Party. The Joe Reed-Nancy Worley faction was now directing the Alabama Democrats. The radical left had severely diluted the multiracial profile of the party. Furthermore, knowing that Republicans would be accused of racism, black Democrats had a greater tendency to vote a straight ticket based solely on race. And this: Joe Reed once objected to the appointment of Emory Folmar to the board of trustees of the Alabama State University because he was white. Reed defended the domination by African Americans of the party structure and repeatedly battled attempts to elect moderates to leadership positions.

The call for ethics reform

With the defeat of Democrats in the legislature, on the night of the election, Governor-elect Dr. Robert Bentley said it was time for ethics reform, promising to call a special session during the first regular legislative session in 2011. The supermajority meant that Democrats could no longer derail Republican legislation. Strangely, Bentley said that Republicans wanted to make sure that voters knew where candidates were getting their campaign money. Reform would come more quickly than Bentley anticipated. In a bit of ethical irony, at the approach of the general election, media revelations entangled Dr. Bentley with rival Democrats and hidden campaign expenditures by the same bad guys that Republicans had just defeated in the historic election (reference chapter 25).

But it was Riley, not Bentley, who insisted on immediate change. "The obstacles to reform have been removed from office, and Alabama has its best opportunity to pass reform," Riley's press secretary, Todd Stacey, stated on behalf of the governor. Riley had made two attempts to convene a special session for ethics reform in 2004 and 2007, but Democrats defeated the initiatives. Public pressure for quick action arose out of scandals and controversies that compromised the state's education system and revealed the sinister connections between numerous legislators and Alabama's gambling empire.

The suggestion that Gov. Riley call a special session for ethics before leaving office quickly caught on with how the GOP could best exercise its new mandate. Mike Hubbard said that the ethics issue was so "hot" that Bentley and Riley needed to agree on calling a special session now, with the energy and impact of the election behind the issue. The same sense of urgency was also picked up by the *Montgomery Advertiser* that questioned the wisdom of waiting until the next regular session of the new legislature.

On Thursday following the election, an *Advertiser* editorial encouraged the governor to call for a special session on ethics. "There is no good reason to wait," Jim Sumner, executive director of Alabama's nonpartisan Ethics Commission, said. "We have all of the catalysts we need to have true ethics reform in Alabama."

Dr. Bentley did not object to the new Republican-led legislature getting in the first licks at reigning in the myriad of the state's financial and ethical problems. Freshman Senator Dick Brewbaker (Pike Road) said that Republican senators were "on the hook" for ethics reform. Governor-elect Bentley volunteered to "lead the parade."

Calling a special session before the next administration was sworn into office was a rarity, even in Alabama, and had occurred only once. During World War II, Gov. Frank Dixon (D) called a special session on November 16, 1942, asking the legislature to fund extended school terms and for the authority to pay temporary state employees during wartime. (*House Journal*)

"Republicans have vowed to pass ethics reform," reported the *Montgomery Advertiser* in the lead article following the GOP sweep, reminding readers about state officials who had been arrested, then and now. The night of the election in Bryant-Denny Stadium, Dr. Robert Bentley told a cheering crowd of supporters, with the strains of "Sweet Home Alabama" blaring throughout the celebration, that a special session for ethics reform "was long overdue."

Sebastian Kitchens, reporting for the *Montgomery Advertiser*, responded the next day with a column accusing Bentley of contradicting his personal behavior, especially during the Republican runoff with Byrne. Bentley had been broadly accused of misrepresenting the extent of the Alabama Education Association's (AEA) Machiavellian role in Republican elections. Bentley denied involvement with AEA spending huge sums on attack ads against Byrne.

Yet, later, Bentley and AEA made modest amendments to their campaign reports for the July runoff that showed the teachers union spent only $21,000 for telephone calls with Bentley's message to "clean up the mess in Montgomery." Furthermore, during the November general election debate, Democrat nominee Ron Sparks confronted Bentley about his secretive dealings with AEA. Bentley made no response.

Gov. Bob Riley had been frustrated during his two terms by the failure to pass ethics legislation. The previous January, Riley had made another attempt to pass ethics legislation, specifically banning PAC-to-PAC campaign contributions and giving the Alabama Ethics Commission subpoena power. Riley had proposed changing ethics and campaign finance laws, only to have them buried in the committee without a hearing. The Alabama Senate, where Democrats held twenty of thirty-five votes, was especially hostile to Riley.

New Republican legislative leadership was careful to comply with Alabama's election laws. Gov. Bob Riley, at the urging of Speaker of the House Mike Hubbard and Senate President Pro Tempore Del Marsh, recommended a seven-day special session for December 7, 2010—barely a month after Republicans took control of the legislature. Gov. Riley told the *Montgomery Advertiser* that Republicans could put an end to the state's broken and corrupt political system: "This is a defining point in the history of Alabama."

Aware that Democrats would intentionally misinterpret the special session, the House and Senate scheduled public hearings in the historic House chambers the day before the special session convened. The governor's office made additional postings of the proposed bills online. Once the session got underway, Republicans went to work crafting and passing a package of seven ethics bills. Ironically, Democrats were forced to rewrite their own legislative charter. The existing charter had been written when they were the majority party.

Dems want Bentley (not Riley) to lead reform

Democrats agreed that ethics reform would be good for Alabama; nevertheless, they wanted Governor-elect Robert Bentley to lead ethics reform after being sworn in January 17, and the new legislature was organized March 1, 2011. Democrats angrily insisted that the special session was not an emergency. Joe Turnham, chairman of the Alabama Democratic Party, 2005–2011, protested that the called session was little more than "political chest-thumping."

The extent of the seven ethics bills was designed to correct "loose" ethics laws: subpoena power for the Alabama Ethics Commission; restrict legislators from holding two state jobs; Pac-to-Pac transfers; pass through pork; ethics training; ban payroll deductions; and limit the amount of money that lobbyists can spend on legislators.

The media saw banning dues deductions not as an ethics bill, but Riley's way of settling the score with the teachers union for its underhandedness in Bentley's campaign. So did teachers and state worker organizations, who stalled the legislative process for fifteen hours trying to kill the legislation banning dues deductions by the state. It was also the closest vote of all the ethics bills. The House voted 52-to-49 in favor, and the Senate voted 22-to-12.

Marsh and Hubbard said that legislators on both sides of the aisle in both chambers passed more ethics reform in seven days than Democrats had for decades.

In the Senate, Del Marsh and Jabo Waggoner asked former senator and two-year college chancellor Bradley Byrne to draft the law on "double-dipping" that prohibited public officials from holding more than one state job. Byrne had fought that battle with AEA while chancellor and prevailed. The bill gave the Ethics Commission subpoena power and reduced the $250-per-day threshold for lobbyist spending on entertainment to $250 annually, a daily cup of coffee. Byrne also helped revise the dues check-off bill after it was introduced.

Just as importantly, PAC-to-PAC transfers that had hidden the source of political contributions during Bentley's campaign for governor was struck down, another blow to the hide-and-seek trickery of Democrats. Finally, to ensure compliance with the new ethics regulations, a law was passed that mandated ethics training for all state employees.

Republicans were not reluctant to tackle the contentious issue of changing the teacher tenure law. As a union organization, AEA defended its worst-performing members, sometimes after criminal conduct sent them to prison. AEA had traditionally defeated attempts to reform the state tenure law. But the conservative power shift had weakened the opposition, and Republicans passed a more responsible, "streamlined" tenure process for educators.

AEA protested loudly while Republicans made shambles of their political empire. The teachers union unleashed a torrent of public criticism about the reformed legislation. An AEA press release claimed that the special session was not about corruption but was about "political payback" against the union, calling the session "draconian."

The special session would have made Edmund Burke, England's original political conservative, proud. The legislative revolution was a signal honor for Gov. Riley and victorious Republicans. By the conclusion of the political reform and realignment, the *Montgomery Advertiser* editorialized thusly: "*The special session on ethics should cement Gov. Bob Riley's reputation for openness and promoting ethical standards.*"

Indeed, the special session was an exclamation event for Bob Riley's eight-year tenure as chief executive of Alabama that further facilitated greater success for the reemerging Alabama Republican Party.

The special session continued into the early hours of Thursday morning when both Houses of the legislature were gaveled down for the final adjournment. Riley invited excited but worn lawmakers to join him at the Governor's Mansion for a well-deserved celebration. A few decided to drive home, but most piled into vehicles for the five-minute drive down Hull to the Governor's Mansion on South Perry Street.

The driveway was jammed with cars that cold winter night when hungry but happy Republicans gathered around the long dining table set with food and drinks (no booze). First Lady Patsy Riley and her staff had waited up to host the wee-hours-in-the-morning victory celebration. Legislators congratulated one another and relived the entire victorious experience, anticipating what they would be doing under new leadership in the next regular session of the Alabama Legislature.

Gov. Bob Riley signed the anticorruption bills into law Monday, December 20, 2010, in the historic old state archives room in the state capitol. Riley was surrounded by the new Republican majority that had worked in earnest to restructure the way Alabama did business.

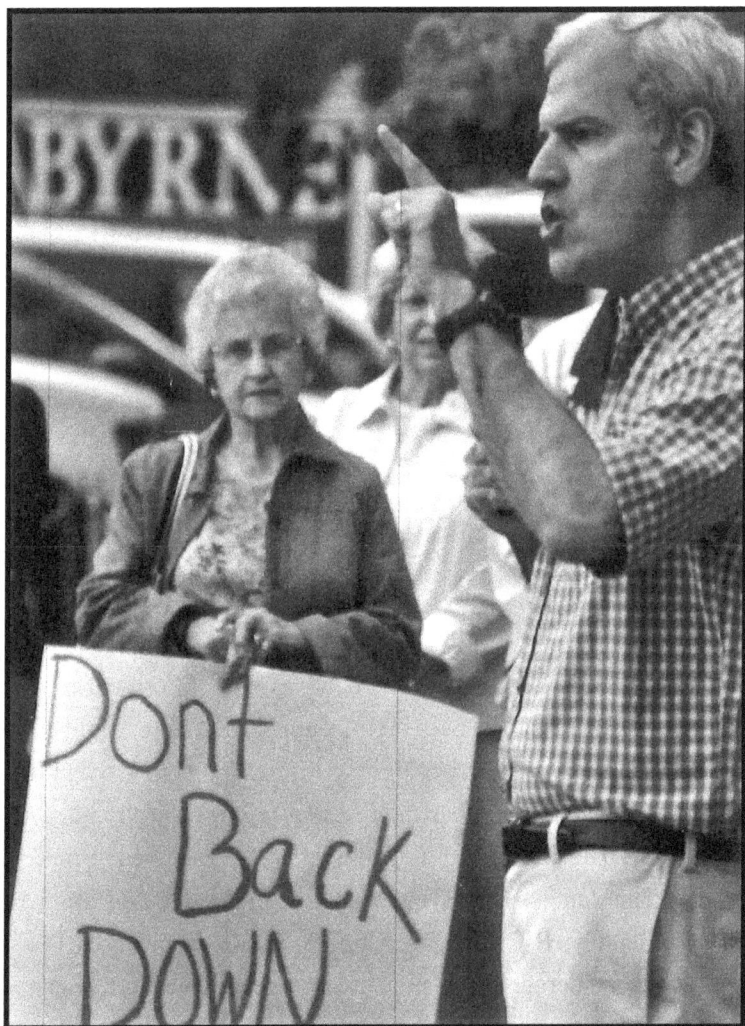

Bradley Byrne in full campaign mode

CHAPTER TWENTY-FIVE

Dr. Paul Hubbert (D) sacrificed the last of his nine lives to help elect Dr. Robert Bentley (R) governor

The 2010 gubernatorial election is better understood as the concluding chapter.

The 2010 campaign for governor was equally critical to the Republican surge to take over the Alabama Legislature. Eight candidates qualified for a run at the top office, and the race had the promise of electing another trendsetting reformer in the likes of Bob Riley. The list of Republican candidates included: Bradley Byrne, Tim James, Kay Ivey, and Roy Moore in the top tier; Robert Bentley, Bill Johnson, Charles Taylor, and James Potts were not considered serious contenders when the election began a year out from the primary.

From the onset of the 2009 campaign, Bradley Byrne was regarded by party insiders and the media as the top candidate to continue the Riley legacy. Byrne brought the most distinguished public service record to the race, a member of the state board of education, state senator, and chancellor of the two-year college system. At the same time, he had similarly engaged in running battles with the Alabama Education Association (AEA).

Quin Hillyer, writing for *The American Spectator*, said that in the state Senate, Byrne "never wavered under unrelenting pressure from liberals who controlled the chamber," and often filibustered against their "big-government" agenda. Byrne had a reputation as an uncompromising conservative that earned him the endorsement of major Alabama newspapers, complemented by numerous business organizations. His emphasis on reforming the state government long controlled by Democrats put him in good stead with Alabama's business and education interests. Early polling data showed Byrne with a 28–30 point lead for the top spot.

Also, at stake was the 2010 congressional redistricting. Three Alabama districts were vulnerable to electing a Democrat should the new governor have a cozy relationship with AEA, the political pseudonym for Alabama Democrats. With AEA honchos Paul Hubbert and Joe Reed manipulating the party structure, a fair redistricting plan was out of the question. It could have crippled the Republican business-education agenda for another decade.

Byrne's solid lead meant that he caught the brunt of the initial political attacks, including cheap shots from his old antagonist, AEA. At the same time, Byrne's campaign team did little in the way of effective media advertisements that featured his stellar political accomplishments. His television commercials did not rise above the ordinary, nor did they persuade voters to support his candidacy. Still, his dynamic speaking style and aggressive campaigning kept him atop the polls despite lackluster media advertising.

Dr. Paul Hubbert (D) sacrificed the last of his nine lives to help elect Dr. Robert Bentley (R) governor

Roy Moore of Ten Commandments fame aired ads that accused Byrne of being a liberal, that he supported teaching evolution, and that he didn't believe all the Bible—all of which reflected Moore's fundamentalist viewpoint of Byrne's Episcopal faith.

But it was Tim James, son of former two-time governor Fob James, who created the biggest media sensation. James's "English Only" ad created an uproar that went viral with a bit of cultural humor. James criticized the state for giving written driver's license tests in twelve languages. "This is Alabama; we speak English," James said in the commercial. The ad had minimal effect in Alabama, but it became an instant social media controversy on the internet—especially among liberals.

James was accused of ethnic coding and was hammered by the *New York Times* as "the candidate from Xenophobia." The thirty-second commercial was created by Fred Davis, described by the press as a Hollywood advertising guru. Interviewed by Bill O'Reilly for Fox News, James was asked if he was indeed pandering on the immigration issue. James categorized the media fuss about his commercials as "political correctness gone amuck." One article compared him to slow-witted Forrest Gump. Certainly anyway, with the growing concern (since President George W. Bush) over the immigration crisis, James struck a raw nerve with liberals already positioned as staunch defenders of immigrant rights.

Around the time the campaign season was heating up, Republican insiders realized that Lieutenant Governor Jim Folsom Jr. did not have strong Republican opposition and could be reelected. Folsom faced only nominal opposition until Bradley Byrne suggested that one of the less competitive candidates with low poll numbers could consider switching to the lieutenant governor's race.

Byrne approached two candidates about switching races: Dr. Robert Bentley and two-time state treasurer Kay Ivey. Bentley rejected the suggestion outright, twice, but Ivey considered her options until late March. Two days before the qualifying deadline, Ivey announced that she would challenge Folsom for lieutenant governor.

"There is an eight-candidate field for governor, and it's all jumbled up right now," Ivey said in an interview with the Associated Press. Cheers went up in Republican ranks across Alabama. Ivey was a legendary speaker and spirited campaigner with an excellent record of public service. She had spent $1.7 million of her own money in the governor's race and had taken in only $87,000. In Ivey, the GOP had a candidate with a reputation for trading punches with Folsom in the general election. For many Republicans, it was the most intelligent political decision of the election cycle.

The governor's race went along, as political races are wont to do, with candidates plugging away at one another until Dr. Robert Bentley released his first television commercial with a folksy approach. Bentley leaned across a tricked-up split rail fence and promised that he would not take a salary until Alabama achieved full employment (5.2 percent), concluding with his tag line: "Alabama is sick and needs a doctor." Bentley's ads were nonconfrontational and positive. He presented himself in a caring, bedside manner that convinced people he was a nice man who could be trusted. Even though his poll numbers were low and at the time were single digits, his personal appeal in the television ads eclipsed the entire field—both parties.

Bentley's ambition to be the first governor willing to work for nothing attracted attention, but even that failed to keep him among

Dr. Paul Hubbert (D) sacrificed the last of his nine lives to help elect Dr. Robert Bentley (R) governor the top three leaders. The no-salary promise was clearly an act of desperation. For months, he had trailed Byrne, James, and Moore badly in the polls. Further, the leaders had plenty of cash, especially Byrne and James, and Bentley was woefully shorthanded to continue his statewide television campaign in major markets. Bentley's staff understood his frustration over the inability to attract big donors, and they advised the doctor to consider dropping out of the race. "The critics were right. I couldn't raise money," Bentley explained to George Talbot, a reporter for the *Mobile Press-Register*. "It was kind of a low point for us."

The Bentleys campaigned in a modest, understated style, traveling together most of the time. Diane Bentley, a sweet, grandmotherly woman, drove their big white pickup truck from town to town, so her husband could speak to mostly small audiences. (Bentley met and married Martha Diane Jones of Montgomery during his first year of medical school.) Bentley impressed people as humble and genuine, but insiders felt that he could not win. In the legislature, his committee assignments were respectable: Education Appropriations, Agriculture and Forestry, and vice chairman of House Internal Affairs. Yet, during his two terms in the House, many legislators remembered him walking the halls in near anonymity and expressed surprise that he ran for governor. They didn't expect voters to give him a second thought.

In an interview with *Business Alabama* (Birmingham-based business magazine), Bentley talked about preparations for bigger things in Alabama politics. He said that he had been a delegate for Arkansas Gov. Mike Huckabee to the 2008 Republican National Convention and served on the Platform Committee. The McCain-Palin ticket was eventually nominated, but the Huckabee connection remained as an important relationship for Bentley.

By May 2009, after serving two terms in the House and a narrow loss in a Senate race, Bentley announced that he was running for governor. With Diane Bentley and a cluster of grandchildren around him at Capitol Park in Tuscaloosa, Bentley told a small audience that he would bring both parties together and "create a government that works." He felt that his close relationship with Democrats would enable him to reach across the aisle and lead the state as a Republican working with Democrats. Admitting a lack of name recognition, Bentley explained, as a chartered bus idled nearby, that he was beginning a two-day bus tour to introduce himself to Alabama voters.

All too soon, the Bentley campaign ground to a halt, if it had any momentum in the beginning. In January 2010, he had hired Bob Wickers from San Francisco as his media consultant to help generate fresh ideas, but Wickers had been unable to create real enthusiasm for the doctor. That's when Bentley took a break to evaluate his campaign. He spent time alone, bush hogging around his home property in residential Tuscaloosa, mulling over the governor's race. He still believed that he could win, but it was critical that he return to advertising with his original political tease to work-for-nothing.

He needed money badly. He said that some people "gave me money because they felt sorry for me, or they gave me a little money because they were friends." Conferring with his wife, Diane, they agreed to withdraw money from their retirement accounts and take out a second mortgage on their home—considerable risks for a campaign down in the polls.

With money in the bank, Bentley returned to television in early May with the primary only four weeks away. Employing the same nice-guy appeal, Bentley saw his poll numbers immediately begin a steady climb. The central message didn't change—as governor, he would not take a salary—but this time, it resonated with voters weary of the negative back-and-forth media brawl that erupted between Byrne and James. The contrast had an immediate impact on voters. Bentley was most effective among independent white voters in the eastern and western rural areas of the state, the regions where Folsom and Wallace had populous support.

Bentley's campaign peaked at the right time. "Voters were looking for an alternative to James and Byrne, and they found it in Bentley," explained Brad Moody, a political scientist at Auburn-Montgomery. Bentley parlayed his casual personal style, future retirement income, and mortgaged home into political capital. He was confident that he could convince people to vote for him if he campaigned hard enough and presented his case for governor.

On June 1, 2010, the results of the Republican primary gave Bentley his big break. The final election tally released by the Alabama Republican Party on June 8 showed that Bradley Byrne won 27.89 percent of the vote, mirroring late campaign poll numbers. The shocker was that Robert Bentley edged Tim James for second place by a whisker-thin 167 votes. Roy Moore placed fourth with 19 percent. Money spelled success, and Byrne had more in the bank than the other top candidates with $4.7 million, followed by James at $4.4 million, compared to Bentley with $1.4 million. More importantly, state GOP officials reported that Republicans topped Democrats in the total number of votes cast, only the second time in recent history.

The primary created an entirely new and unimagined race for Byrne, Bentley, and James. Tim James called for a recount in counties where vote totals could make a difference and paid counties to retabulate the original ballots. The Republican process called for county GOP chairs to coordinate the vote recount with the local probate judge and county sheriff.

Recounts were not a new experience for Bentley. He had agonized through a previous recount in 1998 when he ran for state Senate. He finished fifty-eight votes behind Democrat Phil Poole. Recounting the ballots didn't change the outcome, and Bentley gained only eight votes out of more than 45,000 cast. In the process, he spent some $446,000 on a losing race.

Bentley's close call in the Senate race no doubt galvanized his concerns about losing close elections. Bryan Sanders, Bentley's new campaign manager, immediately questioned the professionalism of recount officials despite veteran poll workers. Bentley joined the criticism with concerns about methodology. Attorney General Troy King added to the confusion when he issued an opinion that the law didn't allow for a recount until after the runoff. Nevertheless, amid complaints and opinions, the recount went on, and Bentley increased his small lead over James to some 270 votes out of more than 492,000 cast. James's recount gamble served only to elevate Bentley's name recognition.

For GOP Chairman Mike Hubbard, the statewide recount was an unfamiliar and unexpected responsibility. The process consumed three of the six weeks during the July 13 runoff cycle. It also occupied two weeks for Chairman Hubbard and the headquarters staff. Deliberate about neutrality in primary and runoff elections, the GOP headquarters in Birmingham, already cramped for space, soon had a large contingent of Bentley and James people underfoot, sure of their own suspicions, watching and listening for a hint of anything that might compromise Bentley's very thin lead or give James the second runoff spot.

Hubbard said supporters representing both sides repeatedly

DR. PAUL HUBBERT (D) SACRIFICED THE LAST OF HIS NINE
LIVES TO HELP ELECT DR. ROBERT BENTLEY (R) GOVERNOR
"berated" the staff and frayed nerves. One legislator practically
camped out in the office of Executive Director John Ross. But
their worst fears were unfounded. By the end of the recount, there
were no complaints against the state party, either by James or
Bentley.

Pressing on during the recount, Byrne's vote totals in the primary did not exactly give him a comfortable edge, leading Bentley
by only 14,000 votes. In the run-up to the primary, Byrne's poll
numbers routinely topped 24 percent while Bentley barely broke
8 percent. But that would change. AEA recharged the runoff with
more negative ads that entangled Byrne and James in their own
battle. With both camps in the dark about the source of the negative ads, each suspected the other of mischief-making. That AEA-
contrived quarrel alone would ultimately cost Byrne a sizable
chunk of James's supporters in the runoff.

The primary changed Bentley

Politics can change people. The surprising second-place finish in
the Republican primary definitely changed Dr. Robert Bentley.
Those close to him said he was different when he realized that
Paul Hubbert had trapped Byrne, and he could meet Byrne one-on-
one in the runoff with the collective support of other Republican
candidates. Bentley was gripped by the possibility of winning the
nomination for governor and meeting the Democrat nominee in
the fall election. Alabama voters were fascinated by his willingness to work for nothing.

Bentley was adding more consultants during the recount. He
hired a new campaign staff with a national reputation, quickly
and crudely dismissing the core leadership group that had helped

him win a surprising second-place finish, only 3 points behind the front runner. Without a hint of warning, Bentley sacked his campaign manager, communications director, and news-media director. Sally Albright, the news-media director, returned to her former position with the Alabama Democratic Party.

Bentley's hatchet job on the very people who helped get him into a winning position, according to spokesman Stephen Berry, was abrupt and ruthless. Berry said the shake-up came as a shock, and that Dr. Bentley turned a deaf ear on their request for references. The firings confirmed how quickly Bentley was willing to abandon his good-natured behavior when he realized that he was on the brink of claiming the Republican nomination for governor.

Robert Bentley's upbringing was a Depression-era story of a family living in near poverty. The youngest of six children living on the wages of their sawmill worker father, the Bentleys lived on a forty-acre farm near Columbiana, Shelby County. Robert Bentley graduated at the top of his class at Shelby County High School in 1961, attended the University of Alabama, and earned his medical degree from the University of Alabama School of Medicine (UAB) in 1968. His family said that he had always wanted to be a physician.

Attaining success through the medical profession had been a monumental achievement for Bentley, evidenced by continually touting his medical degree during the campaign. He reminded voters in his television ads that Alabama was sick, and "we need a doctor." Feedback after the election told a different story. The promise to work for free, not his medical profession, was the pivotal factor in voting for him, especially with rural, independent voters.

DR. PAUL HUBBERT (D) SACRIFICED THE LAST OF HIS NINE
LIVES TO HELP ELECT DR. ROBERT BENTLEY (R) GOVERNOR

The tale of the firings was not forgotten and for a good reason. Charles Dean's article in the *Birmingham News* illustrated Bentley's cruel intent in the heartless firings and his grasping quest for the nomination. Two of the three employees issued a clarifying statement on June 16 about their dismissals. Steven Berry and Sally Albright released a three-page statement through Tuscaloosa attorney Ralph M. Clements III, calling the firings "callousness unusual even in political campaigns." The letter stated that Berry and Albright suddenly found themselves shunned at the big victory party. When told that their services were no longer needed, the three were also turned down for the customary letter of recommendation. They asked to speak with Bentley before leaving headquarters. "All we wanted was a thank you note that we could show our children someday," Albright said in the letter. "Apparently, even that was too much to ask." Bentley rejected their request and coldly refused to speak with them.

But it was Ralph Clements who put in proper context the startling contrast between the old and new Bentley. Clements said, "What was so disappointing about this is Dr. Bentley has presented himself as a Southern gentleman, as someone above the nastiness of politics." Referring to the deep disappointment of Bentley's former employees, Clements further stated, ". . . these people who worked so hard to take him from a really joke of a candidacy to second place is at odds with that image."

Bentley had moved quickly, hiring Bryan Sanders as his new campaign manager in time for the recount. Sanders had been the top aide to former Arkansas Gov. Mike Huckabee during his presidential campaign. He eventually married Sarah Huckabee, the governor's daughter. Bob Wickers, another Huckabee strategist, was hired as Bentley's press contact. Closely aligned with

Huckabee brought new respect for Bentley. Mike Huckabee topped the field in Alabama's Republican presidential primary.

AEA *lurking in the shadows*

Dr. Bentley would need every advisor that he could keep on the payroll. Revelations about a series of troubling compromises soon called attention to his willingness to thoughtlessly drop his civil behavior and throw himself in exactly the kind of dirty politics that he had promised to clean up in Montgomery.

Almost comedic but certainly clumsy, early in the primary, Bentley asked the Republican Party to include his medical title on the ballot. He wanted to appear on the ballot as Dr. Robert Bentley. But Republican Party rules did not allow candidate nicknames or titles. The GOP ruled against Bentley and also against Roy Moore, who wanted to be listed on the ballot as Judge Roy Moore. A third candidate, Dale Peterson, asked that his name be listed as Cowboy Dale Peterson. Del Marsh, a member of the GOP Steering Committee, explained to the press that including titles on the ballot would set a bad precedent.

Bentley wasn't entirely satisfied with the decision, still convinced that his medical degree was an important marketing tool. On March 30, Bentley made the ridiculous decision to change his first name to "DR" to skirt party rules and advertise his medical profession. When the Republican Party made the same ruling, he changed his name back to Robert Bentley. At this point, Bentley was not about to give up his obsession with leveraging his medical education to impress voters.

By then, the press uncovered yet another contradiction. Bentley had to explain misleading references to his military

DR. PAUL HUBBERT (D) SACRIFICED THE LAST OF HIS NINE
LIVES TO HELP ELECT DR. ROBERT BENTLEY (R) GOVERNOR
service in TV advertisements. In a campaign ad, "A Man's Word,"
Bentley spoke of serving his country with "honor and integrity."
The video showed a military aircraft and the words, *Hospital
Commander Vietnam War.*" A closer examination of his military
record by the press revealed that Bentley was again up to his old
tricks of misleading the public. He joined the Air Force in 1969
with the rank of captain. His military service had been medical
officer, then commander of a hospital at Pope Air Force Base in
Fayetteville, North Carolina.

Bentley initially denied embellishing his military record, a
temptation that often trips up ambitious politicians eager to portray themselves as veterans. Angry Vietnam veterans called a
news conference in Montgomery and challenged the false claims.
Bentley eventually admitted to the *Montgomery Advertiser* that he
had been the interim commander at a military hospital for "about
three months." And he had never been to Vietnam.

However, there was a major revelation coming at Bentley.
Major state newspapers reported that the Bentley organization and
campaign staff were in a secretive collaborative relationship with
Paul Hubbert and AEA to defeat Byrne.

Bentley, quick to boast about being a lifelong Republican, began taunting Byrne in debates about switching parties in 1997.
(Byrne had a historic family background as a Republican as early as the 1920s.) Bentley's relationship to the Republican Party
was anything but loyal, as he claimed. He often voted against
Republicans in the legislature, and he stood with Paul Hubbert and
AEA to defeat Gov. Bob Riley's education reform bill to establish
charter schools in Alabama. Further, Bentley tended to avoid any
negative comments about Hubbert and the teachers union, sometimes voting with them, sometimes against them. All of that was

bush-league politics compared to the extent of Bentley's under-handed pursuit of the Republican nomination for governor.

Early in the campaign, AEA began their media assault of Byrne, who they claimed was antieducation despite serving two terms on the Alabama Board of Education and chancellor of the two-year college system. In both roles, Byrne had taken a hard line against many of AEA's power grabs with the education system. AEA seethed with hatred for the immovable Byrne, and Byrne faced them in unflinching defiance. Compared to the intractable Byrne, Bentley seemed more accommodating to the AEA agenda. Hubbert and Reed knew they could trust him in Montgomery, where cutthroat politics was the norm.

Hubbert and company were incensed that Byrne branded AEA a "corrupting influence in state government." For over six months, AEA kept public pressure on Byrne with an unrelenting series of covertly funded false TV ads. Neither Byrne nor Hubbert slackened their fast pace of criticisms and accusations, the fieriest of the 2010 election. Byrne said that he was not backing down from AEA, and Hubbert turned his propaganda campaign up a notch.

Especially egregious was Hubbert's "Conservative Coalition for Alabama. PAC" that drew the Alabama Republican Party into the media brawl with James. Republicans were shocked by the revelation that the ads were being funded by the Marengo County Republican Party, chaired by Andy Renner with lobbyist Claire Austin. Marengo County was a majority black county, and the GOP wasn't sure the party had an organization in that part of West Alabama. With Paul Hubbert and Joe Reed working with Renner, money began flowing through a series of PAC-to-PAC transfers. AEA's handprint was clearly on the attack ads.

DR. PAUL HUBBERT (D) SACRIFICED THE LAST OF HIS NINE
LIVES TO HELP ELECT DR. ROBERT BENTLEY (R) GOVERNOR

State GOP Chairman Mike Hubbard, with the agreement of other candidates, went public with information that Democrats were investing heavily in the Republican primary through a PAC created by a Republican county chairman. Renner, Hubbard reported, confessed to contacting Democrats and AEA, which led to Renner's immediate resignation as chairman of the county Republicans. On that single media transaction alone, AEA poured some $1.4 million in negative advertising to distort Byrne's record and drew him into a dispute with James.

But that was not all. AEA stepped up union attacks against Byrne throughout the Republican runoff. Paul Hubbert claimed that AEA was simply trying to defend itself, insisting that Byrne wanted to "burn our house down." But that claim was as bogus as the advertisements. "He started the fight, and we sat still for months and months," Hubbert said.

"When he declared for governor," Hubbert added in an interview with the *Birmingham News*, "he really declared war on us." It was a phony excuse for AEA's aggressive opposition, but Hubbert had strong incentives to keep Byrne from succeeding Riley as governor.

It was then that Paul Hubbert, cochair of the Alabama Democratic Party, finally admitted to conspiring against Byrne. One of the ads questioned Byrne's claim as a reformer in the two-year college system, which ended the practice of "double-dipping" that had been the first strike for ethics in the Alabama Legislature. An infuriated Hubbert struck back at Byrne with a vengeance, scolding the man who cost Democrats plenty of easy money in the community college system.

Byrne correctly argued a week before the primary runoff that "Our party is being hijacked by the liberal Democrat machine."

Only then did Hubbert publicly acknowledged that the union was involved with PACs but stopped short of disclosing further information or identifying donors.

Bentley's "innocent bystander" alibi

The big shocker was still to come. When guilt indicated a link between Bentley and AEA, Bentley vigorously denied AEA's involvement in the Republican primary and runoff. He kept telling the press that he didn't know anything about AEA's complicity in Republican elections. Initially, at least, he did, for the record. Bentley offered a feeble defense, saying one thing while his campaign was doing the opposite. The evasions and denials proved useless until Stan Pate, a Bentley insider and big-money contributor, mailed packets of explosive emails to major newspapers around the state.

The assorted emails revealed that on the morning of July 8, Bob Wickers sent a message to Stan Pate asking for his help. The back-and-forth messages eventually led to an agreement for AEA to place robocalls before the runoff. Pate's role in the Bentley-Hubbert relationship became a critical factor in exposing Bentley's lack of truthfulness—start to finish.

Pate immediately became the intermediary between the Bentley campaign and AEA. He said that Bob Wickers wanted to make arrangements for Bentley to record robocalls through AEA's phone network. Shortly after the initial contact, AEA public relations manager David Stout emailed Pate with instructions for setting up an account with AEA's calling service and attached a script for Bentley.

Pate said he forwarded the email to Wickers and Bryan

DR. PAUL HUBBERT (D) SACRIFICED THE LAST OF HIS NINE LIVES TO HELP ELECT DR. ROBERT BENTLEY (R) GOVERNOR Sanders, who arranged for Bentley to record the script. According to Pate, the next day, Sanders sent Pate an email thanking him and informing him that "Doc" would soon record the third phone message. Sanders had more good news; his father-in-law, Mike Huckabee, had recorded a call on Bentley's behalf.

The reason for the urgency? Bentley and his strategists became alarmed when polling showed Byrne steadily closing the gap between them. Even more troubling, Byrne reported more than $2 million in cash, three times Bentley's bankroll. Byrne criticized Bentley in the media for his known ties to Democrats and the AEA and was gaining ground by the day.

Byrne made a hard choice for the runoff. He could change to a less confrontational campaign style against the easygoing Bentley, or he could continue his aggressive criticisms of Hubbert and the AEA for their insidious role in the Republican primary. The Byrne team agreed to remain consistent by exposing AEA's dirty tricks. It was a risky decision that gave Bentley an emotional edge with exasperated voters.

To ensure that Bentley didn't lose the election only days from victory, Sanders and Wickers contacted AEA to help slow Byrne's late surge. Like the Andy Renner arrangement, it was another opportunity to continue crippling Byrne's campaign. Paul Hubbert was more than pleased to oblige Dr. Robert Bentley, his political ally.

AEA took it from there. Over the next three days, the teachers union made more than 500,000 recorded phone calls daily for Bentley. In the calls, Robert Bentley said that he would "clean up the mess in Montgomery and run an open administration with high ethical and moral standards." Later, when evidence of his hand in hand relationship with AEA began to surface, Bentley repeatedly emphasized that he was an "innocent bystander" in the matter. Bentley was anything *but* innocent. The next week, he released a written statement that claimed, "No member of my staff nor any of our hired consultants have ever been authorized by me to make a negative ad. There is no connection between our positive robocalls and negative attack ads." Parsing words did not redeem Bentley from his old habit of cooperating with Hubbert and the teachers union.

The statement glared with compromise. AEA had been a Bentley mainstay during the campaign and had agreed to all of Bentley's requests. The hush-hush arrangement allowed Bentley to continue playing the happy talker while AEA created more attack ads that enabled Bentley to take the high road while Byrne was getting beat up trying to defend himself.

After the election, Bentley revealed in an interview that during the runoff, Byrne attacked him for two weeks without affecting his poll numbers and that his internal polling had him from 12-to-14 points ahead of Byrne in the final week of the runoff. Jess Brown, a professor of political science and justice studies at Athens State University, said that Bentley had been "unbruised" going into the runoff. Byrne wasn't even putting a dent in Bentley's campaign. Strangely, some voters felt that Bentley's burst of generosity qualified him to be governor.

The Republican runoff was almost anticlimactic. Polling data had rightly reckoned with the will of the people. Robert Bentley won the Republican primary runoff 58-to-44 percent. He had the combined support of Tim James, Roy Moore, Paul Hubbert, Joe Reed, and enough Democrat crossover votes to swamp Byrne. Furthermore, he had escaped numerous media revelations to win the nomination. The historic capture of the state legislature would

Dr. Paul Hubbert (D) sacrificed the last of his nine lives to help elect Dr. Robert Bentley (R) governor further ensure that Republicans would win across the board in November.

And, yet, Bentley did not report AEA's robocalls as required by the Alabama Fair Campaign Practices Act. It wasn't until October 14, three months later, that the Bentley campaign eventually filed an amended finance report with the secretary of state. The report showed that AEA's political action committee provided $20,769.19 in-kind advertising.

But Stan Pate had more compromising evidence. He released a taped phone call made during the runoff, showing that AEA had given Bentley $150,000 through PACs. The September 23 conversation between Pate and Paul Hubbert discussed the large donation. Hubbert revealed that the money was funneled through Tuscaloosa lobbyist Ryan deGraffenried III. When pressed about the contribution, Bentley acknowledged that AEA gave him $10,000 once in 2009. However, there were estimates that AEA may have invested millions in defeating Byrne.

In state newspapers, Pate explained his change of heart. He said that he turned against Bentley when it became apparent that he was lying about his relationship with Democrats. But his disgust went further. Pate ordered Bentley and his campaign staff to immediately vacate their Tuscaloosa headquarters in a building that he owned.

The cumulative evidence of Bentley's wrongdoing served as the basis for a lawsuit filed by former Birmingham city councilman Jimmy Blake, who wanted to remove Bentley from the ballot. The lawsuit cited the robocalls and a list of six corporate contributions exceeding the legal limit allowable by law. Bentley returned the checks, and Circuit Judge Nicole Still ruled that she did not have the jurisdiction to halt an election.

By then, the general election was in full swing, and Ron Sparks, who had defeated Artur Davis for the Democrat nomination, took up the crusade to expose the Bentley-AEA connection. Sparks pointedly asked Bentley in a debate if he had accepted contributions from AEA. Bentley denied it, although evidence by his own supporters indicated otherwise. "He has lied to me and to the people of Alabama this entire campaign," Sparks said.

Dr. Robert Bentley won the 2010 general election 58-to-42 percent, despite obvious evasions and ethical wrongdoing in the Republican primaries and general election. Bentley received 860,472 votes to Ron Sparks 625,710. His promise to work for nothing won the top office in the state, but in his quest for power, Bentley compromised himself to the extent that his character and motives were suspect to all who had watched his campaign of deceit and outright fraud. In no time at all, the people of Alabama would discover, much to their regret, that they had been short-changed.

Index

Abernethy, Tom, 21–22, 37–38

Adams, John Q., 142, 144, 146

Aderholt, Robert, 170

Alabama Democrat Party, reorganized, 8–9; 10–11, 1901 Constitution, 13–14; first Democrat Party primary, 16; drop the conservative title.

Alabama Education Association (AEA), Wallace coalition, 29; 103–04, Hubbert and Reed, 103–04; Barron and Windom, 125; 161, changing the legislature, 178; 180–82, 186, ethics reform, 188; 190–97, 198–200

Alabama Republican Party, organized, 1–7; Rosenwald Schools, 17–18; civil rights champions, 22–23; Anne Manie, 26–27; Frank M. Johnson, 29–30; resurrecting the Alabama Republican Party, 33–37; Martin-Hill race, 40–46; Martin and Wallace, 48–52; Goldwater, 50–52; disastrous 1966 election, 53–60; wilderness years, 61–67; first GOP primary, 63–67; Denton wins Senate, 74–81; Folmar race, 85–87; Hunt elected, 92–96; Martin saves oil leases, 99–100; Hunt convicted, 107–10; Sessions-Shelby, 111–16; James's second administration, 116–20; Windom's nonscandal, 122–24; Siegelman's final folly 125–30; the Riley doctrine, 130–34; Magnolia Springs,

Sources consulted

The formative period of the Alabama Republican Party has been well-documented. In the post-Civil War era, state newspapers clashed with the ideals of a new liberal political party. Leah Rawls Atkins wrote about the period in her book, *The History of the Deep South*. Sarah Woolfolk Wiggins provided descriptive profiles of scalawags and carpetbaggers, rightly dividing traditional perceptions from the truth. Margaret M. Story described the extent of Union involvement in Alabama in her book, *Loyalty and Loss: Alabama Unionists in the Civil War and Reconstruction*. The author published a dramatic story about multiple hangings during Reconstruction in *Death at Cross Plains* (University of Alabama Press). Also consulted were: Heather Lehr Wagner, *The History of the Republican Party*; Lewis L. Gould, *Grand Old Party*; Heather Richardson, *To Make Men Free, A History of the Republican Party*.

The second phase of Republican Party history is the rather lengthy beginning with Gov. W. H. Smith (R) to George Wallace (D). The website, Our Campaigns, provided an original listing of Alabama gubernatorial elections from statehood in 1819. The site included Republican candidates from 1867–'68. Information about each candidate was gathered from multiple records and historical sources. The state press rarely reported on Republican activities, which made it difficult to develop Republican activities and leaders fully. Nevertheless, sufficient information was developed to create a brief profile of little-known Republican gubernatorial candidates.

Among sources consulted for this section: *Alabama Governors*, published by the Alabama Department of Archives and History; *From Civil War to Civil Rights: Alabama 1860–1960*, an anthology from the *Alabama Review* edited by Sarah Woolfolk Wiggins; *Alabama: The History of a Deep South State*, William Warren Rogers, Robert David Ward, Leah Rawls Atkins, Wayne Flynt; *Southern Politics in State and Nation*, V. O. Key; *Encyclopedia of Alabama*, "1901 Constitutional Convention," Sarah A. Warren. Heather Cox Richardson, *To Make Men Free*: *A History of the Republican Party*; Samuel L. Webb, *Two-Party Politics in the One-Party South: Alabama's Hill Country, 1874–1920*.

Other sources consulted for this section: *From Civil War to Civil Rights: Alabama 1860 to 1960*, Sarah Woolfolk Wiggins. William Warren Rogers, Robert David Ward, Leah Rawls Atkins, Wayne Flynt, *Alabama: The History of a Deep South State*. V. O. Key Jr., *Southern Politics in State and Nation*. Sarah A. Warren. "1901 Constitution Convention." *Encyclopedia of Alabama*. The author's book *Patterson for Alabama* addressed the Folsom-Patterson-Wallace era of state politics. Newspapers from major Alabama cities, Huntsville, Birmingham, Montgomery, and Mobile, helped develop background information.

From the George Wallace administrations forward, there is more than ample information about Alabama politics. The rise of the Alabama Republican Party had been reported in the major newspapers. Interviews with party leaders helped in discussing the weaknesses and strengths of the GOP. Also providing insights were: James D. Thomas and William H. Stewart, *Alabama Government and Politics*; Bob Ingram, *That's the Way I Saw It*; James G. Stovall, Patrick Cotter, Samuel H. Fisher, *Alabama Political Almanac*; Darrell Prescott (Anne Manie), *The Harvard Crimson*; George E. Sims, *The Little Man's Big Friend*; Jack Bass, *Taming the Storm*; Dan Carter, *The Politics of Rage*; the oral histories of Bass and DeVries, *The Civil Rights History Project*.

The brief attempt to resurrect the Alabama Republican Party in the early 1960s relied heavily on newspaper accounts of convention proceedings and the many failed Republican elections. The research involved interviewing many of the principal people of that era and consulting newspaper coverage of Republican summer conventions. James Martin, John Grenier, and Mignon Smith were the driving forces in reactivating the languishing Republican Party. There was no real progress in the party between 1966 and 1986. Summer conventions were the primary sources of party activities. Multiple Wallace administrations completely overwhelmed Republicans during this period. I also reviewed James L. Sledge's dissertation on the history of the *Alabama Republican Party from 1867 to 1978*; Auburn University, 1998. Dr. Wayne Flynt was Sledge's faculty advisor.

Alabama's 1986 election has so much recent history reported by state and national media. Personal interviews with state and local Republican leaders and historical accounts about the emerging Republican majority from the Ronald Reagan era served to paint an accurate picture of how Alabama became a red state.

Kevin Phillips, *The Emerging Republican Majority*; Alexander P. Lamis, *Southern Politics in the 1990s*; Edmund Morris, *Dutch: A Memoir of Ronald Reagan*; Byron E. Shafer and Richard Johnston, *The End of Southern Exceptionalism*; Earl and Merle Black, *The Rise of Southern Republicans*; Robert D. Novak, *The Agony of the G.O.P. 1964*; "Southern Oral History Program Collection, 1973–2013" (Ray Jenkins and John Grenier interviews), University of North Carolina; Jack Bass and Walter DeVries, *The Transformation of Southern Politics*; Eddie Curran, *The Governor of Goat Hill*; Samuel E. Webb and Margret E. Armbrester, *Alabama Governors*; James M. Glaser, *Race, Campaign Politics, & the Realignment in the South*; Allen Tullos, *Alabama Getaway*.

The battle for the Alabama Legislature was easily plotted through personal interviews and newspaper accounts of the historic 2010 election drama. Major newspapers gave concise reports of both parties as the election unfolded, first in the primaries and Republican runoff, then the November general election.

For Southern background, I tend to reference Clarence Cason's *Ninety Degrees in the Shade*, University of North Caroline Press, 1935, and W. J. Cash's *The Mind of the South*, Alfred A. Knopf, 1941.